"*Rachel and Steven teach from their heart and will touch your soul. They will make a lasting contribution to your life.*"

-Jack Canfield, author, Chicken Soup for the Soul, The Success Principles

"*Rachel and Steven pursue their mission with integrity and competence.*
I appreciate their commitment to excellence and their support of the highest quality learning for their participants."

-Robert Dilts, author and NLP Developer

"*Rachel and Steven are outstanding trainers of NLP and Hypnosis. I give them my highest recommendation.*"

-Stephen Gilligan, author, The Courage To Love

NLP:

A Changing Perspective

By Rachel B. Hott, PhD and Steven A. Leeds, LMHC

ISBN-13: 978-1495997549

ISBN-10: 1495997545

To our children, Daniel and Maya

Contents

Acknowledgments

In August 2011, we made the commitment to write this book together. Now we have a moment to look back and see how far we have come. Yes, we wrote this book, but we could not have written it on our own. So besides acknowledging each other for our contributions, teamwork and love, we want to acknowledge those who have helped us get to this completion point.

Thank you to our parents. Both of us are fortunate to have had parents that gave us the message that we are loved and we are loveable. We both want to especially thank Dr. Jacqueline Hott for her tremendous guidance and support before, during and after the writing of this book.

As a married couple and parents of two adult children, we have learned so much about ourselves from their feedback. As Daniel, our eldest son, has stated, he was the experiment. Yet as our daughter Maya knows, we are still experimenting. And it never ends. Thank you for being part of our lives. It continues to be a rewarding experience to be your parents. And whether we are communicating effectively or not, please remember you are both loved.

Thank you to our NLP and Hypnosis students. This book is written for you, your family and friends. We appreciate that you want to improve and make a difference in others' lives. You make a difference in ours. Because of you, this world is a much better place to live.

We also want to thank our NLP Center of New York training team. Over the years we have had wonderful trainers, some who have moved on and other who are still part of our staff. Thank you to Josh Davis, Gail Heimberg, Kathy Mazetti (first in our trainers training and first in offering feedback on our book), Rob Schwartz, Leilani Siri and Trudy Steinfeld for all your help and support.

To our NLP and Ericksonian Hypnosis teachers and colleagues, you have touched our lives and contributed to our work either by training us, connecting at conferences or having a social visit. Thank you to Steve Andreas, Connirae Andreas, Andrew Austin, Richard Bandler, Roberts Dilts, Judith Delozier, Tom Dotz, Charles Faulkner, Stephen Gilligan, David Gordon, Brent Geary, John Grinder, Chris Halbom, Tim Halbom, Leslie LeBeau, Anne Linden, Doug O'Brien, Bill O'Hanlon, Shelle Rose Charvet, Virgina Satir, Suzi Smith, Frank Staas and all the others in the NLP Community. And a special thank you to Jack Canfield for your inspiration end encouragement. You have all made a lasting difference in our lives.

We also want to acknowledge Milton Erickson, who we never got to meet, but whose wisdom we received through his writings and his students.

Thank you Mark Gabor for your time and guidance in helping us get started.

We want to especially thank our editor, Lisa Kennelly, who demonstrated the need for an editor.

Lastly, we want to acknowledge you, the reader. Thank you for being curious before, during and after reading this book. May your perspectives never stop changing.

Rachel Hott and Steven Leeds

The Magician's Story

A young man and young woman knocked impatiently at the front door. After some time, the door opened and a tall man wearing a purple robe appeared before them. "Yes?" he asked the visitors. "We have come to see the magician," they replied in unison. "What is the purpose of your visit?" inquired the man. "We want to learn more tricks. We want to get better at fooling our friends," said the young man. "And we want to learn the art of deception. We want to dazzle and manipulate our customers so we can make lots of money," said the woman. "I do not think you will find what you are looking for here," said the man. "Stop wasting our time, old man. Take us to the magician. We have come prepared to pay him whatever he wants. And we want to see him now," demanded the young man. The man at the door smiled. "You have seen him," he said, and closed the door.

Later that evening, there was another knock on the door. Another young man and young woman waited, patiently. The door opened and the magician appeared at the doorway. "Yes?" he greeted the visitors. "Are you the magician?" inquired the young man. "Yes, I am," he replied. "We would like to study with you," said the young woman. The magician studied their faces for what seemed a lot longer than the few seconds it actually took. Then he smiled, bowed and said, "Please come in."

The magician led them to the parlor and offered them some tea. "We have heard and read so much about you and we were hoping that we could study with you," began the young man. The magician, who appeared to be looking right through them, rejoined, "Before I respond, I would like to tell you a story."

Many years ago there was a performance at the Grand Palladium. The huge crowd came to see the Great Maltoni perform his magic. In the final act, the Great Maltoni asked for a volunteer from the audience. A young boy who had come with his older sister raised his hand. The Great Maltoni gestured for him to approach the stage. "And now, ladies and gentleman, watch carefully as I turn this boy into a rabbit." As he waved his magic wand, sparks flew and purple smoke filled the stage. He recited some incantations, pointing the wand at the boy and right before their eyes the audience witnessed the transformation of a boy into a rabbit. There was wild applause. Everyone was impressed except for one, the boy's sister, who approached the stage and asked the magician bring back her brother. The Magician apologized, saying that he only just recently learned how to turn a boy into a rabbit, but not the other way around. The audience laughed, but the girl could tell that the Great Maltoni was not joking. At first she began to cry, pleading with him to do something. But he just laughed and the audience laughed with him.

The Great Maltoni then handed her his magic wand and suggested that she might have a go at it. She held it for a moment, tossed it aside, picked up the rabbit, sat down in the middle of the stage and gazed deeply into her brother's eyes. She turned and looked at the audience and pleaded with them to be quiet. The laughter dissipated.

She knew there must be a way to bring him back, but she did not know how. So she closed her eyes and visualized her brother. Something stirred deep within her soul and she began feeling a powerful energy surge throughout her body. As she continued to summon up this newly found inner strength that had been awakened, she conjured up a vivid image of the bunny transforming back into her brother. Dropping deeper and deeper into this powerful trance, she heard the words coming from her lips, "Turn this rabbit back into my brother. Turn this rabbit back into my brother. Turn this rabbit back into my brother." But instead of sounding like the voice of a young girl, it became the voice of a Crone or Wise Woman. People in the audience heard a strange other worldly hypnotic voice uttering the ancient words, "Abracadabra," sending shivers down their spines. And although they were familiar with the word, they all heard it as if they were hearing it for the first time in their lives.

And before their very eyes, the rabbit transformed back into a boy.

"So now you have heard my story," said the Magician sitting in the parlor with his prospective students. The young man and young woman who were sitting, listening, spellbound by the magician's tale, looked around the room, remembering where they were. The magician, looking deeply into their eyes, said, "If you are here to learn the magic of The Great Maltoni, the theatrical tricks, the pretentious displays and the slick appearance, you have come to the wrong place. But if you would like to learn the magic of the sister, the magic of wonder, of love, of going deep within ourselves and of empowering others, then I am here at your service."

This story with many embellishments is based on a story we first heard from Susan Pitzele, a friend from our early days of NLP.

Introduction

There have been many NLP books written over the years discussing the history of Neuro-Linguistic Programming, its basic skills, its advanced techniques and the people who have contributed to the field. There are also many varied opinions, understandings and misunderstandings of NLP circulating the Internet. Having taught, practiced and lived Neuro-Linguistic Programming since we began our NLP studies in the early 1980s, we decided it's time to present both our version and our vision of NLP.

For us, NLP is about being effective communicators and influencing with integrity. It is about taking responsibility for the impact we have on others as well as our selves. And it is about recognizing how we limit our potential and can discover choices we did not know we had available. NLP has been and continues to be a cutting edge human technology that produces powerful long lasting changes in the people who have studied it or have worked with someone who has. And it is transforming the lives of people all over the world.

The first book written by Richard Bandler and John Grinder, the developers of NLP, was <u>The Structure of Magic</u>. The word "magic" conjures up all sorts of associations: enchantment, wizardry, tricks, fascination and glamour as well as skill, expertise and talent.

These early developers sought out the therapeutic "wizards" of their time: Fritz Perls, developer of Gestalt Therapy; Virginia Satir, leading family therapist; and Milton H. Erickson, developer of a unique style of hypnosis known today as Ericksonian Hypnosis. Bandler and Grinder's goal was not to learn "why" their methods worked, but to learn "how" they did their "magic."

While each of these therapists had their own perspectives, theories and methods, they all shared a common purpose, which was to help people actualize their potential as human beings. And all were effective at producing results. The "magic" they employed was used to heal past wounds and help people live emotionally healthy lives. They recognized that we are each under the spells (the illusions) of our society, our culture, our family and the institutions we live in. They wanted to help people break free of those illusions, not control them with more spells. NLP is about dispelling old self-limiting notions about who we are and what we are capable of thinking, feeling and accomplishing.

"Our" story is a story of two individuals who met through NLP, fell in love, embraced the ideas of NLP, created a center in New York City for learning NLP and Ericksonian Hypnosis and decided after 30 years to write a book in an attempt to distill our experiences into a manageable and useful format. We are Rachel Hott, PhD, and Steven Leeds, L.M.H.C., co-founders and co-directors of The NLP Center of New York.

We met in 1981 at the New York Training Institute for NLP, married in 1984 and started The NLP Center of New York in 1986. Since that time, we have raised two children while continuing to grow as individuals and as a couple, taught NLP and Hypnosis to thousands people from all over the world, provided training for small and large corporations and maintained a private practice working with individuals and couples. Steven is a Licensed Mental Health Counselor, with a Master's Degree in Education and another in Humanistic and Transpersonal Counseling Psychology. Rachel, who has her PhD in Clinical Psychology, is a licensed Clinical Psychologist. She also holds a Master's degree in Dance/Movement Therapy. As a team we bring together our individual specializations and have integrated our experiences in psychology, spirituality, education and business into our teaching.

The NLP Center of New York has been like a child and our participants have become like family. We know that effective communication is essential for healthy couples, functional families and thriving businesses. We are perpetual learners, searching for new ways to improve our personal and professional communication, building upon and going beyond the NLP model and teaching from our experience. Recently, as we practiced Bikram Yoga (a form of hot yoga that we have both been doing regularly since 2006,) our yoga teacher referred to us as, "The Power Couple." But we like to think of ourselves as an "empowering couple." We believe that if we are going to teach people how to be excellent, we need to model it in our own lives. Our dedication to our relationship, our family, and The NLP Center of New York is a part of our commitment to help ourselves and others learn to live life fully and develop our greatest potential.

Our goal in writing this book is to guide you through each part of our NLP Coach Practitioner Certification Training for both professional development and personal transformation. While coaches, psychotherapists, body workers and other health care professionals frequently attend this training, so do business professionals, artists, lawyers, educators, IT workers and anyone else seeking to enhance their communication skills and learn new empowering abilities and techniques. We would like to be your guides to learning NLP and discovering better ways to live a happier and more fulfilling life.

As you read this book, we suggest that you maximize its benefits by periodically pausing to reflect and "try on" the suggested practice exercises.

Whether you are a newcomer to NLP or someone with prior NLP knowledge, we hope you will find it to be as meaningful and valuable an experience as we have.

CHAPTER 1

NLP: Now Let's Play

"It's not what you know, not even who you know; it's how you know."
-Steven Leeds

Do you think you know what NLP is all about? That's what *you* think. And that's what NLP is all about. It is about "What you think and how you think it."

Most attempts to succinctly define NLP fall short of the mark. While we have yet to find one definitive definition, we do have some useful ones. Here are a few.

Neuro-Linguistic Programming (NLP) is a model of communication and change.

NLP is a model about influencing our own thoughts, feelings and behaviors.

NLP is a model about influencing other people's thoughts, feelings and behaviors.

NLP is a model of models. It is a modeling process.

NLP is the study of the structure of subjective experience.

The last definition comes from the title of the book, NLP Volume I: The Study of the Structure of Subjective Experience by Bandler, Dilts, Delozier and Grinder. NLP essentially concerns itself with discovering the structure of consciousness or that of our subjective experience. There is an objective world "out there" that we know only through our senses. And there is our subjective perception of the world that contains the meaning we give it.

NLP is not concerned with studying objective reality; we are interested in perceived meaning and its influence on both subjective and objective reality. For example, if someone steps on your toe and you perceive it as a deliberate attempt to cause you pain, your reaction might be to become angry and aggressive, resulting in a fight. But if you perceive it as "an accident" with no ill intent, you might only feel the sensation of pain. In other words, "how" we perceive things (the meaning we make) influences our emotions, our actions and the responses we get from others.

Using NLP, we learn "how" to listen to verbal and non-verbal language patterns so we can recognize how other people understand the world and how it is uniquely different from our own. In this way we can truly understand others and in understanding them, we begin to understand ourselves. With this awareness, we can influence and transform the way we think and how others think.

In 1975 when NLP developers were exploring these concepts, computers were so large they filled an entire room. Since that time period, just as computer technology has changed drastically, we have been refining the NLP skills and processes, making them more compact, more user friendly and more accessible. NLP provides us with simple yet powerful tools that we can use to "update" our existing neuro-linguistic programs and thereby give us access to new possibilities.

One more definition of NLP that we like to use is "Now Let's Play."

So let's get started.

CHAPTER 2

Bold Characters: Our NLP Journey

"When you come to a fork in the road, take it."
-Yogi Berra

There are moments in our life whose significance can only be seen when looking back.

It was 1981. Rachel Hott was helping non-verbal communication researcher Martha Davis organize her bookshelf, when a book with a colorful Peter Max-like cover got her attention. It was Frogs into Princes by Bandler and Grinder. Yes, she read it for its cover. She read the book and got hooked on NLP. She remembered having seen a flier for an NLP workshop in New York City the year before, so she "called information" to get the only NLP phone number in NYC. Upon enrolling in her first NLP workshop, she was struck by how much fun she could have learning this powerful transformational model.

Two years earlier, Steven Leeds was studying for a master's degree in psychology through the New England Center for Wholistic Education under the mentorship of Jack Canfield. At the time Jack, who is now one of America's leading authorities on creating success and personal fulfillment, was director of the center located in Amherst, Mass. Knowing Steven's interests, Jack suggested that he read The Structure of Magic by Richard Bandler and John Grinder. Steven and his buddy, Bruce Gill, who was also studying at the center, read it and spent hours together deciphering and practicing the linguistic tools known as the Meta Model. The following year, he saw a small ad printed in the New York Times, advertising an NLP Practitioner Training in New York City, where he could get to train with Bandler and Grinder. The next month he enrolled in the course. His final paper was on the effectiveness of NLP.

The rest is our history.

Rachel and Steven found their way to the New York Training Institute for NLP in Manhattan, where they met at a Metaphor Workshop led by NLP developer David Gordon. In 1986, they founded The NLP Center of New York where they have been co-directors and co-trainers, as well as psychotherapists, hypnotherapists and coaches.

About Rachel Hott

Prior to learning NLP, I was working for the American Management Association (AMA) as a non-verbal and verbal communication coder. I had already received a Master's Degree in Dance Movement Therapy and was trained to observe non-verbal behavior. My job was to observe managers behind a screen where they would do role plays and knowingly have a video camera record their interactions. The coding was based on a book called Management Competency, by Rick Boyatz. I was trained to observe and listen to the participants' interactions and rate them according to the 18 competencies method. Fortunately for me, when that program ended, AMA started an NLP course titled, *Building Better Working Relationships*. I was in the right place at the right time. In 1984, I began working as a professional trainer for the AMA and would lead three-day NLP courses for the next 10 years in New York City, Chicago, Atlanta and Washington, DC. In addition to leading the NLP courses for AMA, I also led the Achieving Professional Excellence classes that were designed by Jack Canfield, with whom I had been trained in 1994 and 1995 in his Self-Esteem workshops.

In the Achieving Professional Excellence classes we worked on setting goals. At this time in 1995, I was aware that I had a personal goal that I had not yet achieved. That was the goal to obtain my PhD in Clinical Psychology. I was aware that I was leading people in our NLP training and in the AMA training towards achieving their outcomes, but I was not doing the same for myself. So in 1997 I began studying for my PhD in Clinical Psychology at The Union Institute. By 2004 I had my New York

State license. Also in 1997, I had another challenge, one I had not chosen. I was diagnosed with breast cancer. Fortunately I was able to use my NLP skills during my chemotherapy and radiation treatments. I will share more of that in the chapters about being resourceful.

My NLP adventure began in 1981 with three workshops; *Metaphors* with David Gordon, *Fabric of Reality* with Anne Linden and *Hypnosis* with Robert Dilts. Next I began my NLP Practitioner Certification Training, followed by a one year NLP Master Practitioner Certification Training and a two-year NLP Trainer Training. Between 1996 and 2006, I did additional training with both Stephen Gilligan and The Milton Erickson Foundation.

In 1986, Steven and I decided to create our own NLP training center. At that time our advertising was all phone calls and bulk mailing. We rented a small office overlooking Washington Square Park and when that got too small, we started renting space from the Isadora Duncan studio that gave us the experience of nice open indoor and outdoor spaces. After renting an apartment in the East Village, where our students worked in each room including the kitchen, we found our current location at 24 E. 12th St. I find that helping others to unlock their potential continues to move me to be committed to my clients and students.

About Steven Leeds

"When I went to school, it was right after the Sixties and before this general wave of practical purposefulness had set in. Now students aren't even thinking in idealistic terms, or at least nowhere near as much. They certainly are not letting any of the philosophical issues of the day take up too much of their time as they study their business majors. The idealistic wind of the Sixties was still at our backs, though, and most of the people I know who are my age have that ingrained in them forever."

-Steve Jobs from a 1985 Playboy interview

During the sixties and seventies I was seeking to "find myself." I was on a personal quest looking for the path to "enlightenment." Although I had never travelled to India, followed a "guru" or committed to a specific spiritual path, I did study many spiritual and psychological disciplines including meditation, Tai Chi, Buddhism, Taoism, Gestalt therapy, transactional analysis, psychosynthesis and family therapy. The first of my many transformative training experiences took place in 1973 when I enrolled in est (Erhard Seminar Training), an organization that eventually became Landmark Forum.

That same year, I graduated from Queens College where I majored in mathematics and began teaching math at a junior high school in Forest Hills. A few year later I found a position working as a math teacher at PM High School, a New York City alternative school in downtown Brooklyn, whose students were comprised entirely of high school dropouts who dropped back in. Most of them worked in the morning and came to school in the late afternoon and evening. I loved working there. The staff was excellent – creative, alternative and deeply committed to their students. While I loved math, I did not love teaching long division, adding fractions with different denominators or solving for x, which my favorite college teacher Dr. Metas referred to as "pencil pushing" back when we used pencils. The school gave me the incredible opportunity to create a course in which I could apply all of the transformational tools and skills I was learning. But while I loved working there and found it incredibly challenging and rewarding, I was still searching for something different.

Richard Bandler and John Grinder created NLP in the mid 1970s. A few years later in New York City, Anne Linden founded the New York Training Institute of NLP where she and her partner, Dr. Frank Stass, organized an NLP Practitioner Certification Training in Soho, NY. So began my studies with John Grinder, Richard Bandler, Robert Dilts and David Gordon. I was excited to be a part of an exciting new field that opened up a world of possibilities. By employing these new NLP skills with the alternative high school students, I developed the confidence and competences that would help me to take my next professional steps – working with people of all ages and all cultures, helping them become aware of their limiting beliefs and getting them to actualize their fullest potential.

After completing my NLP and Hypnosis training at the New York Institute, I started working there as a psychotherapist and trainer. That's when I had the fortune to meet and fall in love with my coauthor Rachel Hott. Since that time, in my roles as NLP trainer, coach, psychotherapist, hypnotherapist, business owner, husband and parent, I have developed a profound understanding of how people think, feel and act, consciously and unconsciously. And each day, I do what I can do to use my knowledge and experience to make a difference.

CHAPTER 3

Hidden Depths: How learning NLP is Like Learning SCUBA Diving

"The best way to observe a fish is to be a fish."
-Jacques Yves Cousteau

When I (S.L.) received my SCUBA diving certification in the 1980s, I completed four distinct learning phases. First I needed to read and memorize some very important information, like the physics of breathing compressed air, calculating the maximum time we can spend underwater at specific depths, and how fast we can ascend without getting the bends. Then I needed to "immerse" myself by practicing in the controlled environment of a swimming pool, learning how to attach the regulator to the tank, to breath underwater, and handle things like clearing my mask with air if it accidentally fills with water. Next, I went to the Rockaways to do a shore dive. And finally, I did a boat dive a few miles off the Jersey shore, where I finally got to do a backflip into the cold choppy ocean waters.

Having completed each of these four stages of my certification, I was prepared to safely explore an awesome underwater world and enjoy many amazing adventures.

Learning NLP also happens in these four distinct segments. First there is gathering the information about NLP: its language, definitions, underlying presuppositions, skills, and techniques. Then there is having the direct experience, watching and listening to NLP demonstrations, engaging in dynamic interactive exercises both as guide and explorer, making lots of mistakes and being part of an NLP learning community. Next, there is finding and creating opportunities in our lives where we get to put into practice the skills and techniques before returning to the training environment to discuss what worked, what didn't work and receive meaningful feedback from seasoned trainers. Finally, there is our final testing weekend, where participants are placed in challenging situations in both simulated roles plays and real life situations where they get to demonstrate what they have learned.

This book will provide the NLP "information" that we teach in our Level I NLP Practitioner Coach Certification Training. The chapters of this book are consistent with the flow of the training and follow the guidelines of the International Association of NLP (IANLP). We will be introducing you to the NLP attitude, concepts, life skills and techniques that are part of becoming an effective communicator, resourceful human being and successful coach.

Although there are no prerequisites or degree requirements for reading this book or taking the NLP training, there is one essential element that will determine how successful you are in learning and practicing NLP. That ingredient is developing and maintaining an attitude of "wonder and curiosity." Doing NLP requires this ability to remain curious when you do not understand, when the response you are getting is not the one you expected, when you become confused or when you are facing a challenging situation. Milton Erickson, one of the geniuses who Richard Bandler and John Grinder modeled, often began his sentences with, "I wonder" or "I am curious" or "I don't know." He was so full of wonder and curiosity, especially when what he was doing wasn't working. While we suggest maintaining this frame of mind, we realize how easy it can be to lose it. Losing curiosity in and of itself is not the problem as long as we recognize that we have lost it and know how to find it again.

Through NLP, people learn how to influence their thought patterns, feeling states and external behaviors. In reading this book, you will have opportunities to work on making changes in the way you think, feel and act. Take small incremental steps. Many people want to work on their most serious issues first. This is a mistake. We may be born to run, but first we must learn to walk. And we do not learn to SCUBA dive by suiting up and jumping into the ocean. In our training, participants are carefully guided through a sequence of steps, building their perceptions, developing flexibility and becoming more secure with their skills so that they can start working on the "heavier" issues.

In our training, as in this book, we refer to the people who are leading the exercises or techniques as "coaches" or "guides" and the students who are working on their issues as "clients" or "explorers." Throughout the book, we will be sharing client and student stories from our psychotherapy/coaching practice and our NLP training. All names have been changed to maintain confidentiality. Between the two of us we have logged in hundreds of thousands of hours exploring human consciousness. The more we have practiced, the more we have been richly rewarded. We wish the same for you.

So, let's get started.

CHAPTER 4

NLP Presuppositions: How To Think Like an NLP Master

"Man often becomes what he believes himself to be. If I keep on saying to myself that I cannot do a certain thing, it is possible that I may end by really becoming incapable of doing it. On the contrary, if I have the belief that I can do it, I shall surely acquire the capacity to do it even if I may not have it at the beginning."
-Mahatma Gandhi

To understand any model, you must first know its underlying assumptions. The NLP Basic Presuppositions presented in this chapter lay the groundwork for everything that will follow. You do not have to believe them. But to learn the NLP Model and to get the results described in this book, you do need to begin by "acting as if" they are true.

As NLP practitioners, we are not interested in arriving at or claiming knowledge of some Ultimate Truth; we are interested in what is possible for each individual. By inviting people to "try on" the NLP Presuppositions, we have helped thousands to go beyond their perceived limitations. We now ask you to see for yourself how they will make a difference in the way you perceive the world and in the rewarding results you get.

To know how an NLP master thinks, you will need to understand his/her underlying assumptions. Implementing an NLP technique without understanding the NLP Presuppositions is like playing a sport without knowing the rules. When traveling to a foreign country, we inevitably encounter some very different cultural beliefs and values. If we don't recognize these distinctions, we will become confused and a series of miscommunications will follow.

Entering into an NLP classroom is a bit like stepping into another world, so learning the NLP presuppositions will prepare you for the journey. But if you take these presuppositions as written in stone as universal truths, then you run the risk of becoming a fundamentalist – rigid, defensive and thinking you know what's best or right. Only by remembering that they are useful assumptions will they promote increased flexibility, openness to change and enhanced communication.

As we previously indicated, NLP was first developed by modeling the excellence demonstrated by leaders in the field of psychology and interpersonal communication, Milton Erickson, Fritz Perls, Virginia Satir and Gregory Bateson. These NLP Presuppositions come from the beliefs they held and the methods they used. We invite you to "step into" each one of the following presuppositions and consider how the world looks, sounds and feels when you do.

The NLP Presuppositions

I. The Meaning of Your Communication is the Response you Get-No Matter What Your Intentions

According to this presupposition, the "meaning" of our communication is all about how the other person responds to us. If the other person is insulted, then that is the meaning of our communication. If the other person becomes delighted or inspired, then that is the meaning of our communication.

It we are typing on a computer keyboard and aiming to hit the letter "z" but instead hit the key to the right, then "x" is the meaning of our communication. While teaching in Europe and typing on the computers there, I (S.L.) discovered that every time I went to hit the "z" key, a "y" appeared on the screen. After awhile I realized that the European keyboard had the "x" and "y" keys reversed. Interpersonal communication works the same way. It involves the realization that every person we meet has his/her internal keyboard configured differently. Our ability to figure that out is the "key" to effective communication.

A common response to the computer-key reversal, when you are not using this presupposition, is to blame the foreign keyboard, thinking that it is broken, that something is wrong with it or that it's not working properly. Or we can blame ourselves, thinking that we are the problem. Of course, we can also fault the "foreigners" who built it.

Of course, a computer doesn't have a will of its own (at least, not yet). So let's leave the metaphor and return to human interactions. When we do, we see another person who is responsible for his/her part. So while we are not suggesting that we take responsibility for the other person's behavior, we are proposing taking full responsibility for ours, since it is really the only thing that we can directly do something about. But we caution you here. Responsibility, as we are defining it, is not about blaming or feeling guilty. It is about accepting the response you are getting while generating other ways to get the response you are looking for. This is the idea behind this presupposition.

When we communicate, we often we get the response we're looking for, as when a comedian gets laughs or a storyteller inspires wonder. But there are times when a comedian gets silence or a storyteller elicits boredom. The best comedians and storytellers are excellent communicators who pay close attention to the responses they are getting. If a response doesn't match what they are looking for, they recognize it and use their flexibility to modify what they're doing until they get the response they want. While this flexibility can come from being well prepared - having practiced their skills for many hours, days, months or years - it must also come from their ability to think on their feet and be spontaneous.

What if you tell a joke and one person laughs and another gets angry? Does that mean the meaning of your communication is different for each person? Yes. It does. To be effective means to be responsive to each individual.

Milton Erickson looked forward to the times when he was working with a client and the technique he usually used didn't work. He remained incredibly curious. And while in this state of wonder, he gathered more information, varying his approach until he got the intended response.

Resistance is a statement about the inflexibility of the communicator.

When I (S.L.), started learning NLP in the 1980s, I was also working as a mathematics teacher at an alternative high school in Brooklyn, New York. I had a student, Maritza, who was doing outstanding work. But when I attempted to pay her a compliment she responded, "I am a terrible math student." Even after I tried to prove her excellence by quoting her test scores, she continued to protest and again resisted the complement. At this point, it was clear that the meaning of my communication was not matching my intended communication. Recognizing that I was becoming frustrated, I shifted my state of mind to one of curiosity and found myself saying to Maritza in a calm soft voice, "For someone who considers herself to be a terrible math student (LONG PAUSE), you are doing really, really well." A big smile appeared on her face. "Thank you," she responded, as she drew in a deep breath along with the compliment. To get the response I wanted, I had listened attentively for what was true for *her*. Instead of disagreeing, I joined Maritza's experience by accepting her presupposition as "her" truth and leading her to a place where she could, in turn, accept what I was saying. (I also realized that further work might be required for her to let go of her self-limiting belief and create a more positive opinion of herself.)

The inherent beauty of this presupposition is in its effective and efficient "guilt free" approach that develops greater flexibility of behavior resulting in the response we want. And even when we are not getting the response we want, we still benefit. The presupposition gets us to be creative, by coming up with new solutions. In the process we get to build a vast repertoire of stored possibilities for future use. For NLP Practitioners, it is a new definition of responsibility that is light, energizing and liberating – not heavy, pressurized and blameful. Responsibility in communication is not seen as a burden, but as an empowering core value that gives us the opportunity to transform relationships.

But even if you choose to adopt this presupposition, not everybody will. Which means, "Be prepared to be blamed" by people unaware of or unwilling to take responsibility. When they do, you can either join them in the "blame frame" or you can maintain an NLP perspective. In other words, you are either going to revert back into a "stuck state" or stay resourceful. And in doing the latter, you will be modeling a healthy way of communicating. But be forewarned, most people don't like to be left alone in the blame frame. They will try to pull you in. And some can be very persuasive. Then again, maybe you can persuade them.

What if we do attempt to have another person accept what we have found to be a very useful presupposition and he/she still declines, resists or refuses? If he/she does, then his/her behavior is the meaning of our communication and we can explore other ways of communicating. Some of us can become so enamored with our own "useful" maps, that we might find ourselves "pushing" our ideas on others. When this happens, we frequently stop listening while the other person feels ignored. People have the choice to reject our premises. Understanding their choice will contribute to making you a more effective communicator.

If you ever find yourself introducing a wonderful, excellent, positive, healthy idea to someone and getting frustrated and angry when they resist, then you know it's time to take on this presupposition. You will be amazed at how much more influential you'll become – not to mention how much better you'll feel – when you adopt this presupposition and model it for others.

NLP Momentary Practice
How do you learn this approach if it's not something you do automatically? Here's one way to practice with another person when you get an unintended response, e.g. hurt feelings. First, you have to know what response you are after. The question an NLP practitioner asks is, "What is my outcome?" Let the other person know you can see that they have been hurt. And pause. Let him/her know that you did not intend to hurt him/her. Since you did nothing "wrong," you need not defend yourself. And be compassionate.

II. There is No Such Thing As Failure, only Feedback

"The Journey is the Reward"
-Steve Jobs

When a child takes his/her first step, it is the result of months of movements that include pulling, pushing, turning, lifting, rolling, sitting, falling, balancing and standing. He/she has spent much more time "failing" to walk than "succeeding." But it does not matter; the ideas of success and failure do not exist for him/her. He/she is learning to walk, receiving feedback all along the way. And when he/she finally takes his/her first step, he/she doesn't need to celebrate his/her success (maybe his/her parents do). He/she also did not worry along the way about failing. For the child, there is no such thing failure; there is only feedback. It's called learning.

As adults, we "learn" about the existence of success and failure and we learn to associate failure with all sorts of bad feelings. As a consequence, we spend quite some time worrying about failing and trying to avoid it. If we don't paralyze ourselves in the process, we may still move with a fear of being punished, criticized or abused for making a mistake. And if we are "successful" in avoiding these failures by procrastinating, distracting ourselves or being disorganized, we miss out on the valuable feedback that we need to achieve our goals. Even if we reach our goals in spite of it, it certainly does not make for a very enjoyable journey.

As human beings, we are designed to go through a natural learning process called trial and error. We succeed when we pay attention to the feedback. But if we start interpreting errors as personal failure, then we interfere with this process. And without feedback, we will continue to make the same mistakes over and over. A variation of this presupposition is there is no such thing as failure, only not enough time. We have not failed. We have just not yet succeeded.

In the mid-1980's, I (R.H.) worked for the American Management Association (AMA) as a trainer for the course entitled *Building Better Work Relationships.* One day I was given constructive criticism about my presentational style. Although it was meant to be constructive I felt criticized and worried that my job would be in jeopardy. Then I realized that it was an opportunity for me to learn about training the way the AMA wanted. Even though it was a long time ago, I still remember sitting with the manager at the chalkboard, learning about clear applications for the managers attending the course. If I hadn't received that feedback I would not be the highly experienced and excellent trainer that I am today.

Instead of thinking, "I failed," I turned it around and asked myself, "What is the feedback?" "What I am learning right now?" "How can I do things differently?"

These experiences can happen at our job if we don't get the project we wanted or the promotion we expected. They can happen with someone we just started dating and learn that he/she isn't interested in continuing the relationship. Although we can't always get the promotion or the potential date, we can always change our attitude.

Some people think that we are recommending a cavalier attitude. We are not. When something we do or say results in someone getting hurt, we can feel remorse and be compassionate without beating ourselves up and feeling guilty.

As you look at and listen to the people you are communicating with you are getting continuous feedback from their eyes, their facial expressions and body posture, their breathing, their words, their voice, etc. And this feedback is the meaning of your communication. If you are not getting the response you want, you have not yet succeeded.

When Thomas Edison was asked if he felt like a failure and ready to give up, he replied, *"Young man, why would I feel like a failure? And why would I ever give up? I now know definitively over 9,000 ways that an electric light bulb will not work. Success is almost in my grasp."* And after over 10,000 attempts, Edison invented the light bulb.

NLP Momentary Practice

Take a moment and reflect on this past year. As you do, think about something you have labeled as a failure, a screw up or a huge mistake. If you cannot think of one, congratulations, you are already using this NLP presupposition. As you think about that memory, ask yourself, "What did I learn?" If and only if you have waited at least 60 seconds and no answer has arrived, then ask, "If there was something valuable to learn from the experience, what might it be?" If you keep a journal, write down what you learned so that it will be useful in the year to come. If not, just sleep on it. We ask that you continue to imagine what it will be like to look back at things you once considered to be a failure and think of it now as a valuable learning experience that will be an asset in the future.

As we say in our NLP universe, "Live long and get lots of feedback."

III. Each of Us Has the Resources We Need to Meet our Next Developmental Challenge

"In the depth of winter, I finally learned that within me there lay an invincible summer."
-Albert Camus

When we are in a resourceful state, we have access to the many qualities and attributes that we need to fully realize our potential, achieve the goal we set and meet the challenges we are facing. These inner resources improve our effectiveness. What comes to your mind, when you think of the qualities you possess, the attributes you admire in others or the strengths you want to develop? Patience? Inner strength? Confidence? Love? Courage? Resilience? Trust? Centeredness? Calm? Acceptance? Determination? Believing in your self? Curiosity? Compassion? Humor? All of these are all examples of Inner Resources. You can think of resources as mental, emotional or spiritual states that allow you to think, feel and act in ways that are empowering.

This presupposition is suggesting that no matter who you are and where you are, you can develop and activate these inner resources. Many of us do not believe we have or can develop these inner resources. Sometimes all it takes is remembering a time when you have already experienced them or acting as if you have them now. Later on in the book we will refer to the ability to model other people as another way of gaining access to these resources. We will also discuss how to break down the resource as we may do with a chemical compound and re-experience each of the "elemental resources." For example, if you need self-love, but don't believe you have ever had it, you may think about what elements make up self-love, perhaps "confidence, self-acceptance and compassion." This technique, which you will be learning in

Chapter 22, is called Chunking Resources. With it you will learn how to put these elemental resources together to create a more powerful resource.

We once went to the New Age Health Spa, in Neversink, NY, for a weekend getaway. After arriving, Steven felt like he had signed up for the wrong weekend. All the meals came in measured portions and the atmosphere was slowed down to the slightest heartbeat. However, he became very excited when he discovered that there was a ropes course. We signed up and discovered that this ropes course concluded with standing atop a telephone pole (there was a harness), and reaching for a brass ring. Steven was happy with this turn of events, but I (R.H.) had some trepidation. I didn't believe that I had the adequate upper body strength needed to manage the climb. As we were first hoisted onto a rope fence, I was convinced that I was going to have a difficult time. While on the platform, waiting my turn to stand on the tip of the telephone pole I found myself becoming frightened. I asked myself what resource did I need and "courage" came to mind.

At that moment I began to cry because I had felt that I had used up my courage during my breast cancer health crisis. I had gone through a lumpectomy, chemotherapy and radiation. I had been courageous throughout. But now I felt I had used up all of my courage. At that moment, I thought about this presupposition of having all of the resources and I imagined that my inner resources (unlike natural resources) were limitless and would not be depleted. I imagined a vast well within myself containing all the courage that I needed and reconnected to courageousness. Then I jumped.

Although I did not reach the brass ring, I found that by successfully reconnecting to the belief that I had all the resources within, I had grasped something far more valuable.

NLP Momentary Practice

Identify a situation coming up in the near future and ask yourself what resource you will need. Now think of a time when you had that resource and spend some time reliving that memory, now. If stepping into a memory and reliving it is something you do naturally, this task will be easy for you to do. If not, it is a skill that you can learn to master. You can read about it in Chapter 21 on "Association and Disassociation." Isn't it nice to know that we can learn to activate the resources that exist within?

IV. Every Behavior is Motivated By a Positive Intention

When we receive calls for individual psychotherapy, potential clients often ask if we can help them can get rid of a problem associated with a negative thought pattern or an unwanted behavior. These include things like cigarette smoking, overeating, substance abuse, being late, procrastination, shyness, worrying, anxiety, "negative" self-talk, etc. The request usually sounds reasonable. Why would anyone want to be anxious, repeat a bad habit or engage in negative self-talk?

People often call these unwanted behaviors self-sabotaging, self-destructive, negative and bad. They also refer to these behaviors as lazy, crazy, stupid, childish, irrational, etc. They are quick to point out the negative consequences of the behavior, which can vary from not accomplishing what they set out to accomplish to being overweight, feeling upset, hurting others, becoming untrustworthy, wasting time, pushing other people away, etc. When we hear these statements, we introduce the idea of the "positive intention" and how it is different and distinct from its "negative consequences."

For example, smoking cigarettes may cause cancer, but the intention may be to relax, to fit in with one's peers or to rebel (to be an individual). A critical voice may make us feel incapable or unworthy, but its intention may be to motivate us or to learn new things.

A client came in to work on her weight issues. She wanted to stop overeating at night. When asked what the positive intention of continuing to eat after she was no longer hungry, her unconscious responded, "to be nurtured." For another person, the same behavior of overeating at night could have the positive intention "to feel safe." People are often pleasantly surprised and pleased to discover the positive intention. In Chapter 23, in the reframing section, we will discuss techniques to help transform these problems.

From Breakout to Breakthrough

In our early dating relationship, my (R.H.) face was breaking out with acne. Of course I was 26 and devastated that my face would have not only one but several pimples. Steven asked me what was the positive intention of the pimples. Although it was an unusual question to be asking about pimples, I decided to take a moment and imagine becoming the part responsible for breaking out and the answer I received was that it got me attention. When my face broke out I couldn't hide. I was being seen and receiving attention. Steven lovingly said, "Well, how about if I give you even more attention when you are not breaking out." I said that would be great. Of course it seemed like magic when my face cleared up. But I couldn't always rely on someone else giving me attention, so I had to find other ways to ask for attention or to give it to myself. It was within my control to learn new ways to give myself attention even when my face was clear. Over these 30 years that I have been involved in NLP, a pimple occasionally erupts. I now use it as an opportunity to check in with myself to make sure I am getting the attention I deserve and remind myself to take better care of myself when that occurs.

This presupposition about positive intention can often be confusing and require clarification. Trainees often bring up the most horrific crimes and ask what could the possible positive intention be. It may be difficult to encounter violence and see anything good about it. When we use the phrase, "positive intention" we are not implying that the behavior is "good." We are saying that it has a purpose for the individual (protection, safety, motivation, fun, survival, etc.) but in fact might not actually produce any useful results and on the contrary can in many cases be harmful.

When we think of our own behaviors as having a purpose, we can be more accepting and become more curious and creative in developing alternatives that will better satisfy the intention.

NLP Momentary Practice

Identify something you do that you want to stop doing, but haven't. Ask yourself, "Am I open to there being a 'positive intention?'" If yes, ask yourself, "What is the positive intention?" and wait for an answer. Then ask yourself, "What other ways can I better satisfy the positive intention?" If, on the other hand, you are not open to there being a positive intention, ask yourself, "What is the positive intention of not being open?"

V. Every behavior (internal and external), every symptom and every communication is useful and meaningful in some way (in some context).

The question here is, "Where, when and with whom (in what context) would this behavior be useful and appropriate?" Take procrastination, for example. Procrastination is often perceived as a behavior that interferes with doing things that are important. Can you think of a time and place where delaying a decision and sleeping on it would be useful? There would be a lot fewer people in jail and a lot fewer suicides if people had just waited and given themselves time to think things through.

On the other hand, if we always did everything right away and never gave ourselves time to think things through, we could be accused of being impulsive or reckless. Can you think of a time and place where acting spontaneously without thinking would be useful? Imagine an improvisation comedy group only acting with forethought. Not funny!

All children behave. They just have no idea about context. You may have heard the terms "indoor and outdoor voices," when speaking with children. The indoor voice is the quiet voice you use "indoors" and the outdoor voice is the loud voice you can use "outdoors." The kids are being taught about context. This concept is quite different from the prevailing one passed down from generation to generation, where kids are told that are doing something "bad" or that they are being "bad". If you want to teach kids that they are bad, you punish them for being bad. If you want to teach them that every behavior is appropriate given some context, you teach them that there are consequences in life for doing a behavior that is not appropriate for a given context. It can also be quite lucrative to find the right context. Many a class clown has found a niche in stand up comedy.

We have some friends who are loud talkers and who frequently interrupt conversations. When they are eating out, their voices can be heard throughout the restaurant. More than once we have heard diners ask the host to move to a table further away. We could not exactly "hear" it. But it "appeared" that way. Take these same friends to a sporting event or a rock concert and their loud voices fit right in. Now it's fun.

Another example is anger. We have had people tell us that they do not want to get angry. They explain that it is negative and they want to eliminate it from their life. Most of us can think of times when we got angry and wished we hadn't. Now, think of a time when anger would be an appropriate and useful response.

On the train to Brindavan a Swami sits beside a common man who asks him if indeed he has attained self-mastery, as the name "Swami" implies.

"I have," says the Swami.
"And have you mastered anger?"
"I have."
"Do you mean to say that you have mastered anger?"
"I have."
"You mean you can control your anger?"
"I have."
"And you do not feel anger."
"I do not."
"Is this the truth, Swami?"
"It is."
After a silence the man asks again, "Do you really feel that you have controlled your anger?"
"I have, as I told you," the Swami answers.
"Then do you mean to say, you never feel anger, even-"
"You are going on and on – what do you want?" the Swami shouts.
"Are you a fool? When I have you –"
"Oh, Swami, this is anger. You have not mast –"

"Ah, but I have," the Swami interrupts. "Have you not heard about the abused snake? Let me tell you a story.

"On a path that went by a village in Bengal there lived a cobra who used to bite people on their way to worship at the temple there. As the incidents increased, everyone became fearful, and many refused to go to the temple. The Swami who was the master at the temple was aware of the problem and took it upon himself to put an end to it. Taking himself to where the snake dwelt, he used a mantra to call the snake to him and bring it into submission. The Swami then said to the snake that it was wrong to bite the people who walked along the path to worship and made him promise sincerely that he would never do it again. Soon it happened that upon the path a passerby saw the snake, and it made no move to bite him. Then it became known that the snake had somehow been made passive and people grew unafraid. It was not long before the village boys were dragging the poor snake along behind them as they ran laughing here and there. When the temple Swami passed that way again he called the snake to see if he had kept his promise. The snake humbly and miserably approached the Swami, who exclaimed, "You are bleeding. Tell me how this has come to be." The snake was near tears and blurted out that he had been abused ever since he was caused to make his promise to the Swami. "I told you not to bite," said the Swami, "but I did not tell you not to hiss.""
-Rolling Thunder by Doug Boyd

NLP Momentary Practice

Think about some annoying behavior that one of your family members or friends does often. Ask yourself, "In what context would this be appropriate." Imagine them doing the behavior in that context and evaluate the difference.

VI. The Map is not the Territory

There is reality. Then there is our map of reality.

We get to know reality through our senses. We perceive what is happening "out there" through our eyes, our ears, our skin, our nose and our taste buds. Our senses filter our perceptions. In addition to these perceptual filters, we have our individual filters that delete, distort and generalize our experiences. In other words, we construct "maps" of reality that give meaning to our experiences and to navigate our way around. It is the meaning that we give to the experience, not the experience itself, that determines how we respond to people and situations. It is our maps, not external reality that limits us.

Everything that we think, everything we read or write, everything that we hear or say is a representation of experience. All words, music, letters, numbers, images, symbols, dance, photos and movies are representations.

The study of NLP is the study of our maps, our subjective experience. By identifying and enriching our impoverished maps of the world, we can perceive more possibilities. And by being aware of these possibilities, we can better meet life's challenges. Alfred Korzybski, founder of General Semantics, who wrote the book Science and Sanity in 1945, coined the phrase, "The Map is Not the Territory". By making this distinction, we get to focus our attention on updating our "map of reality." It's like updating a computer operating system from an earlier version to a current version. A system (or map) is not good or bad. Any system is both useful as well as limited. Updating our maps expands their limitations and makes them more useful.

Some people follow the rule, "If it ain't broke, don't fix it." In NLP, we do not consider anyone to be broken. So we are not trying to fix anything. But when we find ourselves in an old pattern, using an outdated map, it might be time for an upgrade. The reason we do the same thing over and over again and expect different results is that we are still using the same old map. It's not insane; it's in vain. To change we need to continually recognize that our map is only a map and only by developing new maps can we grow and evolve and get different results.

Knowing this will also transform our interpersonal relationships. Rather than spending our time making our friends, family and colleagues wrong, we can learn about their map, how it is uniquely different from our own. Understanding another's map will make us more effective communicators. So when someone asks for our "support," we must first understand what he/she means by "support" and how he/she wants to be "supported." Only then can we respond effectively to what he/she is asking for.

Some other examples of "The Map is Not the Territory" are "The Menu is Not the Meal" and "Language is not Experience." Have you ever gone to a restaurant, looked at the menu and said, "That looks good, I think I will have some of that." What were you seeing? Was it words on the menu? Was it something you were picturing in your mind's eye? Maybe a memory of something you once ate. Whatever you were thinking about, it was not the actual food. And when you are served, does the food match what you imagined it to be. The food is the territory. Similarly language is not experience. Take the word "Elephant" spelled, E-L-E-P-H-A-N-T. It is not an "elephant." The spoken word or the written word is a representation or map of some experience.

We would like to conclude with an application for working with someone suffering from performance anxiety. A client makes the statement, "I get anxious whenever I have to speak in front of people." This is a statement reflecting his/her map of reality. To accept his/her map as a reality is to accept that this is something that "always" happens and that there is an expectation that it will continue to happen. But if we were to view it as an impoverished map, then we can do something to modify or update it. We can ask, "Has there ever been a time when you spoke in front of people and did not get anxious?" If the answer is "yes," we have begun to change his/her map to, "Sometimes I got anxious speaking in front of people and sometimes I did not." This could be followed by, "So in the past you sometimes got anxious when you spoke in front of a group (This is pacing his/her new map). How do you want to respond in the future when you are speaking in front of a group?" (This introduces a new map that offers the possibility that the future can be different from the past). A further question might be, "And what inner resources will allow you to consistently respond in this way?" (This map introduces the existence of inner resources and the belief that he/she will no longer feel anxious when speaking in front of group.) What we are attempting to do is expand his/her limiting map by introducing new ways of looking at things.

Each of the NLP Presuppositions introduced in this chapter is an example of a map that can be used to recognize more possibilities and enrich our experience.

NLP Momentary Practice 1

Pick a word that describes something that is important to you. Some examples may include, "success," "love," "fairness," "trust," etc. Over the course of the week, ask three people what they mean by that word, what does it mean to be a success, to be loving, etc. As they answer pay attention to how their way of thinking differs from your own. In this way, you will be learning about their maps as well as your own.

NLP Momentary Practice 2

If you were going to add your own presuppositions to this list, what would they be?

NLP Momentary Practice 3

Can you think of a time and place when one or more of the NLP Presuppositions would not be useful? If you can, you are really starting to think like an NLPer.

CHAPTER 5

No Problems: Only Solutions

"I Tell Them There's No Problem – Only Solutions."
-John Lennon

We make assumptions. Often these assumptions are communicated through language.

When I (S.L.) ask someone, "When will you be free for dinner?" I am assuming that they will be free to have dinner with me and that they want to have dinner with me. If I ask, "Do you want to have dinner with me?" these assumptions are not present.

If I ask, "What is your all-time favorite TV series?" I am assuming that you have watched TV for some time and that you have a clear favorite. Or if I think, "I have to start taking care of myself," I am assuming that I have not been taking care of myself and that it is something I "have to" do as opposed to something I "want to" do. These assumptions not only have a profound effect on how we think, feel and act, but also on the responses we get from others.

Many business communication trainers are fond of saying, "Do not assume (ass-u-me). Because it makes an 'ass' out of 'u' and 'me'." While the saying has been often repeated, it is not particularly useful or realistic. It's not about "not" assuming. It is about awareness and utilization. When we speak, it is useful to be aware of our assumptions and use them purposefully and strategically. For example, we ask our clients "What will it be like when you have made the change?" rather than asking "What would it be like if you could change?" We also pay careful attention when we listen to other people's presuppositions, so that we can better understand their model of the world and how it is distinctly different from our own. For example, if a client says, "I get anxious when I meet new people." We do not want to "buy in" to their assumption that they will continue to be anxious in the future, so we might respond by saying, "I understand that in the past you have experienced being uncomfortable when meeting new people. What do you want your experience to be when meeting new people in the future?"

Presuppositions in language lead people to think and feel negatively or positively? Do your questions inspire and motivate? Do they lead to creative solutions? Or do they perpetuate negative thinking and reinforce helplessness?

Do you focus on the Past or do you look to the Future? Let's explore the power of presuppositions with a simple exercise.

Take a moment and identify something that you want to change about yourself.

Here are some examples:

To learn a foreign language
To resolve an internal conflict
To be more focused
To be motivated
To stop smoking
To be more assertive
To trust your intuition

Have a pad of paper nearby or a writing tablet, because we will ask you to record your experience after the exercise.

Problem vs Outcome Frame Exercise

Select one thing that you want to change about yourself or something that you want to learn. When you have made the selection, ask yourself the questions from Part I (see below). Pause after each question and pay attention to your thoughts and feelings. Do not read the next question until you have finished answering.

Part I Questions
What's my problem?
Why can't I fix this problem?
What are my limitations?
What's wrong?
Who is to blame?
Whose fault is it?

Reflections:
Now ask yourself, "What am I experiencing right now?" What words or phrases capture your feelings or the state of mind you find yourself in? If this were a movie or a song, what would the title be? Write down the title of that experience and any additional words that describe your experience.

Important: Now take a few deep breaths and move your body around, and do the "NLP Shake." Basically you are breaking the state and getting ready for the second part of the exercise.

Go back to what you wanted to learn or change about yourself and ask yourself the questions from Part II (see below). Pause after each question and pay attention to where your thoughts and feelings go.

Part II Questions
How do I want to be different?
How will making this change affect my life?
What inner resources will I need to access in order to accomplish this?
Having made this change, how am I seeing differently?
Having made this change, how am I speaking differently?
Having made this change, how am I thinking?
Having made this change, how do I feel?

Now again ask yourself, "What am I experiencing right now?"
What words or phrases capture your feelings and state of mind? If this were a movie or a song, what would the title be? Write down the title of that experience and any additional words that describe your experience.

Compare the two sets. Typically our students have described the first set of questions with words like:

Negative
Feeling Bad
Heavy
Stuck
Overwhelmed
Constricted
Anxious
Depressed
Dark
Past

While the second set is often described with words like:

Positive
Expansive
Freedom
Possibilities
Lightness
Excitement
Opportunity
FutureCreative
Inspiration

Generally, the first set of questions takes people to a place that feels unpleasant and unproductive, while the second set takes people to a place that explores possibilities and is more conducive to finding solutions.

The state of mind evoked by the first set we call the "Problem Frame" and the one conjured up by the second set as the "Outcome" or "Solution Frame."

We have found that there are some people who feel more comfortable with the Problem Frame because it is more familiar, while the Outcome Frame can bring about uncertainty or fear of the unknown. They are of the belief "better the devil you know than the devil you don't." For them a better question may be, "What inner resources would allow you to be comfortable with 'not knowing'?"

Most people have heard the first set of questions repeated far more often than the second set, whether they have been spoken aloud or silently to themselves. If you suspect you are one of them, ask yourself, "What will it be like when the second set of questions becomes more familiar than the first?

Problems vs. Outcomes

The first set of questions emphasizes limitations, problems, blame, what's past and what is wrong. We call the first set of questions the "Problem Frame." We all make assumptions or presuppositions when communicating. The first question, "What is the problem?" presupposes that a problem exists, which for most people implies that there is something wrong. When people think of the thing they want to change as a problem, they generally feel badly. The problem frame has us look to the past, which is not necessarily where we will find the solution. It is predictable that using the presuppositions from the first set of questions (i.e. you have a problem, you are limited, you can't change, it's someone's fault, etc.) will create negative feelings. Although people asking these questions may have a positive intention, the meaning of their communication is usually a non-resourceful state.

The second set of questions we call the "Outcome Frame" or the "Solution Frame." These questions presuppose that you can and will change and that you have the resources you need to make the change. The results can vary from recognizing new possibilities to feeling inspired and uplifted.

The NLP model is oriented towards the future. But this does not mean we ignore the past. On the contrary, we carefully examine "how" we think of the past and learn how to look at it in a way that promotes healing and facilitates change. Benjamin Dover once said, "It is okay to look back at the past, just don't stare at it."

By becoming aware of the presuppositions contained in our questions as well as in our statements, we can chose the presuppositions that will get the responses we want. There was a student who told us that nobody at her office would help her, even when she asked. When we learned that she was asking questions like, "Why is it that you never have the time to help me?" or "Why can't you help?" we suggested that she ask her questions in a way that presupposed that people would help. So she began asking, "When can you be available to help me on this project?" or "When is a good time for you to lend me a hand?" This made a huge difference.

To communicate effectively and to achieve our goals, we need to know our outcome and use the presuppositions in our mind and in our language to get us there.

NLP Momentary Practice

1. Think about something you want to do that you are not doing. Ask yourself the "Outcome Frame" questions.

2. When interacting with others, notice if you are about to ask a "Problem Frame" question like, "What's wrong with you?" and replace it with an outcome question like "What do you want?" or "What would you like to happen?"

3. Identify the presuppositions in the following questions.

Why can't you just listen to me?
When would be a good time for you to talk?
Where did we go wrong?
What can we do to get ourselves back on track?
What's wrong with me?
How will I learn from this?
What did I do to deserve this?
What can I do to show you how much I love you?

CHAPTER 6

Inside Moves: How To Change The Way We Think Using Submodalities

"You only have control over three things in your life: the thoughts you think, the images you visualize, and the actions you take."
-Jack Canfield

Many years ago we heard a story about a cyclist traveling from France to Switzerland carrying a large sack over his shoulder. When he arrived at the border, the border guard looked at him suspiciously and told him to stop and get off his bike. The guard proceeded to open the sack and discovered that it was full of sand. As there was nothing illegal about bringing in sand, the cyclist was allowed to proceed on his journey. Two weeks later, the same man on a bike with a sack over his shoulder arrived at the border crossing. Again the guard checked the bag and only found more sand. For two months, every two weeks this ritual played out until, exasperated and at his wits end, the guard said to the cyclist, "Okay, I know there is something going on here." Then he led him into his office, took off his badge, placed it on his desk and said, "I want to speak frankly with you and off the record. And I promise I won't press charges against you, but please tell me what are you doing?" The cyclist seeing that he was sincere, smiled broadly and said, "I am smuggling bicycles."

As you will see, when our mind gets focused on one thing or looking for one thing, we do not see other things that are right in front of us. There is a wonderful video created by Christopher Chabris and Daniel Simons that beautifully illustrates this point. If you have not seen them, we suggest that you watch the videos at theinvisiblegorilla.com. If you have not seen the video, we do not want to spoil it for you.

There are many examples of this phenomenon. When I (S.L.) attended the World's Fair that took place in Queens, NY, from 1964-65, I visited the General Cigar's "Hall of Magic" Pavilion. Next to the structure they built a machine that lofted huge smoke rings high above the fair grounds. Part of their advertising was giving out buttons that read:

MEET ME
AT THE
THE SMOKE RING

Most people did not notice that the word "the" appeared twice. (They were also oblivious to the connection between smoking and cancer. It was just "smoke and mirrors.")

Now let's talk about other things that are right in front of us that we are not noticing.

First, we would like you to think of an animal.

How are you thinking of the animal? Do you have an image of the animal? Do you hear any animal sounds? Do you feel any feelings related to the animal?

Take a moment to describe to yourself what you are thinking or feeling. You might want to write it down.

In describing the animal, you probably described the type of animal, perhaps its name if it has one, its features, its behavior, the scenery or some other facts about the animal and its surroundings. We refer to this description as the "content."

But did you describe where you saw the animal (in front of you, to the right or left), whether the image was moving or still, two-dimensional (2D) or three-dimensional (3D), framed or panoramic, color or black and white, larger or smaller than life, close or far away? If you did, you probably already have some experience with NLP. This is a description of the "form."

The distinction here is "how" we think as opposed to "what" we think. When we get lost in the content, which is what we usually do, we do not notice the form. And as you shall see, this has some very significant ramifications, since it is the form that has a greater impact in our experience than the content does.

Now let's do an experiment. Think again of the animal. We will now ask you to change the form, making one change at a time. It is important to make one change at a time, because you might not like the results you get and may want to immediately reverse it to return to the prior experience. If this does not make sense, it will shortly.

If your original image was a still image, make it into a movie.
If your original image was a movie, make it into a still.
Stop and experience the difference.

If your image is panoramic (seeing through a wide angle lens), put it into a rectangular frame.
If your image is already in a frame, make it panoramic.
Stop and experience the difference.

If your image is 2D, make it 3D.
If your image is 3D, make it 2D.
Stop and experience the difference.

Are you seeing both yourself and the animal or just the animal?
If you are seeing both, move into your position and see the animal through your own eyes.
If you are already seeing the animal through your own eyes, move out of the picture and see both you and the animal from the outside.
Maybe you even want to see what it is like from the animal's perspective and step into its "shoes."
Stop and experience the difference.

See what happens when you make it brighter.
Then see what happens when you make it darker.
Stop and experience the difference.

Now move the image farther away.
Then bring the image closer.
Stop and experience the difference.

In each instance we are keeping the content the same, only changing the form.

How did making these changes affect your experience? Did your feelings change? Did the intensity change? Did the change make it feel more real and alive or less real? Did making one change result in other changes?

We call these distinctions "submodalities." And the ones that we are now "focusing" on are visual "submodalities."

Did you find some of the changes were not to your liking? Did you change them back to the way they were? Changing submodalities can put life into your experience or just as easily take it out. Making the image panoramic, moving and 3D as well as brighter, closer and larger usually intensifies the experience and makes it come alive while putting it into a frame, making it still and 2D as well as making it darker, moving it farther away and smaller will, in most cases, make it less emotional.

So if your animal is a grizzly bear, you might prefer to keep it as a photo that you are holding in your hand instead of being in the moving, 3D scene with it bearing down on you.

This also explains why you can tell the same story to two different people and one person will have a strong emotional reaction (either pleasant or unpleasant) while the other's reaction is neutral and unemotional. They may both be listening and picturing what you are describing, but how they are picturing it is quite different.

Reflecting on Visual Submodalities

Visual Submodalities:

Still and Moving
Framed and Panoramic
2D and 3D
Color and Black and White
Distance: Close and Far
Size: Large and Small
Perspective/Angle
Focus: Blurry and Sharp

Foreground and Background
Brightness: Light and Dark
Associated (in the experience) and Disassociated (outside the experience)
Location: Above and Below, Left and Right
Speed: Fast and Slow

Certainly "what" we think about (the content) impacts us. For example, thinking of a dolphin will usually produce a different response from thinking of an alligator. But how we think (the form) about it determines the intensity of the experience. So no matter what animal you chose, when you see it in 3D, moving, in color and panoramic, the effect will be quite differently from seeing it in 2D, still, in black and white and in a picture frame. As long as these submodalities are out of our conscious awareness, we will have no control over them. Bringing them into conscious awareness and learning how to alter them will have a profound and powerful effect on how we experience what we experience.

When thinking of an animal or thinking about any of the things we might ordinarily think about during the day, we typically do not consciously decide which submodalities we will use, but that does not mean we do not have a choice. With awareness comes choice. And with choice comes responsibility. "Flexibility" in NLP means flexing these mental muscles as well as the physical ones.

There is a story about two monks who belong to a special order where touching a woman is forbidden. Once day as they are walking down a country road after a torrential downpour, they come upon a young lady in distress. She is trying to navigate her way across the road that is filled with rainwater. One of the monks walks up to her and offers to help her across. His friend, watches in disbelief as he lifts her up and carries her across to the other side. Then as if nothing happened, he returns and they continue on their way. For over an hour, they walk in silence. All the while the monk who observed this indiscretion is replaying in his mind the details of the scene he had witnessed while getting more and more irritated and upset. Finally, he could not contain himself and burst out, "How could you do that? How could you be so cavalier? You know that there are rules about touching women?" To which his friend replied, "Yes, I did that. I broke the rule. I picked her up and then I put her down. But you, my friend, are still carrying her with you."

We all carry stuff (content) with us, but it does not have to be heavy. We can learn to lighten our load (using form).

Changing Submodalities of the Past

I (R.H.) had a client who was troubled by his past. When I asked him "where" he experienced his problems, his eyes defocused and he said they were directly in front of him. This particular client was a construction worker and I used the image of a crane because I knew he would relate to it. I suggested that he imagine a crane lifting all of the past problems located in front of him and swing them around far behind him and deposit them there. As he did this, he felt much lighter and had a greater sense of ease.

Changing Submodalities of the Present

Right now as you are reading this, see what happens if you "expand" your awareness by slightly defocusing your eyes, becoming aware of your hands and your peripheral vision. We are not asking you to "shift" your attention away from what you are reading by moving your head or your eyes. What we would like you to do is include more and more of your surroundings as you continue reading. And you can relax your eyes, while gradually including more and more of the space around you (left and right, above and below). You can also expand your awareness deep into your body, to your heart, to your lungs and to your belly. This might seem strange and unusual if you have never done it before. The idea here is to explore what happens in your consciousness when you change the submodalities of focus and location. Having this kind of flexibility can create an altered state of awareness where we can focus comfortably on what is important without becoming rigid and restricted.

Changing Submodalities of the Future

I (S.L.) worked with a man who was complaining that he was overwhelmed by the things he had to do. He told me that he understood that he could only do one thing at a time, but that he was still feeling stressed. He then said, "I am feeling oppressed and burdened. It's as if everything is hanging over my head." When I heard this I suggested that he look up at all those things above his head and slowly move them down to the ground by his feet. Upon making this maneuver, he exclaimed, "Wow, I am suddenly feeling on top of things" and he proceeded to have a great week accomplishing what he needed to accomplish one thing at a time without feeling burdened or pressured. He literally "put" things in perspective. He had been unaware of the "form" of his thinking. This is also an example of how listening to the words people use will provide the cues to which submodalities need to be changed to produce a more desired response.

Speaking about Auditory Submodalities

Another client of mine (S.L.) reported that whenever he made a mistake, he heard an inner voice saying, "You f#*ked up." Which made him feel guilty and ashamed. I asked him to describe how the voice "sounded." It was harsh and loud, emphasizing each word. The tone was deep with the emphasis on the middle word. I then asked him to use a higher tone, "soften" the words "f#*ked up" and add an inflection and emphasis to the word "up." It now sounded like he made a simple forgivable mistake instead of a grave unpardonable error.

Changing auditory submodalities can be useful with obsessive thinking and habitual internal dialogue. Not surprisingly, when people have obsessive thinking they only notice the content. So rather than paying attention to the content, we explore the form of what is being said. Is it loud? Fast? Slow? Low? High? Where is the voice located? When there is obsessive thinking it is helpful to think, "content is irrelevant." When we explore the form we will find more choices in our thinking. By finding the submodalities that make a difference, we can transform "worry into concern" or "fear into caution."

Auditory Submodalities

Volume
Location: Inside/Outside, Left/Right, Front/Back
Tone
Tempo: Fast and Slow
Rhythm

Inflection
Clarity
Mute/Silence
Gender: Male and Female
Distance: Near and Far
Mono/Stereo/ Surround Sound
Cartoon Voice

Connecting with Kinesthetic Submodalities

In a recent Bikram Yoga class, the teacher suggested to me (S.L.) that I breathe from my belly, not from my chest. By shifting my physical awareness to a different location, my abdomen, my breathing deepened. I felt more relaxed and I had more energy.

Every so often, we hear someone giving someone the suggestion "Breathe!" We are obviously breathing. But he or she is noticing something about "how" the person is breathing. What they are really saying is, "Change the way you are breathing!" either by slowing it down, lowering it to the belly, deepening it, or making it continuous and rhythmic. Some of the benefits of changing these breathing submodalities can lead to greater relaxation and increased energy.

As with the visual and auditory submodalities, changing kinesthetic submodalities will change the way we think and feel.

Here are some examples you might want to explore.

When eating: Chew your food slowly.
When shaking hands: Use more pressure (or less pressure) and for a longer (or shorter) duration.
When giving a hug: Make fewer movements with your hand. Keep them still.
When giving a presentation: Extend your hands away from your body, change the speed of the movements and change the direction your palms are facing.

Sometimes we change submodalities to get specific results. Other times, we can do it to expand our repertoire, learn new movements and develop greater flexibility.

It is our tendency as human beings to get into fixed habits so that we do not have to think about everything we do. Breaking out of these patterns requires doing "something" different. In NLP, that something is often a visual, auditory or kinesthetic submodality. When you change submodalities, keep in mind that the resulting experience may be unfamiliar, since you are exploring a new way of moving, thinking or feeling.

Kinesthetic Submodalities

Intensity: Strong and Weak
Pressure: Light and Hard
Location
Temperature: Hot and Cold
Humidity
Duration: Short and Long
Speed: Fast and Slow
Vibration
Tension
Numbness
Texture: Smooth and Rough, Dull and Sharp
Flexibility and Rigidity
Depth
Movement and Stillness
Spin: Clockwise and Counterclockwise
Balance
Weight: Heavy and Light
Breathing: Deep and Shallow, Slow and Fast, High and Low

Enhancing Positive Thoughts

Many of the examples we have given refer to using submodalities to reduce or eliminate negative feelings. But that is just one way of using submodalities.

Choose something positive that you might say to yourself. For example, "I love you." Identify how you hear the voice: the submodalities. Now change them one at a time: move it closer, vary the tone and tempo, place the emphasis on different words and pay attention to the resulting feelings. Which submodalities increased or enhanced the positive feelings?

Now take a positive image. Picture something you achieved, like a pleasurable memory or a desired goal. And play with the submodalities, learning how to increase or further improve upon it.

Isn't it nice to know that you can make an enjoyable experience even more satisfying!

When people are motivated, they are not making a flat, distant image with dull colors. Their images are bright, 3D and colorful. The more familiar we are with the structure of our thinking, the more empowered we will be.

Reducing Negative Thoughts

So many of our clients come to us tormented by negative thoughts. Their inner voice badgers them about why they aren't good enough, how they don't work hard enough, or what they should have done differently.

Choose something negative that you might say to yourself. For example, "I hate you." Identify how you hear the voice: the submodalities. Now change them one at a time: move it closer, vary the tone and tempo, place the emphasis on different words and pay attention to the resulting feelings. Which submodalities decreased or diminished the negative feelings?

Now take a negative image. Picture something that you failed to achieve. And play with the submodalities, learning how to decrease the negative feeling or find a more positive way of looking at it.

Worrying and Planning

Worrying and planning are two ways in which we think about the future. In both, there is usually internal dialogue accompanied by internally generated pictures. When we worry, we might ask ourselves what can go wrong or picture worst-case scenarios. When we plan, we also talk to ourselves and visualize, but instead thinking about what will go wrong, we ask ourselves what it is we want to happen and prepare ourselves for situations that might arise. Since we are all unique, we do not know exactly how each person goes about worrying or planning, but we can find out.

For this exercise, we would like you to worry about something.

Think about the worried voice. What type of tempo (speed) and tone does it have? Where is the worry voice located? What's the volume? Note anything else about the quality of the voice. If you are making pictures, pay attention to the visual submodalities. Are the images close, big and bright? Or are they distant, small and dark? Are you watching yourself or seeing what you are seeing?

Now prepare for something or think about something you are in the process of planning.

Compare the auditory and visual submodalities of planning those of worry.

As you notice the differences, explore what happens when you change the submodalities of worry to the submodalities of planning. Do your feelings change? If you like the changes, keep them.

You can do the same exercise with the kinesthetic submodalities of worry and planning.

Now it's Your Turn to Control the Mind

Even though we have been paying attention to how we can change the thoughts and images in our mind, there is another very useful way to use submodalities. We have worked with several clients who spoke to us about their intimidating bosses towering over them. They often describe their bosses as having big egos or looming large. Sometimes they feel small and insignificant. The submodalities of size and height are being highlighted.

When I (R.H.) started studying NLP, I was also practicing Aikido, a Japanese martial art. There was one particular student who was very aggressive and rough when he practiced with me or with the other students. I did not like practicing with him. However, in the dojo we were required to turn to whomever was next to us, bow and start practicing together. I decided that the next time we were paired together I would change a visual submodality and miniaturize him to the size of an ant. Visualizing him in this way, I was no longer intimidated, and when we practiced together I felt comfortable and powerful.

I (R.H.) also used the same technique with a boss of mine at the American Management Association. I had been feeling uncomfortable around him until I began imagining him inside a picture frame. Every time I saw him I would see him inside this frame, which gave me a sense of boundaries that allowed me to be more comfortable working in his presence.

A client of mine (R.H.) described having an internal dialogue in her head that related to her food craving. She called this voice "the food addict." The voice would say things like, "You can have anything you want." My first suggestion was to have her create a "word salad" by rearranging the words. (This was intentional to say word salad, so there was a double suggestion for using submodalities as well as suggesting something healthy). The client came up with variations, "have anything, you want, you can", "anything you want you can have," "have can you want anything you," "can you want have anything, you," etc. We call this, "The Yoda technique." She was also taught how to change the tone of the words, as well as adding background music. She learned that changing the form, not the content, made the biggest difference. She liked having a specific tool that she could effectively use.

Submodalities are the building blocks of our experience. Working or playing with them is a creative process that develops flexibility of the mind, body and spirit. It is something that you can practice regularly to train your brain to think about something in a new way. Sometimes awareness accompanied by a shift in that awareness leads to permanent changes, while other times the change is temporary. As you will see, the goal of NLP is to create powerful, long lasting changes that will have profound consequences.

NLP Momentary Practice

Think of someone with whom you work. How do you represent him/her in your mind? Imagine him/her much bigger and notice how you feel. Now imagine him/her smaller and again notice how you feel. Experiment with other submodalities to determine the way you would like to influence your internal thoughts and images.

Think about an argument, a conflict or a disagreement that you have had recently that you want to let go of, but you find yourself still holding onto.

And do the following:

Imagine that you are an audience member sitting in an orchestra seat of a Broadway theater watching yourself and the other person interact on stage. If you like you can move to the balcony.

Now change it from a drama to a musical and hear the orchestra playing. If nothing changes, switch to a movie theater and create a soundtrack using the first song that pops into your head.

Now imagine stepping onto the stage or into the movie and becoming the other person, viewing the scene from his/her perspective.

Lastly, as you read these words, become aware of your actual posture and your breathing. Change it so that you are sitting upright and relaxing your breathing. Breathe deeply and comfortably. Relax your shoulders. Drop your arms and hands and adjust your head so that it is comfortably resting on your shoulders. And sit or stand so that both feet are placed firmly on the ground. Then step into the scene and imagine the interaction from your own perspective, but this time make the same adjustments in the scene that you are making with your current posture, breathing, head, shoulders and feet. And continue to breathe this way as you go through the interactional sequence.

When you now think about the interaction, what has changed? What have you learned?

CHAPTER 7

Acting "As If": What is It Like Having Already Achieved Your Goal?

"You can pretend anything and master it."
-Milton H. Erickson

Did you ever ask someone what he/she wanted and instead of telling you what he/she wanted, he/she described the future he/she didn't want. Some examples of this are, "I don't want to fail," "I don't want to be afraid," and "I don't want to be so negative." In each of these cases, the speaker is describing what he/she doesn't want.

Many people spend a lot of time imagining very clearly what they do not want to happen. When someone describes his/her goals this way we ask, "Now that I know what you don't want, will you tell me what you do want?" or "What do you want instead?"

So now we ask "you" to think about some personal and professional goals that you "do" want. And take a few minutes to record them. Imagine what it will be like to actually achieve each goal. Do this before continuing to read on.

If you are already in the habit of doing this, you are familiar with the benefits. But now we are going to add another step that will not be as familiar. It is called the "As If" frame.

When you use the "As If" frame you are giving yourself the opportunity to become one with your goal and experience it "as if" you have already achieved it. So instead of imagining what it might or will be like, you are experiencing what it is like.

There are many times that we suggest something to a client and the client says, "But I can't do that." When we hear this response we often suggest, "Act as if you can," or "Just pretend you can." Surprisingly, when someone acts as if he/she has already accomplished what he/she says he/she wants to accomplish, something meaningful happens. People who are in the habit of using affirmations will speak as if they have already achieved what they want. When I (R.H.) was studying for my clinical psychology licensure exam, I would say to myself, "I am a licensed New York State Psychologist," before I actually had the certificate. I was acting as if. Many people know this approach from childhood. We pretend to be someone different by creating a future reality with all the submodalities of the present moment. Once the idea has been created, it is stored in our brain and can motivate us to achieve our goal.

One of our former trainees, Ariane Hundt, did this exercise at the start of her NLP Coach Practitioner Training as she was dreaming up her ideal business. Her dream was to have her own business as a personal trainer and nutritionist and to start a boot camp. Five years later we went to her launch party to celebrate her DVD and success of her Brooklyn Bridge Boot Camp. Ariane has created a very successful boot camp program literally on the Brooklyn Bridge. At the launch party there was a life size cardboard replication of her, and a video showing her workout. Many of her fellow students were part of the huge turnout. At the party Ariane told us that this was the dream that she had created in the "As If" exercise. She said the exercise gave her the opportunity to pretend, to dream and to create a business plan to follow and accomplish. We laughed together as we reflected on the power of using this technique.

Live Your Goal and Work Backwards

Take this moment to dream. Use this opportunity to identify a goal, but instead of simply saying, "I would like to be doing X," "I want to have Y," or "I want to be Z," state it as if you have already achieved the goal. So rather than say, "I want to have a healthy, loving relationship" or "I want to write a book," or "I would like to become a coach," say: "I am in a healthy, loving relationship," "I have completed my book," or "I am a well established coach." Make sure to use present tense verbs. Don't just think it. Say it out loud.

As you say it, live it fully. How does your life look, sounds and feel when you have already accomplished this goal. Experience the world through this filter. What are you doing? How are you moving? How you are interacting with the world? How have you changed? Really consider each question.

As you continue to think about where you are, ask yourself what did you need to do to get to this point. Go ahead. Make up some memories.

Remember what had occurred that got you to where you are now. What had you been thinking about prior to achieving your goal? What steps did you take along the way? What feelings and emotions came up for you? For example, if your goal was to write a book, think about how you planned and created time in your schedule to write, what new habits you developed, how you continued to remind yourself about your commitment, how you had to overcome distractions and nagging doubts about whether or not you would ever get to finish, how you had to revise what you wrote multiple times, how you struggled and eventually found the words that described exactly what you wanted to say and the satisfaction of accomplishing what you set out to achieve, how you coached yourself though it all, what, if anything, you had to give up or postpone and whether or not it was worth it. And remember the day it all began, when you did the "As If Frame" exercise.

Before coming back to the present moment, ask yourself, "What is it about this experience that I want to bring back with me?" Then reorient to the present moment. It is important to remind yourself that you are back in the here and now. Look around, seeing the environment you are in right now. Remember the current day and year, so you know you are fully reoriented. And reflect on what you have learned.

As IF Frame

In our NLP training class, we guide participants into the future and have them describe their "as if" experience out loud. We ask questions and have them answer using present tense verbs, so that they remain firmly rooted in the future time frame as they share their experiences. Some students and clients easily slip out of the "as if" frame and revert back to, "If I were to have accomplished this goal" or "When I do accomplish this goal." If this happens we guide them back to, "I have accomplished my goal and I am now enjoying..." After doing this, we reorient back to the present moment and reflect on our experiences and discuss what we have learned. As with many of the exercises in this book, being guided through the process by a well-trained NLP professional will keep you on track so that you will receive the maximum benefits. Also, doing this particular exercise in a group will often amplify the experience.

After going through the experience, ask yourself the following questions:

What did I learn?
What's different?
How has my representation of the outcome changed?
What am I going to take away from this experience and begin to implement?

Following this exercise, people's comments have ranged from, "Wow, that was powerful," and "I am excited to get started" to "I can make it happen." I (R.H.) had worked with a client who did the "As If frame" exercise for creating a family. She had a partner, but she was having difficulty conceiving. In her "As If" moment she saw herself with her partner and a baby walking with a stroller and feeling like she had finally achieved her goal to become a mother. This was not an easy process for her to do, as she was afraid that if she asked for what she wanted, something bad would happen, as was the case so often in her childhood. Doing this process helped her realize that one of the steps that she needed to take prior to conceiving was learning how to handle her fear. This was something she then worked on in her individual sessions. She is now happy and living with her husband and two children.

NLP Momentary Practice

Before closing this chapter, take a moment and look again at the goals you recorded at the start of the chapter and choose a second goal and go through the "As If" frame with it.

CHAPTER 8

Think and Grow Different: Aspects of an Effective Communicator

"If you want others to be happy, practice compassion. If you want to be happy, practice compassion."

Dalai Lama

When NLP first came on the scene in the mid-1970s, it was described as a model for effective communication and change. At that time, "communication" had a very different meaning than it does now. It was a time before we communicated via text messaging, video conferencing, power point, email, Facebook, Instagram and Twitter. We only used speaking, writing, printing, photocopying, telephoning and faxing, having recently outgrown Morse coding, telegraphing and smoke signaling.

While communication technology has come a long way, we can still find ourselves with no cell phone, no computer or tablet and no way to communicate other than in the old-fashioned way, in the flesh, where all we have to rely on is our voice, our language, our eyes, our hands, our facial expressions and the rest of our body posturing. We used to call it interpersonal communication, because it was between persons, but the term itself now seems antiquated. We can't even call it face-to-face, since that might imply using Skype or Facetime. Perhaps we should call it bare bones communication or hands free communication or maybe "naked communication" since that's how it feels for some people when they have to put down their handheld devices for a few minutes and be "exposed" to another human being.

Communication is something that we all depend upon for our survival and to influence the world around us, from the loudest cry to the faintest sigh. We refer to some people as being good or great communicators while other are considered poor listeners or incoherent speakers. There are people who know how to "listen" and those who don't, some who can't get enough of it, while others shy away from it.

And yet, we are always communicating. Even when we are silent, we are communicating something. If we avoid communicating, that communicates something. If we speak continuously without pausing, that communicates something. If we do not look at people when they speak, that communicates something. We can't not communicate.

We are always communicating something. But is that "something" actually what we intend to communicate? Are we actually communicating and getting the response we want?

The international distress signal, SOS, which can be communicated as a series of three short beeps or flashes, followed by three long beeps or flashes, followed by another three short beeps or flashes, communicates "I am in distress and in need of HELP." There are very few universally recognized signals. And even these signals are no longer universally recognized. Therefore much of what passes for communication is mostly miscommunication. But miscommunication itself is really not the problem. The problem is that most people think they are communicating effectively, when they are not.

To use the metaphor of archery, communication is like shooting an arrow into the air and not noticing or not caring where it lands. That may be fine for Cupid, but for the rest of us poor mortals, it is our Achilles heel.

Some of us aim to hit the "bulls eye" of a target and notice when the arrow hits or misses its mark. This is definitely an improvement since we are now paying attention.

But what happens if we miss the target? Do we then look to find excuses or assign blame? "Somebody must have moved the target" or "Something is wrong with the bow," or " I am simply bad at archery." And if we do attempt to shoot again, we pretty much do exactly what we just before without having learned anything from our prior attempt.

Or do we see it all as a learning process, paying attention to the feedback, noticing how we are holding the bow and arrow, the angle of the bow, the tautness of the string, the direction and velocity of the wind. When we remain curious and see what happens when we make adjustments, we vary our behavior until we eventually succeed. There is no such thing as failure, only feedback. We identify our target. We pay attention to relevant information in the environment. And in the process we develop greater flexibility. These are some of the essential skills for effective communication.

Effective communicators are moving in the direction of getting the responses they want. Ineffective communicators either have no clear target, do not pay attention to the responses they are getting, do the same thing over and over again and blame themselves for doing it wrong or find fault in someone else.

What else do you think is important for an effective communicator? This is a question we ask our students in training. Some of our students' responses have been know what you are talking about, make eye contact, speak clearly, be confident and listen. Of course these are all important ingredients. We would like you to create a list of what you believe makes an effective communicator and see how it compares to our NLP list. The following discussion will include the five aspects of an effective communicator, which we refer to throughout our NLP training.

Aspects of An Effective Communicator

By incorporating the following five aspects of an effective communicator, you will boldly communicate where no one has seen or heard you go before. They are: Knowing Your Outcome, Flexibility of Behavior, Sensory Awareness, Respect for Another's Model of the World and Recognition of Being

I. Knowing Your Outcomes: What do you want?

Obstacles are those frightful things you see when you take your eyes off your goal.
-Henry Ford

When you are an effective communicator you know what you want. You know the response you intend to get. You know your target.

Here are some examples:

I want to be understood.
I want to sound convincing.
I want to make people laugh.
I want to inspire.
I want to be patient with my children.
I want my spouse to feel supported.
I want to be taken seriously.
I want to learn what the other person wants.
I want the customer to be satisfied.
I want to say "no" when I really do not want to do something.
I want to be true to myself.
I want to authentically express my feelings.
I want to stay in touch with my friends.
I want to give myself permission to be happy.
I want to forgive.

As you can see, some of these outcomes are interpersonal (to influence another person's thoughts, feelings and behaviors) while others are intrapersonal (to influence our own thoughts, feelings and behaviors). They may in involve an audience of one or thousands.

In the archery metaphor, the ultimate outcome may be to hit the bulls eye, but it could also be to learn or to have fun.

After working with managers at American Management Association for a three-day *Building Better Work Relationships* seminar (basically an NLP course) I (R.H) would contact them after the course had ended to find out what skills they were still utilizing. The majority of managers would say "Knowing My

Outcomes." One manager explained that whenever he picked up the phone the first thought he had was, "What is my outcome at this moment with this individual." The manager claimed that it helped him to focus and be specific.

Some people when asked what they want will say, "I just want to talk." If this were true then as long as they are speaking, they are successfully hitting their target. But generally, talking in and of itself is not their actual outcome. There are other outcomes, possibly unconscious, such as, "I want to be heard," "I want to be understood," or "I want to be respected." Some other intrapersonal outcomes may be "I want to feel important even when I am being ignored," or "I want to love myself, even when another person is being rejecting." Being aware of your outcomes is the first step in getting what you want.

When we were dating, I (R.H.) had the outcome that my relationship with Steven would be the, "one" – a serious relationship leading to marriage. Of course it takes two. Our relationship was going along very well and I didn't want him to feel any pressure about the M word (marriage). One of my outcomes with my family was to make sure that no one, particularly my 90-year-old grandmother, would ask him when we were going to get married. My outcome with my grandmother, Bubbie Rose, was whenever Steven and I visited her, Bubbie Rose would refrain from asking the marriage question. "Bubbie, whatever you do, don't ask Steven when we are going to get married." When we visited Bubbie Rose she honored my request and never said the M word. Instead she fed Steven as much chicken soup as any human could possible tolerate. A year later he proposed. I happily got my outcome. Apparently it was a mutual outcome. (Or maybe Steven just liked the chicken soup).

II. Flexibility

"If you always do what you've always done, you'll always get what you've always got."
-Henry Ford

Effective communicators are flexible. If what they are doing is not working, they do something else. If what they are doing is working (e.g. moving closer to their outcome) they keep on doing it (unless they get tired of doing it one way and want to be more creative). But if what they are doing isn't working, then it is time to change. Flexibility implies varying your approach. You can be flexible in the way you think, feel and act. For example, you might change your thinking from, "This is not going to work," to "How will I make this work?" Or you might change your behavior from "frowning" to "smiling." Or change your feelings from "frustration" to "curiosity" or "determination." NLP training develops flexibility, making essential changes, effortlessly.

Some of you may be thinking, "I am a very flexible person." Perhaps you are, but then again, how are you when it comes to standing firmly and saying, "No!" Perhaps you can be even more flexible by adding "firmness" to your behavioral repertoire-especially if you are always bending over backwards.

Flexibility of the mind comes about when we discover the generalizations or judgments that we are making about someone or something. It is about "seeing" things from different points of view. If we were to look and listen to people who are different than us with a open mind, we would have a very different society. Think of the Apple slogan, "Think Different."

Changing our Actions

Changing our posture, gestures and voice style are also part of behavioral flexibility. We would like to ask you to stop reading this and clasp your hands together. Which thumb is on top? Now move your fingers so that the other thumb is on top. Most students say it feels awkward, but when they look around no one looks particularly awkward. So the experience of flexibility may initially feel uncomfortable, but those who are looking at you will not think that your variation looks forced or awkward. We would like to challenge you to find your own behavioral flexibility experiment. If you are someone who does not use other people's names when you say "Good morning," see what happens when you do. If you are not in the habit of saying "Good morning," start doing it.

If you always sit in a particular location, pick a different seat. This type of flexibility can be done with dressing differently. We remember a time when an NLP trainee always wore black. Our task for this person was to come to class wearing colors. She came in wearing red and described how strange it felt. This change did not necessarily make her a more effective communicator, but it gave her more confidence in making small changes. What initially started out as being unfamiliar and uncomfortable eventually integrated seamlessly and effortlessly into her repertoire.

Changing our Feelings

So far we have described flexibility of how we think and what we do. There is also flexibility of how we feel. If we are frustrated, we could change our voice by speaking more slowly or use different gestures, but still be communicating our frustration. The same is true when we are being impatience, irritated or outraged. So what do we do? What options do we have? One is to directly express our feelings of impatience, irritation or outrage. Another is to attempt to conceal it. Someone once told me that if you only have one choice, you are stuck. With two choices you have a dilemma. Only with three choices do you really begin to choose.

Most of us are familiar with the first two options, express or repress. Although both these options are quite appropriate for many situations, they do not always help us get what we really want. Expressing outrage when someone innocently and unintentionally says something that opens an emotional wound will not get a positive response. It often gets the opposite response. For example, instead of getting them to understand, we put them on the defensive. And by keeping our feelings hidden, we are often stuck carrying around bad feelings. The biggest obstacle to changing our feelings is the assigning of blame. And it does not matter if we are blaming the other or blaming ourselves. We experience ourselves as victims.

The third option is to take responsibility for our feelings and learn how to change them. With it we are empowered. Without this third option, we are victims. NLP provides us with the "how to", but we must "want to."

Combining Outcome and Flexibility

In the late 1970s I (S.L.) spent most of my summers on Fire Island, an island just off the south coast of Long Island, 32 miles long and only ¼ to ½ mile wide. It is a very peaceful place with no cars or roads, mostly beach, sand dunes and houses. But between Memorial Day and Labor Day, starting on Friday nights, crowds begin to arrive by ferry and the small island is transformed by the energy of NYC residents wanting to relax from the stresses of living in the city and have fun in the sun. But once the last ferry leaves on Sunday evening, the island returns to its calmer and quieter state. So it was on a Monday morning that I left my beach house with a Frisbee in hand to find a companion to enjoy one of my favorite activities on the beach.

But the beach was empty and there was no one to play with. Being determined to play, I threw the Frisbee along the beach and ran to retrieve it. But that was not much fun. For me the challenge was the precision with which I could get the Frisbee to my partner along with the skill of catching it. So I did something different. This time I faced the ocean, angled the Frisbee upward at a 45° angle and threw it. It sailed forwards and upwards then returned like a boomerang, sailing way over my head towards the dunes behind me. So I lowered the angle to about 20°. This time, it sailed directly towards the ocean and dropping into the waves, giving me the opportunity to take my first dip of the day.

I continued to play with the angle until I got the Frisbee to hover over the ocean and return directly to me. From that point on, I continued to experiment with different angles, up and down and left and right along with my arm and wrist speed, and the exact release point, and I found that after some time once the Frisbee left my hand I was able to predict where and when it was going to land. So as soon as I threw it I moved to the exact spot to catch it. It got to the point that I could hurl it as hard as I could, watch its flight path, enjoy seeing it hover in the air high above the ocean, moving up and down with the wind currents and have it return to the place where I was standing. Other times I preferred not to have it come back to the point of release, so I could enjoy getting some additional exercise sprinting or walking to the exact place where I intuited it was going to land just in time to catch it, just as an outfielder tracks a ball on a windy day.

Once having mastered it, I looked for a new challenge. This time as I released the Frisbee, I called out a word that described a feeling state I wanted to have. So I when I heard myself say "effortlessness" I effortlessly threw the Frisbee into the air and effortlessly ran to catch it. I did it again with the words, "playful," "confident," "love," "determination" and many more. As my state changed, I delighted in how many ways I could throw and catch a Frisbee and realized how flexible I could be in shifting my internal state. Without a watch (no cellphones at that time), I only knew from the location of the sun that I had been lost in this timeless activity for most of the day.

After a good night's rest, I was out there again the next morning. But this time, when I threw the Frisbee, it just sailed into the ocean. But how could this be? I spent the entire previous day leaning all there was to playing what I called, "Solo Frisbee." My conclusion was that something was different.

What was it? Was it I? Was I doing something different? Did I already forget how to do it? It wasn't the beach. Nothing around me looked different.

So I sat down. And I silently listened to the waves crashing along the shoreline and the gulls calling overhead. I closed my eyes and felt warmth of the sun and coolness of the wind. What was different? Then I felt the air and the wind against my body. It was not the same as I remembered it. It was coming from a different direction with a different velocity. So I got up. I repositioned myself and threw it again. Much better this time, but still not what I expected. So I just kept adjusting, modifying the throwing angle and tweaking the release speed. After a few more alterations, I returned to my previous form and continued to play "Solo Frisbee."

III. Paying Attention: Sensory Awareness

Question: When do we need to be flexible?
Answer: When we are not getting the response we want.

Questions: And how do we know when we are not getting the response we want?
Answer: By paying attention.

Playing "Solo Frisbee" developed my flexibility, but it was not enough. I also needed to pay attention to the changing territory. By noticing where the Frisbee landed I was able to adjust my behavior to get the Frisbee to return to where I was standing. Or I could determine where it was going to land and be there when it arrived. And finally I was able to get feedback from the environment by feeling the shifts in the wind, which let me know what to do differently.

Have you ever noticed that some people do not pay attention to you when you speak? They have no idea if you are listening or not. If you haven't noticed this, you too are not paying attention. Paying attention is the third essential ingredient of being an effective communicator.

Q: What are we doing when we are not paying attention?
A: We are paying attention to something or someone else.

So we are always paying attention. It just may not be helping us get our outcome.

Uptime and Downtime

Recently, when Rachel and I (S.L.) were practicing in our Bikram yoga class, I found myself zoning out. Instead of paying attention to the instructions, I was thinking about what stories I was going to use for this chapter. The yoga teacher noticed that I was not doing the correct posture and got my attention by saying my name and asking, "Is there a name in NLP for what you are doing right now?" I told him it was called being in "downtime."

When we are in downtime, we are internally oriented, paying attention to our thoughts, our imaginings, our internal dialogue, our feelings or emotions. When we do this we are not paying attention to our surroundings. When our awareness is externally oriented, we call it being in "uptime." We are in uptime when we are completely immersed in what we are seeing, hearing and/or feeling externally.

One of the benefits of Bikram Yoga is learning to stay in uptime. Riding my bicycle to and from work in New York City requires extreme uptime, noticing anything that could cause me injury or injury to others, seeing what's in front of me, beneath me (gratings and potholes) and peripherally (vehicles cutting me off or people in vehicles getting ready to open their car doors), listening to what's around me (honking and sirens) and being on the alert for pedestrians, other bikers and drivers in downtime.

Sometimes we think we are paying attention when what we are actually doing is interpreting (giving meaning to) what we are seeing and hearing. We are defining "paying attention" as the ability to have direct experience of our senses – being sensory based. When riding my bike I may see a car with their rear left blinker on, but to think that the car is going to make a left turn is an interpretation. The driver might have been riding with it on or he may change his mind at the last minute. It is also an interpretation to think that if it isn't on, then he isn't going to make a turn. In uptime, we are responding to what is actually happening right now, in the moment, not what happened, not what we think is happening and not what will be happening. We will be returning to this important distinction later in the book.

While effective communicators do interpret, they know when they are doing it and do not confuse it with sensory-based experience.

Unlike when riding a bicycle, being in downtime during an interpersonal communication will in general not cause bodily harm. But it can hurt the communication as well as the relationship. When we are communicating with people who are in downtime, we are being ignored. We are neither being seen nor heard. But downtime is not a bad thing. It is the source of our creativity and intuition. It is how we make sense of the world. Developing our ability to move between uptime and downtime and finding a balance between the two are essential NLP skills.

In Chapter 4, I (S.L.) I described an interaction I had with Maritza, in my math class. When I complimented her and she did not accept it, I could have interpreted it as meaning that she was someone who could not take a compliment and stopped communicating. But I did not. My outcome was not simply to give her a compliment. It was for her to take it in. So I paid attention to her response as an indicator that I needed to do something different and recognized that she was telling me that she had a belief that she was not a good math student. Accepting that she believed this, I "paced" her experience by saying "for someone who considers herself to be a poor math student" and led her to "you are doing very well." When she took a deep breath and said, "Thank you," I knew I achieved my outcome. If my outcome were to change her limiting belief, I would have utilized one of the advanced NLP techniques for changing beliefs.

Recognizing people's beliefs, limiting and otherwise, will also make us more effective communicators.

Although I recognized that she was operating with a limited belief, I was still respecting that she held that belief. It was her truth. And in doing so I was incorporating the fourth aspect of an effective communicator.

IV. Respecting the Other Person's Model of the World

There are many people who claim to have the right map — the superior map, which they see as the One and Only Truth. They have no tolerance or respect for maps that are not compatible with their own. They are not flexible and do not attempt to understand. They surround themselves with others who share their map, ridicule those that don't and may use whatever means they have at their disposal to impose their map on others.

Perhaps there is a little of this in each one of us. So be vigilant.

The NLP map offers quite a different perspective. It is about respect. But before going further, we would like define what we mean by respect. Most people associate it with agreeing. It is not. Nor is it about approving, sanctioning, condoning, excusing or ignoring.

Respect as we are defining it in the NLP context is recognizing that people are doing the "only thing" that they can do, given their current programming. It is not their fault. It is their default. Our programs are based on the distinctions we have learned so far. We upgrade from a software program version 4.0 to 5.0, because we recognize the limitations of 4.0 and the benefits of 5.0. But when 4.0 came out, it was the current version and the best one available. Respecting ourselves also means that we accept that we are doing the only thing we can at any given moment in time.

When it comes to intrapersonal communication, we unfortunately spend too much of our time getting angry at ourselves for not being the way we want to be or we surrender to the "fact" that we will never change. We are advocating accepting what is, while endeavoring to go beyond our present imperfections. In other words, accepting that our present map is the best we have right now, while continuing to improve and upgrade it.

When it comes to interpersonal communication, we spend too much time getting upset with others for not being the way we want them to be, which usually leads to resistance and stagnation. Whether your intention is to convince people to see your point of view, change their point of view or simply to understand their point of view, respecting their map is essential.

Maritza had a different model of the world from me (S.L.), but instead of arguing that she was wrong, I utilized it to get my outcome.

I (R.H.) remember learning early on with Anne Linden, one of my first NLP teachers, that respect doesn't mean you have to like the person, or that they have to be your friend. And you certainly don't have to agree with the person.

There is an interesting alternative to this idea of "respecting" another's model of the world. It is the "Steve Jobs" model. Steve Jobs, founder of Apple Computers, believed that the things that he wanted to create were always possible and could be created the way he wanted them to be. He was quite persuasive in getting people to believe that the impossible was possible, but if someone insisted that it was not, they were considered a rotten apple to be discarded. And that formula worked quite well at accomplishing his outcomes at Apple.

This formula certainly appeared to work for Steve Jobs in that he successfully created aesthetically pleasing, cutting-edge technology that made a significant contribution to the world. But many who admired his effectiveness as an innovative and successful entrepreneur who got what he wanted would not have used him as a model for creating healthy interpersonal relationships.

A friend of ours, NLP trainer and intercultural communication specialist Brian van der Horst, told us that when he trained business professionals who had been transferred overseas to help them make a smooth transition to the new culture, he would spend a week teaching them about the new culture and a week teaching them about their own culture. In this way they could appreciate the differences. NLPers appreciate, honor and learn from these differences in beliefs and maps and treat each person as if they were a culture unto themselves.

V. Being Recognized and Recognizing the Being

Neuro-linguistic programming uses the metaphor of "computer programming" which compares us to computers that have been programmed and can be reprogrammed. While this may be a useful operating metaphor, where our patterns, habits and programs can be updated, we must remember that not only are we not our programs, we are also not computers. We are not things. We are beings — human beings.

Taking this metaphor to the extreme means people treating each other as objects to be controlled, manipulated and dominated.

We are not interested in promoting this way of communicating. At the same time, we must be prepared to be resourceful when communicating with people who do operate in this way.

Martin Buber makes the distinction between an I-It relationship (a subject-to-object relationship) and an I-Thou relationship (a soul-to-soul relationship). When we relate as the former we remain separate and detached. When we relate as the latter, there is a human relationship. One creates barriers; the other creates bridges.

An auto mechanic can fix a car without having met the owner. A surgeon can save a human life without ever having seen the human, just his/her body. And as you shall see, we can do NLP without recognizing a soul. And in many cases, it may not matter.

But when we are not recognizing the human being, we are not being fully human.

NLP Momentary Practice

Outcome: Write down a specific personal communication outcome for today.

Flexibility: Think of one thing you can do differently to get your outcome.

Paying Attention: Deliberately move back and forth between downtime and uptime when communicating and notice the difference it makes.

Respect: When you encounter someone whose behavior seems bizarre or inexplicable, act as if it does make perfect sense and remain curious and determined to learn how it makes sense.

Recognizing the Being: Ask yourself the following questions:

What is it like when you are being seen as a human being?
How do you know when you are being seen as a human being?
What happens when you are not? What might you do differently?
How do you know when you are seeing another as a human being?
What happens when you are not? What might you do differently?

Building Flexibility and Sensory Awareness

Find a partner.

Person A shares a personal outcome, e.g. "I want to eat healthy foods."

Person B repeats the statement, e.g. "You want to eat healthy foods" using the same tone, tempo, inflection and volume.

Repeat the above 3 times, as person A varies his/her tone, tempo, inflection and volume and person B matches.

Then A and B switch.

When doing this exercise were you seeing your partner? Or were you so absorbed in the words that you were not seeing him/her? If you found yourself being more attentive to the words, do the exercise again. This time soften your eyes and be in uptime. Look into your partner's eyes and see his/her humanness.

CHAPTER 9

See You, Hear You, Feel You: What Language are We Speaking?

"I speak two languages, Body and English."
-Mae West

Over the years, we have worked with many people who have had difficulties communicating with their partners, often getting frustrated and upset when they cannot get their ideas across.

One possible explanation is that they are not speaking the same language. It's not that one person is speaking German while the other speaks Greek. There is a subtler language that exists within every language and it is based on how human beings experience the world- through our five senses: sight (visual), sound (auditory), feel (kinesthetic), taste (gustatory) and smell (olfactory).

And as long as our eyes, ears, nose, taste buds and skin sensors are functioning properly, we are receiving information through all of these senses. At the same time, we are also receiving images, sounds (including self-talk) and feelings that are self-generated (including memories and made up stuff). There is a lot going on.

As you read this book, you are not only looking at characters (letters) forming words, sentences and paragraphs. Your experience right now, whether you are consciously aware of it or not, includes the formatting of the book, the feel and texture of the book or electronic device you are touching, the chair you are sitting in (if you are sitting), the air temperature and humidity, the position of your body, background sounds and images including your peripheral vision, the specific meaning you generate through internal thoughts (pictures and internal dialogue), light sources, physical discomfort and comfort (including things you recently ate). And of all these stimuli, we selectively attend to some while ignoring others. We do this unconsciously and automatically and it forms the basis of the language to which we are alluding. To learn this hidden language we must pay attention to the type of words, particularly the verbs, nouns and adjectives that we use.

There is an exercise in our training where we ask a trainee to describe an interaction with another person, while the group pays attention to the words used by the speaker. Does the speaker use visual words such as, "see, look, view, picture, focus, perspective" or auditory words such as "listen, hear, speak, tell, tune into, click" or kinesthetic words such as "feel, touch, resonate, connect, move, emotion?" Words reveal a "hidden" language." In order to speak his/her language we need to use his/her words when we interact with him/her. We refer to our preferred system as our "primary representational system." By listening to the words the speaker is using, we can determine how he/she is processing information. The term primary representational system implies that there is "one fixed primary system." This *appears* to be true for some people. For many of us, our primary system can and will change from one context to another and is more variable than the developers of NLP originally thought. This means that we must be extremely careful not to label someone as a visual, auditory or kinesthetic person. It also means we must remain in uptime, paying attention to the changing predicates and nouns along with the changing contexts and not relying only on what has been previously observed.

Speaking In Different Modalities

The following example takes place in the context of "loving and being loved."

Jamie and Kris are speaking

Jamie: "You never *tell* me you love me".
Kris: "Of course I love you, Are you *blind*? Can't you *see* that I love you? I send you flowers, I buy you gifts, and I *show* you that I love you in so many ways.
Jaime: "But you do not *say* the words. I need to *hear* it."

The conversation could also go the other way.

Kris: "You never *show* me that you love me?"

Jamie: "Of course I love you, I am always *telling* you 'I love you'; I leave *voice* messages; I *whisper* it to you in bed. Sometimes I *shout* it out loudly. I even *sing* it."

Kris responds, "*Talk* is cheap. I need to *see* it. You need to *show* me you love me."

The Golden Rule is "Do unto others as you would have them do unto you."

Perhaps if we understood that not everybody thinks the same way that we do, we would change the rule to, "Do unto others as they would have us do unto them." But to follow this rule we would have to pay attention and recognize how their map is different from ours. In other words, we would have to recognize that our own idiosyncratic way of perceiving is in fact only one way.

In this example, there are two types of languages being spoken. Jamie wanted to be told (an auditory preference), while Kris wanted to be shown (a visual preference). Another preference is "kinesthetic". I want to *feel* loved. I need *affection*. I need you to *take me in your arms, hold me close* and *kiss me,* otherwise I don't *feel connected.*

When you use visual words with a visual person he/she will have the experience of being "seen."

When you use auditory words with an auditory person he/ she will be "heard."

And by using kinesthetic words with a kinesthetic person he/she will "feel understood."

In our own experience as a couple, we discovered that Steven is more of an "I want to *feel* loved," type of person, and Rachel is a mixture of "*Show* me and *tell* me you love me," type of a person. So hugs and caresses work for Steve and cards and being told directly, work for Rachel.

When we introduce this topic to our NLP class, we ask our students to identify the representational systems of people in their life. One of our students, who discovered in class that she was, in most cases, kinesthetic, went home *feeling* certain that she would find her husband, a composer, using auditory words. To her surprise, all his words were visual. When she expressed her confusion, he said, "When I compose a song I always *see* it first. It is not until some time afterwards that I *hear* it." Another student broke in, "My boyfriend is also a composer. And last night when I listened to his words, he was using all *feeling* words. Then he explained that when he composed, he first *feels* the music."

Do you know how you want to be loved? Do you know how the people you love want to be loved?

How do you communicate your understanding? Do you say, "I *hear* you?" Do you say, "I *see* what you mean?" or do you just take it in, *feel* it and say nothing.

There also exist some finer distinctions in each category. Not all auditory people are alike. Some are more attuned to the spoken words and often remember exactly what was said, word for word, while other auditory people may not remember the specific words, but they do remember the tone of the conversation and if the other person was speaking quickly or loudly. The same is true for visual people. Some people can recite the sentences and paragraphs that they saw written in a book, while others are more likely to remember and describe the scene that they were picturing while reading.

Examples of Visual Predicates

See
Look
View
Perspective
Reflect
Color
Shine
Mirror

Examples of Auditory Predicates

Hear
Talk

Speak
Listen
Sound
Click
Tune
Conversation

The Kinesthetic category also has its finer distinctions:

Emotions: happy, excited, fun, sad, angry, afraid, etc.
Movement: walk, sat down, take a step back, moving forward, grasp, push, hold, etc.
Visceral Sensations (Inside the body): relaxed, tense, tight, loose, knotted, energetic, etc.
Proprioception: sensing the position and location of the body and body parts, head, hands, legs, feet, etc.
Tactile Sensation (On the skin): rough, smooth, soft, hard, hot, cold, warm, etc.

Of course many words can overlap, describing more than one category. For example, "embrace" can include both touch and movement, while "being touched" can be tactile or emotional. Or it may be ambiguous – the word "clear" could refer to an image or a sound.

Finally, there are words that do not specify any particular modality, such as understand, know, think, believe, remember and plan. When the speaker uses these "unspecified" words, the listener has no way of knowing by the words themselves how the speaker is processing. If we do not ask clarifying questions, we will by default use our own system to make meaning. So if the speaker asks, "Do you understand me?" The visual listener might respond, "Yes, I *see* what you mean" or "No, I am not getting a *clear picture.*" The auditory listener may say, "Yes, I *hear* you" or "No, I wasn't *listening.*" And the kinesthetic listener may say, "Yes, I *grasp* your meaning" or "No, it doesn't *resonate.*"

Be careful not to generalize. As we said, the primary system will change from time to time and context to context. You might be kinesthetic when it comes to love, but visual when it comes to food. You might assume that if the person is speaking in visual words, then they will be most receptive to visual words. While this is usually the case, sometimes our output system is not the same as our input system. This requires us to be attentive all the time.

One of our students was having difficulties communicating with her boss. When they both attended a "train the trainer" meeting about representational systems, they discovered that they each had a different primary system. She wanted to *discuss* everything and *talk* it through. She preferred meetings so they could discuss the issues. He wanted her to have a *clear picture* of what he wanted and to *show* him that she understood his *perspective*. He preferred sending e-mails with lengthy descriptions of the task. This awareness helped both of them become more flexible and resulted in developing better ways of communicating.

Building Rapport and Motivating Others

As NLP professionals, when we ask people what they want we not only listen to the content; we also listen to their predicates (the words that indicate the representational system; visual, auditory, kinesthetic, olfactory and gustatory). Here are a few examples of statements clients have used. Can you determine which system they are using?

" I *see* myself *looking* confident and successful in my new business"
" I keep *telling* myself that I am going to be successful in my new business."
" I will *feel* so proud and *excited* when my new business is successful."

And let's not forget the final two senses.

"I can just about *taste* the *sweet smell* of success."

What about...
"I am *thinking* about what it will be like to *experience* being successful."

The words *thinking* and *experience* are unspecified, so the system in not yet known. If you thought you knew it, you were probably using your own representational system. If you wanted to know, you would need to ask, "How are you thinking about success?" "What, specifically, are you thinking?" or "How, exactly, do you experience being successful?"

To these questions, we might get the responses:

I am *picturing* myself becoming successful. (Visual)
I *tell* myself, "I can do it." (Auditory)
I am *stepping* into the future and it *feels* great. (Kinesthetic)

Now that we know his/her language, we can use it to help establish and maintain rapport. There are some people who will use all three systems and so can you. When they use unspecified words, you can ask questions to learn more about what system they are thinking in. Then adapt your language to the present situation.

I (R.H.) had been working with a corporate team, teaching them how to build a rapport using predicates. At one point, the director had an "aha moment" and looked at the manager and said, "No wonder why we don't get along. You are always *talking* about the numbers, and I only want to *see* graphs." The director finally understood what was causing the misunderstanding and what he needed to do to solve it.

Not only will using someone's words help to establish and build rapport, it can also be used to motivate them. Let's go back to the example about the person who wants to be more successful. If he/she reports, "I *see* myself *looking* confident and successful in my new business," you might respond with, "Yes, it is important to have a *clear picture* of where you are going. How do you *see yourself* into the future." But if he/she says, " I can *hear* my *voice* being *loud* and powerful when I am successful in my new business," then an effective response could be, "When you *hear* that powerful *voice*, what exactly are you *saying*?" and "What are the things you can *tell* yourself now that will motivate you to achieve your goal?" For the kinesthetic statement, " I will *feel* so *proud* and *excited* when my new business is successful," you can add, "I am sure it will *feel* great to *seize* the opportunities and *tackle* each of these goals head on." In regards to this last statement, many trainees have stated that they can see (but not feel) the word "tackle." So depending upon your own preferred system, you may interpret the person's word according to how you experience it or as they actually meant it. One way to prevent this from happening is to ask a question about the word. For example, "When you say *tackle*, what do you mean exactly?" If the person says, "Well I mean to *push* ahead and *grab* hold of the prize," then they have given you a kinesthetic response. If they say, "I *see* a lot of issues *appearing* and I want to *look* more carefully at the details," then you can follow up with a visual statement.

When we moved from our home in New Jersey where we had raised our family to an apartment in New York City, we met with a realtor and began to explore what we really wanted in our new place. We were particularly concerned about what kind of *view* we were going to have. We would not be *comfortable looking* out the window and *seeing* another building. After living in the suburbs we knew that not having nature around, not having something *beautiful* to *look* at, would be *unpleasant*. We were also *worried* about the *noise* level. We hadn't lived in an apartment for 20 years and did not want to *hear* the *sound of* people walking above us nor the constant *sound* of traffic. After searching for a few months, we found a *quiet* apartment that *overlooks* a park with the Manhattan *skyline* in the distance. And we both *felt* at home. Our realtor had paid attention to what we were *looking* for, and we had *clearly* communicated our needs. We were surprised and delighted that our visual, auditory and kinesthetic concerns were all satisfied.

Develop flexibility in your own style

Now that you are aware of the different types of language styles, it is time for you to develop flexibility with your language. Being an effective communicator requires flexibility. One way to do this is to expand your vocabulary to include all of the senses. Thinking differently will be useful for your own intrapersonal development as well. *Imagine* if you were reading a book and the author only *painted* a *picture* for you, or only *told* you about the *conversations* people were having, or only described what people were *feeling*. An author's job is to give a full sensory experience to their reader. Whether you communicate with the written word or the spoken word, expressing yourself in all three systems is essential to reach everyone and to give them all a complete multi-sensory experience.

You can learn something new when you open up another channel of communication. If visual is your dominant system, there is something you can learn by paying attention to the auditory. If auditory is your primary system, there is something you will learn by paying attention to something kinesthetic. Discovering what you pay attention to and what you are ignoring will be very important for learning about your inner world.

For example, think about a recent phone call. Although a phone call implies auditory modality, put yourself back in the situation and remember what you are most aware of. Once you identify what you are most aware of, include another channel of experience. And keep adding another sense until you have them all together. Our students find this to be very helpful in expanding their awareness and being more present to their surroundings.

Effective public speakers will use all three sensory modes. It is what effective politicians and evangelical speakers do when communicating to the masses. Perhaps you want a group to be open to a new idea. If you use your own style you could say, "I have an idea that will make your company's *image shine.*" However, you won't get the attention of the auditory and kinesthetic people in the audience. When speaking to large groups give three examples in three styles and say the same thing. For the visual people, "This new idea will make you a *visionary* in your field. You will be a *shining* example. For the auditory people, "Let me *tell* you about this new idea that will have everyone *talking* about your company and *saying* great things. And for the kinesthetic people, "When you *embrace* this new idea, your company will *feel* a burst of new *energy.*" This way you have been able to communicate to all types. Each person will understand your message in his or her own language.

You may also have noticed that many speakers use unspecified words as well. The same idea that we just communicated in visual, auditory and kinesthetic language could also be expressed without reference to any one modality. "This new idea will revolutionize the way you do business, increase product recognition and ensure unprecedented success."

How do you learn best? Do you prefer to see words written in a book or hear them spoken by a teacher? Do you learn best by watching a demonstration or by doing it yourself? Do you need to see, hear and do? Do you learn best by engaging in live discussions where you can speak to a teacher and be heard, or is texting back and forth sufficient?

The more you know about how you learn, the more you can create learning experiences that match your learning style. Similarly, teachers who can detect their students' learning styles can provide corresponding experiences.

But whatever your preferred style, learning NLP requires engaging "all" the senses, especially the ones out of your awareness. As NLP trainers, we provide opportunities for students to *watch* how people move, *listen* to how people speak, and *connect* to their body. We also train people to become aware of how they *visualize,* how they *talk* to themselves, and how they experience their own *movements* along with *visceral* and *emotional* sensations.

People are mostly unconscious. Without awareness, there is no opportunity for change. Only when we realize how we talk can we learn to speak differently. Only when we are aware of our breathing can we learn to breathe differently. And only when we are aware of how we think, feel and move can we learn to more effectively express ourselves.

We begin with awareness of what is, we follow with curiosity of how it can be different, we continue with exploring options and making lots of mistakes and finish when we arrive at our destination. Then we start all over again.

NLP Momentary Practice

Ask yourself, "What am I most aware of after having read this chapter? Identify whether your answer is visual, auditory or kinesthetic. If you would like to add smell and taste, please do so.

Find someone to do the following exercise. Ask him/her to tell you about his/her dream house. As your partner describes his/her dream house, write down as many words that fit into the visual, auditory or kinesthetic categories. Communicate with him/her about his/her dream house, first by using his/her most frequently used category and then with his/her least used category. Do you notice a difference in how he/she responded? Then ask him/her if he/she was aware of any differences.

CHAPTER 10

The Blame Game Changer: The Stuck-Meta-Resource Chain

"Between stimulus and response there is a space. In that space is our power to choose our response. In our response lies our growth and our freedom."
-Viktor E. Frankl

Most of you are familiar with Stimulus-Response. When presented with a given stimulus, we react a certain way.

Some images evoke happiness while others elicit sadness. Some words can make us angry while others scare us. Some places create a feeling of safety, while others cause anxiety. Sometimes our responses are neutral.

Of course, different people have varied reactions to the same stimulus. One person might react to seeing a dog with affection, while another becomes fearful. A certain scent or a particular phrase might turn one person "on" while turning another person "off." One person laughs at a joke while another becomes insulted.

Every day we are presented with stimuli that influence what we think, how we feel and the actions we take.

Some of our automatic programs pose no problem and are part of our productive engagement with the world. Others can interfere with our health and happiness. We might become enraged each time someone speaks to us with a critical tone or tells us what to do. Or we may feel abandoned whenever we are being ignored.

We can spend our lives feeling like victims, blaming other people and things for how we feel and what we do, resulting in our getting angry at them, and frustrated with our attempts to change them. And if we are not defending ourselves, we are instead attacking them, avoiding them or trying to please them. By resigning ourselves to victim status, we not only negatively affect our emotional and physical health, but we hurt our relationships.

But there is an alternative. We can take responsibility (exercising our ability to respond differently) and learn how to reprogram ourselves. NLP gives us precise tools for doing this. But choice to do so and the exact design of these new programs are up to us.

Becoming aware of our "cause-effect" patterns and recognizing a predictable reaction to a given stimulus is essential if we are going to change them.

Programs Gone Wild

One tricky thing about awareness is that the awareness itself or how we become aware can in and of itself become a trigger for another reaction. That is, it can actually become another "cause-effect" pattern. Sometimes when we see or are shown our own stimulus response pattern, we feel guilty, become self-critical, get depressed, or blame someone. In other words, we might get angry for getting angry. Or become critical for being critical. Frequently, we have heard this complaint in our couple's counseling when someone points out the other person's pattern. For example, "Whenever I give you a compliment, you discount it." One defensive response we have heard is, "Well, this is just the way I am. And if you don't like it, too bad." So the "pointing out the cause-effect pattern" becomes the stimulus for feeling attacked and becoming defensive.

Having worked with many couples over the years, we have seen the reaction of one person becoming the stimulus that causes the reaction in the other person which in turn becomes the stimulus that causes the reaction...and on and on it goes, escalating until each person feels like the victim, abandoned, abused or both while seeing the other as the abuser or abandoner. And so it continues, until one person interrupts the pattern often by "stepping back" and non-judgmentally observing what he/she is doing to contribute to the pattern and stops it. But as long as people continue to see themselves as powerless victims (at the effect) looking to be saved by someone external and in no way contributing to or being responsible for perpetuating the problem, there will be no solution. Only when we transcend the victim-perpetrator-rescuer cycle by becoming the observer of our patterns and changing these patterns can solutions be found. One of the stumbling blocks to freeing ourselves of these patterns is that as soon as it is pointed out to us that we are contributing to the pattern, instead of seeing it as an opportunity to be free from the pattern and a chance for healthy change, we react to it as a further attack, feeling guilty, shamed or blamed and we are again back to the familiar role of victim. As long as we remain in that role, other people are potential perpetrators or potential rescuers.

If you are committed to blaming other people – or yourself, for that matter – for your own stimulus-response programs and not prepared to step back and look at these patterns with an attitude of, "I wonder how else I could be responding," then perhaps this book is not for you. But if you are curious as to how you and others can change their programs, then read on.

Good. You are still here.

On occasion our clients and students say, "I can't change this habit." When this happens we become curious and ask, "Do you really believe you are incapable of changing? Or is it that you do not know 'how' to change?" If the response is that they do not know how to change, then we will teach them. If they respond that they do not believe that they can change, we can help them change that belief. Or we might ask them to temporarily suspend their belief and "act as if" they could change. At this point, most people will give up objecting and be open to learning something new.

There is one more possibility. Some people really believe that they *can* change and they even learn *how* to do it, but still do not change. For example, there are people who believe that they can lose and maintain their weight. They have read every "how to" book, attended many weight loss seminars and done "everything" to change. But they either remain fat or they lose weight and put it all back on, perhaps even adding some extra pounds in the process. So believing that you can change and knowing how to change may not be enough. So what's missing? It is called "Congruence." And it is the topic of Chapter 23 titled, "Reframing," If there is a part of you that wants to make a particular change and yet there is another part of you that wants to remain with what's familiar, then you already know what we are talking about.

The NLP model does not pass judgment on whether any particular pattern or habit is inherently good or bad. These "cause-effect" patterns are learned responses that are now automatic and unconscious. The problem with calling these habits, "stimulus-response" or "cause-effect" is the unintended assumption that it is fixed, factual, unchangeable and out of our control. Something is happening in our unconscious mind from the moment the stimulus is introduced to the moment the emotional or physical reaction occurs. And it happens so damn fast that it seems impossible not to react the way we are reacting.

Dogs, themselves, do not cause anxiety. They require someone who perceives them as a threat. For those who experience anxiety, the image or sound is sent to the brain the moment the dog is spotted and a danger alert is immediately sent through the nervous system. And with the speed of the reaction, the conscious mind has no time to stop it. Maybe we can hold back our words or our physical reaction, but our mind and body is still reacting.

There are many NLP techniques designed to change our reactions. The most intense "cause-effect" reactions are phobias and traumas (including PTSD). We will address how to change these reactions in Chapter 27.

For now we will introduce one of many techniques that we teach to interrupt an existing cause-effect pattern and program a more useful one.

The Stuck Meta Resource Technique

We teach this technique at the start of our training to give participants an early experience of what NLP can accomplish. To skillfully guide someone through it requires developing many of the competencies presented throughout our NLP training.

When we teach this technique we ask participants to identify a context in which they get stuck. A context refers to a specific stimulus or set of stimuli that trigger the reaction. Being stuck refers to a non-resourceful reaction where you become upset and reactive (e.g. impatient, frustrated, guilty, negative, closed, defensive, aggressive, etc.)

So think of a specific type of situation in which you consistently react in a non-productive way. Select something that is limiting, but not traumatic. On a scale from 0-10, where 0 is neutral and 10 most intense, we recommend starting with something 4 and under.

Here are some possible scenarios.

Getting angry when you are told what to do.
Becoming defensive when you are being criticized.
Becoming afraid when someone gets angry.
Retaliating when someone rejects you.
Closing down when someone tells you "no."

Only pick a reaction that you really want to eliminate. When there are inner objections or resistance to change, they must be addressed in another way (see Chapter 23).

Once the demonstration has begun and someone has been selected we create three spaces along a continuum on the floor. The first space is called the "Stuck State," the next space is called, "The Meta Position," and the third space is the, "Resource State." We teach this exercise standing and moving across the floor. Depending upon context and space limitations this exercise can be modified.

The Stuck State is the state you enter into when the situation occurs. It is the combination of thoughts, feelings and actions that you want to change. For example, retaliating or withdrawing when someone rejects you.

The Meta Position is a phrase that is used often in NLP. It means something of a higher order and we use it as a place from which we can objectively observe ourselves.

The Resource State refers to our inner abilities and strengths. Remember the NLP presupposition that we have all the resources within. A resource can be compassion, confidence, curiosity, centeredness, calm, creativity, etc. But resources do not always have to begin with the letter "c." There is humor, playfulness, love, and many more.

The Stuck-Meta-Resource Exercise is the first of many techniques involving dyads that we teach in the training. The person working on himself we call the "Explorer" and the person taking the explorer though the exercise we call the "Guide." In the early days of NLP the explorer was called the "subject," and the guide was called the "programmer." We prefer the more humanistic language. In this book we will sometimes refer to the explorer as the client and to the guide as the coach.

For this technique, the guide begins by asking the explorer to think of a situation (the stimulus) in which the explorer gets stuck (the response). He can ask, "How do you know when to get stuck? Or "What do you see or hear that 'lets you know' it's time to go into the stuck state." We are looking for the following form: "Whenever I see or hear x, I become y." For example, "Whenever I ask my children to do something and they ignore me, I become enraged." It is a good idea to ask if this only occurs with his children, to see if the pattern is more general than first stated. Perhaps, it occurs whenever "anyone" doesn't do what he wants him to do.

It is also a good idea to ask if it happens with all his children, because the phenomenon may only occur with his sons and not his daughters. These types of questions can be used in any context to determine the trigger.

Once the explorer identifies the trigger, the guide asks him/her to experientially "step into" the situation, and feel, see and hear what he/she experiences in that context. When he/she does this, the explorer will begin to feel some or most of the unpleasant feelings. (The explorer is now in *The Stuck State*).

As soon as this happens, the guide immediately asks the explorer to "step out of" the experience and move a few feet away, putting some distance between himself/herself and the "stuck self. " Looking back at himself/herself from this perspective he/she describes what he/she *sees* the "Self in the Stuck State" doing thinking and feeling. It is imperative, in this *Meta Position,* that the explorer only "sees and hears" himself/herself from the outside while all the feelings and emotions, including any self-judgments, remain in the self that is being observed in the original situation. One way to make sure this happens it to have the explorer speak of himself/herself in the third person using "he" or "she" instead of "I" and gesturing toward the "other" when speaking about him. Other ways to keep the explorer from "falling" back into the stuck state is to use submodalities, such as putting more distance between the observer and the observed, making the image 2D instead of 3D, putting it in a frame on a screen and pointing to the screen when describing "his/her" feelings. While some people do this step easily without any coaching, others will need significant help from the guide. (The explorer is now in the *Meta Position*.)

The Meta Position is a perspective where we become an objective observer, often a wise, compassionate observer. We are fully on the outside looking in. This point of view is also referred to as being "disassociated." Perspectives such as judgment, criticism, pity, guilt, blame, resentment and disgust are not part of the objective observer. Whenever these types of states show up, it is important to learn how to disassociate from them as well.

When the explorer has achieved the *Meta Position* and has finished objectively describing what the "Self in the Stuck State" is thinking, feeling and doing, the guide asks, "What resource does he/she (the self in the original context) need right now to be able to respond appropriately and effectively?" Is it Self Confidence, Self Worth, Balance, Inner Peace, Lightness, Humor? It is preferable to have the explorer discover the resource himself/herself. The most skilled guides are the ones who lead the explorer to the answers rather than supplying them. The guide waits, encourages and on occasion suggests. However it is the explorer who gets to choose the resource. For this example, let's use "patience" as the resource.

Having identified the resource "patience," the guide asks the explorer to pick a third location for the *Resource State*. The next step is for the explorer to imagine him/herself being patient. It can be a memory or simply be made up on the spot. It does not have to be an example of a time when the explorer was patient in that situation. It is actually better to identify "patience" in a different context. The guide then asks the explorer to "step into the resourceful experience." The skilled guide will use visual, auditory and kinesthetic submodalities, when needed, to assist the explorer in getting fully immersed into the state. This may involve making it 3D, panoramic, colorful with full movement and surround sound. When we are on the inside of an experience looking out of our own eyes, hearing from our own ears and feeling our feelings, we are "associated." We are no longer "thinking about" the resource; we are being resourceful. When the explorer speaks he/she is now using the word "I." The explorer is now fully and completely in the *Resource State*.

At this point the explorer has experienced three distinct states, the *Stuck State*, the *Meta Position* and the *Resource State*. When done correctly, it is not an intellectual exercise; each step engages all of the senses.

At this point, we do something, anything to break state. The explorer can ask the guide to shake his/her body, move around the room or distract him/her with some irrelevant topic. This is called a *"Breaker State."*

What you are now about to do is design a new pattern, create a new habit that will replace the old neuro-linguistic program.

The guide now repeats the previous steps by first guiding the explorer back into the location of the original situation, the *Stuck State*, then stepping back to the location of the *Meta Position* and finally to the location of the *Resource State*. A skilled guide will be able to "see" and "hear" that inner state changes are taking place by calibrating the explorer's external behavior. Then *Break State*.

Go through the steps a second time, and make sure you *Break State* at the end.

Next the guide has the explorer revisit each of the three states while the explorer remains in the same physical location. Typically, the explorer experiences moving through each position as he/she rapidly arrives at the *Resource State*.

The Stuck-Meta-Resource technique introduces you to a way to update your program by introducing and installing a resourceful way of responding. In effect what you are doing is teaching the unconscious to follow a new more satisfying pathway or chain, where the initial stimulus will take the explorer directly to the *Resource State* without having to consciously think about it.

A skilled guide will use language that supports the updated program. For example, he/she can say, "Now step into a situation that 'used to' upset you," instead of "Now step back into the *Stuck State.*"

Remember that the situation (the stimulus) 'had been' linked to the *Stuck State* (the response). So use language presuppositions that reinforce this "unlinked" status. For example, if the context was driving a car and getting cut off by another driver, you can say to the explorer, "Notice what happens now when you put yourself into the drivers seat where in the past you 'used to' feel enraged at being cut off, and tell me what happens now having the new resource available."

This is how we test to see if the new program has been successfully installed. By describing it in this way, you are assuming that the old program is no longer running and the new resource is in place.

When the resource state shows up automatically, you know that you have successfully tested the new program.

Some people are under the impression that it is their conscious mind that is in charge, that they can consciously control their reaction. So before we begin the technique we will sometimes say to the explorer, "If you believe you have a conscious choice about getting stuck or not, then just go ahead and change your reaction." Once he/she recognizes that the conscious mind is not the one in charge, we can proceed to program the unconscious.

Some people tell us that making such a change cannot happen so quickly; that according to their coach, making it permanent requires practice and that changing a habit actually requires 21 days of practice. While we have come a long way since people believed that we required 21 years of therapy, the 21-day requirement is still a limiting belief and not based upon any valid research. While learning to become an effective NLP Coach/Practitioner requires practice and lots and lots of feedback, the techniques are designed to install a new program that does not need further practice.

Although we do the demonstration while moving in space, it can be done sitting in one location. One trainee reported doing it at his desk while he spoke on the phone. Another did it in his car while stuck in traffic. Still another student guided his partner through the steps while skiing in the Swiss Alps. After setting up the three locations, she just skied through each state bringing the resource state along with her as she continued down to the base of the mountain.

While it might seem that the ideal setting is a quiet room with plenty of floor space, you can see that with a little creativity, flexibility or 'snow,' you can practice these techniques anywhere.

You can think of the following technique as dance steps, a recipe or a mathematical algorithm.

The Stuck Meta Resource Exercise Steps

1. Identify a context in which the explorer gets stuck.

2. Briefly, have him/her associate into this *Stuck State*.

3. Step out of the *Stuck State* into the *Meta Position*.

From the *Meta Position* describe the self in his/her *Stuck State*, his/her physiology, voice, feelings, thinking, breathing, etc. Refer to the self in the stuck state as "he," "she," or "him," "her." In the *Stuck State*, there is only curiosity and objective observation — all other feelings are to remain in the *Stuck State*.

4. From the *Meta Position*, Identify an Inner Resource.

Identify the inner resource(s) needed by the self in the original context (e.g. Centeredness, Love, Playfulness, Safety...)

5. From the *Meta Position* turn to a new location for the *Resource State*.

Ask the explorer to see and hear him/herself embodying that inner resource. This should be done in a context different from the original one.

6. Now Step (Associate) into the *Resource State*

Guide the explorer to step into the *Resource State*. You can ask the explorer to "take all the time in the world" to experience fully what it is like to be in this state. You may offer a supportive touch and say the name of this state aloud.

7. Step into a *Breaker State* and review the process.

Guide the explorer to step into a *Breaker State* and review the entire process. You can also distract the person by talking about something entirely unrelated or shaking it out.

8. Repeat the passage from *Stuck State* to *Meta Position* to *Resource State*.

Now guide the explorer to repeat the process, going from *Stuck State* to *Meta Position* to the *Resource State*. Then go to the *Breaker State*.

9. While remaining in the original physical location "move" through the three positions.

While standing in the original "location," have the explorer associate into the original "situation," then immediately guide him into the *Meta Position*, then into the *Resourceful State* while the explorer continues to see and hear what he is seeing and hearing in the "original situation."

10. Test.

You can suggest to the explorer to "try" to get stuck in the initial situation. Pay attention to physiology to confirm that the subject is accessing the *Resourceful State*. If the explorer still feels stuck, you can repeat steps 8 and 9 or have the explorer go back to the *Meta Position* and find an additional inner resource.

NLP Momentary Practice

Take a moment and think about resource states that you have already experienced. And imagine having them showing up again in the future.

CHAPTER 11

Truth Vs. Truthiness: Sensory Specificity and Interpretation

"There are no facts, only interpretations."
-Friedrich Nietzsche

We are always interpreting, except when we are not. And when we think we are not, we usually are. We do not only interpret art and dreams; we interpret behavior-facial expressions, body postures, gestures, eye movements, breathing changes, words and their accompanying tones, tempos, volume and inflections. While some of our interpretations about what people mean turn out to be accurate, many of them are not. Learning to recognize when we are making these interpretations will improve our communication.

Not only are we oblivious to the "fact" that we are making interpretations, but we also confuse, both intentionally and unintentionally, our interpretations with facts. Stephen Colbert, the Comedy Central host of the Colbert Report, coined a name for this. He called it "truthiness." Wikipedia defines truthiness as "a quality characterizing a 'truth' that a person claims to know intuitively 'from the gut' or because it 'feels right' without regard to evidence, logic, intellectual examination, or facts." Although Colbert used it to refer to many political pundits who espouse their opinions, often by beginning their sentences with, "The truth is...", we will be examining how the effectiveness of our interpersonal communication and the health of our most important relationships depend so much upon making this distinction between our "interpretation of what is happening" and "what is actually occurring."

By the way, we have nothing against "gut feelings" or "intuition." We get them on a regular basis when working with clients and trainees. And sometimes they are spot on. But the only way we can really know whether our interpretations are accurate is by checking it out with our clients and trainees, by listening to them and paying close attention to their responses.

Some frequently asked interpersonal communication questions that involve interpretation include:

Why are you so angry with me?
Why aren't you listening to me?
What's wrong?

In each case there is an interpretation of another's behavior and the assumption that our interpretation is accurate. We are convinced that we already know what is true. This attachment to "thinking we know" what another person really means, thinks and feels frequently leads to other people feeling misunderstood, ignored and/or disrespected.

Alternatively, we might say:

Are you angry?
You appear distracted? What's going on?
You haven't said a word. Is there something you want to express?

In contrast to the first set of questions, these responses demonstrate curiosity and openness.

When someone is interpreting my (S.L.) behavior, I want to know the source of his/her interpretation, especially if his/her interpretation does not match my experience. In this way, I can learn something about his/her experience and maybe something about myself.

If someone tells me, "You are not listening to me" and my experience is that I am listening, rather than contradict him/her by saying, "But I am listening," I will ask a question, such as, "What gives you that impression?" I ask the question to learn what it is he/she actually saw or heard that led to his/her conclusion. I am also interested in learning what he/she would need to see or hear that will give him/her the experience that I am listening. His/her response may be as simple as, "You were looking around when I was speaking and not looking directly at me." Or "You were silent and not making any comments," or "Your head was still and I saw no changes in your facial expression. I need some indication that you are listening, like a nod or a smile." By listening to his/her response I am learning exactly what I will need to do to "give him/her" the experience of being listened to.

In my (R.H.) early training days I was given feedback from trainees that when they would ask me a question, I would look judgmental. I had not realized that when I was thinking of the answer to the question, I furrowed my brow (visualize two eyebrows coming together). I was surprised at this feedback, because I genuinely felt curious and not judgmental when listening to someone's question. Upon being given the sensory feedback that my brow furrowed, I went home and looked in a mirror and imagined people asking me questions and worked at keeping my brow smooth as I listened to the imagined questions. This helped me the next time I was in a practice session because now the feedback was, you look interested in what the person is asking. I had changed the facial expression, and kept my brow smooth and widened my eyes. I did this before Botox. Who knew that people in the 21st century would do something to prevent their brows to furrow permanently? Fortunately, I found a way to change my facial expression naturally. The learning from this example is that when you receive or give feedback, it is important for it to be sensory specific and to know that you can change your behaviors.

When we receive or give feedback it is important that the feedback be sensory based. The sensory information is based on what we can see and hear. Another way to say this is behavioral evidence. When we observe someone we pay attention to their posture, gestures, movement or lack of movement, facial expressions which include eye contact, lips upturned (known as a smile) or down turned (known as a frown), breathing, movement (or no movement), muscular tension, and voice tone, tempo and volume.

Let's go back to the feedback that I (R.H.) was initially given. Being told that I was being judgmental was an interpretation. It is not high quality feedback. However, when told that my brow was furrowed, I was getting sensory-based information that I could do something with. My point is that for us to learn we need sensory-based feedback along with the interpretation. But our unconscious processes these interpretations so quickly that often our conscious mind does not have immediate access to it.

When our description is interpretive, we are not being sensory specific. For example, if someone gives us feedback and says that we looked confident, he/she is not telling us what he/she actually saw or heard. To find that out we need to learn what specific behaviors gave him/her that impression. Was it certain movements, facial expressions, eye contact, no eye contact, gestures, posture, breathing changes, lip changes and brow changes (smooth or furrowed) that gave him/her that perception? We can ask for specific feedback about our voice. Was it loud, soft, fast or slow tempo, high or low pitch? All of these questions are asking for sensory-based evidence. While the information may be unconscious and not immediately accessible, it is there nevertheless and can be retrieved.

Here is one more example of the distinction between Interpretive Feedback verses Sensory Based Feedback.

Interpretive Feedback

"I liked your presentation, you were very confident,"

Sensory Based Feedback

"Your voice was loud and clear and you maintained eye contact when participants asked you questions."

An effective communicator will offer his/her interpretation only "after" he/she has described what he/she has seen and heard. This will give the recipient something useful and valuable.

Effective Feedback

Your voice was loud and clear and you maintained eye contact when participants asked you questions. This gave me the impression that you were confident and warm."

On the other hand, when an effective communicator receives a "gut feeling" interpretation from another person, he/she will ask for sensory feedback. We suggested this in the earlier example where someone says, " You are not listening" and the response is

"What is it that makes you think I am not listening?" or "What specifically am I doing to give you that impression?"

In our training we sometimes ask people how they want to be perceived and how they do not want to be perceived. They might say they want to be perceived as caring and interested and do not want to be perceived as cold and distant. Then we make a chart with two columns. One is for interpretations and the other for sensory-based perceptions. Caring, Interested, Cold and Distant would go under the Interpretation column. Then we would ask participants for the sensory-based descriptions for each one that would go in the other column.

In the discussion about sensory-based feedback, we often mention non-verbal communication expert, Dr. Paul Ekman. He has researched facial reading and goes into greater depth about all of the facial muscles (about 43 muscles in the face alone), and what the expressions possibly mean. In regards to interpretation and accuracy his research showed that there are seven facial expressions that are universally known. They are anger, sadness, joy, surprise, disgust, fear and contempt. To learn more about Dr. Ekman, read the article, *Naked Face*, by Malcolm Gladwell, 2002, The New Yorker Magazine.

Whether you are giving feedback or receiving feedback, it will be to your advantage to use sensory-based evidence in your language. When you do practice we suggest that you listen to someone talk for a minute and notice only what you hear and see — that will be sensory-based information. Then take another minute to wildly interpret. After you do these two processes, notice which one feels more familiar to you: sensory-based information, or interpretation. Some of our trainees have discovered that when they have to identify the sensory information it make them more present and focused. Another benefit that our trainees get is in learning how to sequence the information in the way we described earlier. An example being, "You are speaking loudly and your jaw is clenched. That makes me think you are feeling angry." Giving sensory-based feedback can also be important when you are giving compliments. By telling someone, "Your postures and gestures were symmetrical and your voice was loud and clear, which gave the impression of being comfortably in charge."

In one of my (S.L.) first courses with John Grinder back in 1982, a participant asked him, "What about people who have a sixth sense?" I remember John responding that most of us are not paying attention with our five senses and need to open our eyes and ears to the vast amount of information that's available. Much of our intuition (both accurate and inaccurate) is based on a highly developed unconscious processing of the five senses operating at super speed.

Sensory Vs. Interpretation Exercise

In our training program the exercise we use to practice these skills is called "Sensory versus Interpretation." This is a three-person exercise that inevitably results in laughter and having fun. Warning: Do not attempt to do this exercise anywhere outside the context of doing this exercise. People will probably not laugh and you will probably lose rapport.

One person will tell a story. It is more fun if it is an animated story. As he/she tells the story, the second person (at the same time) will describe out loud what he/she sees and hears. Only use sensory-based information. If he/she makes an interpretation, such as "She is relaxed," the third person will gently tap him/her on the shoulder. The person describing the sensory information talks at the same time the story is being told. (3 minutes).

The person who was telling the story now continues or repeats the story and the person who was using sensory-based language now interprets. The third person will now tap him/her on the shoulder if he/she gives a sensory-based description. (3 minutes).

At the conclusion of first round, discuss what it was like to deliberately use sensory language and interpretive language. One of the fun or potentially irritating parts of this exercise is that the storyteller is telling a story while the other person is talking over them. This could also be called the "rude exercise." So once the exercise is over, you can ask the storyteller if he/she would like to tell it one more time without any interruptions. Then switch roles.

When you do this exercise, notice which of the two languages you find easier to do and which is more challenging.

NLP Momentary Practice

Give someone feedback combining sensory based and interpretive language. Before you do, it is probably a good idea to check if they really want your feedback. Pay attention to their response.

When someone gives you a compliment ask him/her for sensory specific feedback. And remember to say "thank you."

There is a technique from "Drawing on the Right Side of the Brain" by Betty Edwards that asks the reader to find a picture of a face and draw it. After completing the task, the reader is asked to turn the original picture of the face upside down and proceed to draw it again. The result is usually a more accurate drawing. The upside down face is disorienting, which allows us to see only what is actually there and not what we think is there. In other words, without our usual orientation, instead of drawing our idea (interpretation) of what a nose looks like, we draw only what we see. Try it for yourself.

CHAPTER 12

Pay Attention: Observing Non Verbal Communication

"All human knowledge takes the form of interpretation."
-Walter Benjamin

There are some people who are easy to read. They express themselves; they make faces and get "read" in the face. There are others who have a poker face; their signals are minimal and subtler. Although there is no such thing as no communication, the poker face, with no discernable movements, no reddening in the skin, eyes that are fixed, will be more difficult to figure out. The observer of the former might comment, "He wears his/her heart on their sleeve." While the observer of the latter might say, "I have no idea what he/she is thinking or feeling." With the plethora of nonverbal communication books, it is obvious that people believe or want to believe that it is possible to read someone's mind by how they look and speak. It is possible to learn about people's unconscious communications when you know what to look and listen for.

As discussed in the Chapter 9, by training your eyes and ears to be more sensory specific, you can match your interpretations with behavioral evidence and more accurately read someone's nonverbal communication. In order to accurately interpret, it is important to recognize repetitive patterns in someone's behavior. When you meet someone for the first time, there is no pattern recognition history with that person. There are cultural patterns. For example, for most cultures a "head nod," is interpreted as a "yes." Whereas people from India move their heads side to side for a "yes." However, if you are paying close attention to people whom you know over time, you will see behavior patterns that reliably repeat themselves so you can learn to accurately interpret. In this chapter we will be talking about the micro cues of nonverbal communication, particularly facial expressions and breath location, depth and rate.

In order to be an effective communicator it is necessary to develop the skill of observation – acute sensory awareness. This was one of the skills of Milton Erickson, MD, psychiatrist and hypnotherapist, who the NLP developers modeled for his own brand of hypnosis, known as Ericksonian Hypnosis. Erickson paid close attention. He appeared to know what people were experiencing. And his accuracy was uncanny. When Dr. Erickson spoke to his clients, he would look for cues that indicated that the person was "going into trance." At these very moments he would make comments like, "That's right" or "That's it" or "Good," which reinforced the person's hypnotic state and reassured the trance subjects that he was paying attention. While he did not exactly know what they were thinking or feeling, he knew that they were going into trance and used this non-verbal information to deepen the experience. In a session this week I noticed that when my (S.L.) client was speaking about being abused, he smiled. The words and facial expression did not match. Once I noticed it, I could not ignore it. So I commented that what he was saying was not a laughing matter. This produced a noticeable shift in which he took himself seriously. There is so much that we are seeing and hearing that passes by without being seen or heard.

Learning To Observe Non-Verbal Signals

The development of your observer's eyes is the art of "calibration." To effectively "calibrate" another's behavior we must train ourselves to be in the state of uptime, which we described in Chapter 8, where all our senses are directed externally. A very simple way to begin practicing is to find a partner who would be available to help you learn these skills and ask him/her to stand in front of you. Look at him/her and memorize everything you see. Then close your eyes. When your eyes are closed, he/she changes something about his/her appearance. For example, if he/she is wearing a sweater with buttons on the first round he/she could have the sweater open, and the second round the sweater is buttoned. Once you open your eyes, you look to identify what has changed. It is an exercise for you to practice your visual skills and become more observant of others. Sometimes you might notice a change that your partner did not even intend. Once you get good at this, it will be up to your partner to make subtler changes, so you can calibrate finer distinctions. It may be a slight tightening of the lips or a relaxation/smoothing of facial muscles. The more flexible he/she is, the more you will learn. And remember, you can't fail. You will only become better and better at "seeing." The more attentive we are to these cues, the better we will become at knowing if and when people are listening, trustworthy, understanding, etc.

Trust Vs. Mistrust Exercise

Here is another exercise we use to practice calibration where we identify the specific cues that determine whether someone trusts or distrusts. We begin by asking a participant to think of someone he/she likes and trusts. As he/she thinks about the person, the class observes his/her appearance. Next, we ask the subject to think of someone he/she does not like and distrusts, and we again pay attention. We look for facial expressions, body movements, muscle tension, lower lip size, eyes, eyebrows and skin color. We are not just looking for overt clues, like big smiles or clenched fists. We are looking for the subtle nonverbal cues. One of the most important things to observe is breathing. We look at the location of the breathing as well as depth and speed.

Then we discuss the differences between the two observations. After identifying these differences, we repeat the procedure, looking for consistent differences. For example, every time he/she thinks of the person he/she trusts the breathing is slow and deep, but whenever he/she thinks of the person he/she distrusts the breathing is fast and shallow.

Now the fun begins. We ask questions, the answers to which will refer to one of the two people. For example, "Which person has longer hair?" or "Which person is older?" or "Who is taller?" The subject remains silent, responding nonverbally, while the observers determine the answer based on the observed cues. The questions themselves are not important. What is important is that the observers "calibrate" the micro cues, the facial coloration, muscular tension or flatness, breathing and any other movements to determine whom the person is thinking about.

After each question we "vote" on whom we think the person is thinking about, and find out if we were on target. We then discuss what indicators we used. We continue the exercise until everyone gets to calibrate the differences.

The previous two exercises were designed to develop "visual" calibration skills. There are similar exercises that develop auditory, kinesthetic, olfactory and gustatory calibration skills.

An exercise we have used to develop auditory calibration skills is one in which we have one person make a statement, any statement. A second person then repeats the statement. At this point, a third person, who has been listening, describes how the tone, tempo, volume, inflection, etc. of second statement was different from the first and teaches the second person how to match both content and form.

How Do You Read Someone Saying "Yes" or "No"

Next we ask a volunteer to answer a series of "yes/no" questions while the group observes the non-verbal cues corresponding to both the "yes," and "no" answers. This is very important for sales people (and who isn't a sales person, really) to be able to calibrate a "yes" and a "no." Calibrating "yes" and "no" will let you know when to stop what you are doing and change your communication approach.

The way to explore "yes" and "no" is by asking the volunteer to think of something to which the answer is a definite "yes" or a definite "no." The questions could refer to an activity, a place, food or a person.

Here are some examples:

Do you enjoy shopping?
Do you enjoy deep-sea fishing?
Are you an avid sports fan?
Were you born in the United States?

Would you enjoy eating a big juicy hamburger?
Would you like to try mud wrestling?

We keep checking in with the person until we have found at least three definite yeses and three definite nos. Sometimes we get responses that are neither one nor the other. These responses will look different from a pure "yes" or pure "no." But for now we are looking for "definite yeses" or "definite nos."

Now, we ask questions to which we know the answer will be "yes" and calibrate. Then we ask questions to which we now know the answer will be "no" and calibrate. Use the observational skills that you have already been working with, observe breathing location and rate, facial coloration or lack of, lips thinning or thickening, eye brows furrowing or smoothing, tightness or lengthening in the muscles of the face or chest.

Now we ask questions that have not yet been asked. For example, "Would you like to go horseback riding?" or "Would you like learn a computer game?" or "Would you like two tickets to a Yankee playoff game?" The questions are asked and answered (silently). Each time the question is asked, the group determine, based on previous calibration, if it is a "yes" or "no." Before going on to the next question, find out the correct answer. Our goal is to develop greater accuracy with our observations.

Sometimes a trainee's own model (generalizations) of the world interferes. He/she may ask his/her partner the question, "Do you like going shopping for electronic equipment?" assuming that only men like shopping for electronics. This is a reminder about how our model of the world can get in the way of seeing. When our beliefs prevent us from seeing, they become liabilities. Whereas "not knowing," "paying attention" and "being curious" are assets. You might also get responses that do not fit into the patterns that you have previously discerned. If you asked Steven if he wanted to go to a Mets game at a time they were tied for first place, you would get a definite yes. If they were 15 games out of first place and playing poorly, you would get a definite "no." Otherwise, his response might be "ambivalence." Ask him to go clothes shopping and you would get a definitive "no," unless it was to buy a gift for Rachel or the kids.

Can You Identify A Liar

Another allure of nonverbal communication is whether it can determine when someone is lying. Paul Ekman, PhD, is one of the leading researchers on lying. In the research on catching lies the basic understanding is that it is difficult to identify a liar. And NLP does not teach specific skills to "catch" liars. At least, we don't. However, as an NLP trainee, the use of trained observation with your eyes and ears will keep you attentive to hearing and seeing what may be unusual or "out of place."

Are You Giving Away Too Little or Too Much About Yourself?

The other side of detecting other people's patterns is determining if we are actually revealing more or less than we think we are revealing or want to reveal.

Some people doing the Trust/Mistrust exercise are shocked to learn that they are not so easily read. They had thought it should have been obvious to their significant others when they felt angry or sad. It wasn't. This means they need to use their words and/or increase their nonverbal cues if they want other people to know what they are feeling.

If you are one of those people who are not easily read, it can be useful to practice exaggerating your facial expressions. Being perceived as a poker face may be interpreted as "unapproachable or insensitive." If you want others to perceive you as interested in engaging in conversation, then the poker face will not support you in getting that response. Of course, if you want to be perceived as aloof, detached and mysterious, it might work very well for you. Typically a smile that forms lines by the eyes known as "crow's feet," projects a friendly face. The more lines, the more the eyes are smiling. This nonverbal communication, although perhaps not universal, is considered by many as welcoming and friendly.

Other people find that they are showing more than they want to show. This is especially true for individuals who are dealing with social or public speaking anxiety where they find themselves blushing, sweating or shaking. Changing the auditory submodalities (how you are talking to yourself) or visual submodalities (how you are viewing yourself) can be quite powerful in reducing or completely eliminating these unwanted symptoms.

One of my (S.L.) clients told me that she was sweating profusely and got anxious when speaking to a group — she didn't like being the "focal point." I asked her to imagine making the people in the audience the "focal point" instead. By shifting the "focal point" to members of the audience her anxiety disappeared, her curiosity increased and her sweating stopped.

NLP Momentary Practice

For those of you who show more than you want to show.

Stand in front of a mirror. Close your eyes and think about someone who upsets you, then open your eyes and observe yourself. Then close your eyes again and move the person further away. Make his/her image smaller and focus on a point in front of or behind him/her instead of focusing directly on him/her. Open your eyes and see (and feel) how you have changed. You can enhance or modify this exercise by changing to a different submodality (e.g. Change the kinesthetic submodalities of breathing, posture or just moving your awareness to different places in your body).

You have now learned "about" calibrating. The next step is learning "to" calibrate.

CHAPTER 13

Reflections On Mirroring: Building, Deepening and Maintaining Rapport

"Mirror neurons are a kind of a 'neural Wi-Fi' that monitors what is happening in other people...this puts us on the same wavelength and it does it automatically, instantaneously and unconsciously."
-Daniel Goleman

Is getting along with others overrated? Apparently not! As humans, we are destined to interact and as social animals our innate nature is to relate with others and develop intimacy. Yet why is it that some people are awkward, while others do it so well? Fortunately, for those of us who have not yet mastered these essential "rapport" skills, it is never too late to learn. Do not ask, "Why can't I develop these skills?" Ask, "How do I develop my ability to establish rapport and maintain it? And when I lose it, how do I get it back?"

In the early 1980s we both had the chance to see Virginia Satir in action. Satir was one of the therapists modeled by Bandler and Grinder when they began developing the NLP model. Satir was considered one of the early developers of the family therapy system movement. At a conference we attended, we saw her simultaneously embrace all three hundred participants. When she looked at you, you felt special. She did not always know how she was doing what she was "doing, " because her natural rapport style was unconscious. Her ability to get rapport with each member of a family was something she just did without thinking about it. There are some people who have what appears to be a "natural" ability to get along with others. For them, it happens effortlessly and spontaneously. Creating rapport, developing relationships and enhancing connection is not something we are born with. It is learned. This chapter offers manageable steps to learn or relearn how to be in rapport with anyone, if you choose to do so.

First let's look at the question, "What is rapport?" When people are "in rapport" they seem to be "in sync" or are operating "on the same wavelength." There is a sense of "understanding and trust" that develops between two people or within a small group. And while rapport may develop and deepen over time, most of us have experienced it happen after just one encounter with someone.

The level of rapport can also vary depending on the relationship. The depth of rapport will not be the same for a new colleague at work as it is for an old friend. But in either case rapport is something that can be lost and regained. But no matter the depth, establishing, maintaining and when needed, reestablishing it, is essential.

When we are in rapport, we are feeling connected, getting along, and relating well. Yet we do not have to agree. Some people think that you must have things in common, like a love for the same music, movies or people, or shared religious or political beliefs and values. These shared values and common interests do bring people together and do contribute to bonding and intimate relationships. But having these things in common does not guarantee rapport.

How many of you meet people who hold very different beliefs, values and interests from your own, and yet the context calls for rapport? This happens with all professional relationships such as in coaching, therapy, law, medicine, the arts, teaching, managing, or selling. So we need to be able to do it in a way that does not involve agreement or having shared interests and beliefs. To do this, as with everything else in NLP, we will pay attention to the "form," not the content. Earlier in Chapter 9, we discussed paying attention to the styles of language, visual, auditory and kinesthetic, to get someone's attention, to engage with them and to ultimately get rapport. When practicing the language styles, you were learning how to mirror language. In this chapter we explore how to use other forms of our communication to build rapport.

When building rapport we use: facial expressions (including eye contact and smiling), gestures, posture, breathing, movement/stillness, and voice qualities, including volume, tempo, pitch and overall rhythm. This doesn't mean that words (content) aren't important. Eventually we want to be able to build rapport with both content and form. In this chapter we highlight using form.

Practicing Mirroring Techniques To Become Socially and emotionally Intelligent

In order to have positive personal and professional relationships, "Social intelligence" is an important character trait to develop. In the book, Social Intelligence: The New Science of Human Relationships (2006), author Daniel Goleman, uses the term *social intelligence*. It is also referred to as *emotional intelligence*. In business, the term "soft skills" is often used when referring to these intelligences, even though there is nothing "soft" about them. These are skills that help us communicate effectively and efficiently, create repeat business, get referrals and maintain ongoing commitments. These skills get results. We see them as "primary skills." If two candidates with equal job qualifications go for an interview, it is the enhanced communication skills that will make the difference (unless one of them is better *connected*). Companies look for people who are both team players and people who can manage the team.

There was a study done in 1997, led by Dr. Wendy Levinson that explored why some doctors were sued less than other doctors (Levinson, Wendy, Dr., et al, *The Relationship with Malpractice Claims Registered Among Primary Care Physicians and Surgery*, The journal of the American Medical Association, Feb. 19, 1997, Vol. 277, no. 7). When they examined what factors influenced patients' decisions, they found that doctors who recognized the importance of the doctor-patient relationship and took the time in their initial consultation to establish rapport were less likely to be sued by a significant margin.

The NLP tools of establishing, building and maintaining rapport are practical and effective for developing social intelligence. The mirroring techniques reflect the English proverb, "When in Rome do as the Romans do." In Chapter 9, when we wrote about the couple that argued about saying or showing love, they needed to learn that when they were in each other's "country," they needed to follow the customs for that individual country. Rather than "Do to others what you want them to do to you," we suggest, "Do to others what they would have you do to them."

When NLP began modeling Virginia Satir and her rapport skills, mirror neurons had not yet been discovered. However, since the early 1990s, researchers have been exploring the theories about whether there are neurons in the brain that respond naturally to another person's movement. If it is true, then the theory scientifically supports the nonverbal mirroring that we have found to be so effective and that we are encouraging you to learn.

Identify Ways To Establish, Maintain and Regain Rapport

There are many ways that you have already mirrored naturally and unconsciously. Think about a time that you were around young children. You probably found yourself literally getting down to their level, either by dropping down on the floor or picking them up. This is a natural way to create the experience of being at the same level. Your voice may have sounded childlike, or you spoke more simply. These are unconscious automatic rapport skills. Being in sync with other members of the community is an ancient trait. If you observe primitive tribes dancing or singing you will see that they are moving together in rhythm and in unison. It is our goal to teach our students to get to the same level with all people so that you can establish, maintain and regain rapport whenever and wherever you want and still be yourself.

Another common way that people mirror is by their attire. When you are invited to a party, the invitation might indicate "casual attire" or "black tie." The invite is asking for the group to share in an event, and in some way be alike. This is also in evidence in religious rituals and spiritual garb. There is a reason a uniform is called a *uni*form. Once when I (R.H.) led a seminar I found myself in an awkward position. I was leading a communication workshop for a company at an offsite event. I didn't realize that offsite was going to be casual. I wore a suit and nylon stockings while everyone else was wearing casual clothes with sandals. Although I found other ways to create rapport, I felt slightly out of sync with the group. There are times when the presenter is expected to be more "dressed," for the occasion, but in this case wearing stockings at a picnic was way too extreme. It did not match. I learned a lesson and remembered to always ask ahead of time about the dress code.

Some of our executives have shared that the boss who is genuinely liked by all his/her employees is the one who can wear a suit when he/she speaks with investors, and can roll up his/her sleeves when he/she visits the workers at the factory floor. When you practice the mirroring skills, you become adaptable and flexible.

There are people, and you may be one of them, who don't care if they fit in because of their clothes or appearance. Maintaining a certain identity may be more important. I (S.L.) remember going to my first interview for a teaching position with shoulder length hair. I knew it might cost me the job, but as it turns out it was not a deal breaker and I was hired. Tattoos and piercings would now fit into the same category. Having no tattoos, I sometimes feel the odd man out at my yoga class. Every generation finds ways to break with the previous generation and find commonalities among themselves. What's next?

What is important is to understand that rapport is a choice variable and each of us is responsible for making that choice. NLP provides the skills for those who choose to use them.

Ways To Mirror

In essence, you can do anything to mirror the person with whom you are speaking. You can wear the same clothes, get on the same level, speak the same language and as we will be suggesting, use the same tone, tempo and volume or mirror posture, gestures and breathing. But do make sure you are not mimicking or parodying another person's behavior. The idea about mirroring is to approximate a similarity and do it without calling attention to it. We also advocate that people think for themselves and express their differences. The movie reviewer team Gene Siskel and Roger Ebert used to express their strong opinions indicating which movies they liked and which they disliked. Even when one gave a movie a thumbs up and the other a thumbs down, they demonstrated excellent rapport. What matters is that you mirror the form which includes facial expressions, gestures, postures, breathing and the predicates of the primary representational system including visual, auditory and kinesthetic.

When you mirror the form you are not attempting to "parrot" or "do an impression" of them. If they scratch their head, you don't scratch your head, or their head for that matter, and especially not at the same time. Instead be subtle and find something to do that is similar.

If you know that you have a fast tempo, slow it down when meeting someone with a slower tempo. Or vice versa. If you tend to speak loudly, lower your voice when speaking with a "low talker." If someone "leans in" to the conversation, you can do the same.

Also pay attention to your eye level. When possible, it is ideal to be at the same eye level. If you are short, invite the person to sit down. If you are tall, sit down, or lean on something. Rather than slouching do your best to get to their level. On occasion, we have students who require a wheelchair. We find ourselves automatically getting down on one knee so we can interact at eye level. Once there was a trainee who was in a wheelchair who commented how she often had to strain her head to look up at people towering over her and how much she appreciated it when we dropped to one knee and how comfortable it was to be seeing "eye to eye."

Also notice how the person with whom you are speaking is gesturing, sitting or standing. Assume a similar position. One of the mistakes trainees often make is moving their hands to mirror those of the person speaking while the person is still speaking. Instead, wait until there is a natural pause and then respond by using his/her gestures. Here again you must be careful not to call attention to it. If they do a lot of talking with their hands and you practically never use your hands, do not attempt to match them exactly. But you can still move more than usual.

And listen to their voice and identify the overall pattern: volume, tempo, pitch and overall rhythm. Select one voice quality to mirror. Then engage in a conversation in which you use transitional phrases to mirror. You might say, "That's interesting. I had a similar experience." Regardless of the content you select, mirror the voice quality. Perhaps a deeper tone will be sufficient.

You can disagree with the content and still mirror the form. For example, take the same transition opportunity, and say, "I have a different opinion on that." You would disagree with content, but you would still maintain their slow tempo. It is interesting to note that when people disagree they will often mismatch the form as well.

An interesting experiment is easily done by mismatching the form (e.g. speaking louder or moving more quickly) while at the same time agreeing and matching the content. If you decide to do this, be forewarned. You will likely lose rapport. So do not do it in a critical situation and remember to get rapport back by matching. One important result of doing this is that it can build confidence in reestablishing rapport, once it had been broken.

At first this may feel awkward because you may typically speak slowly and the person you are mirroring is speaking fast. Trainees have said, "But speaking fast is not me, I am a slow speaker." The trainee has identified with his/her behavior. It is very common for someone to say, "I am someone who is shy; I speak softly and I don't use my hands when speaking," or "It is not me to cross my arms, or use visual words." In these moments, we share our belief that our behavior is not who we are; they are patterns. Behaviors are what we do, not who we are. We are who we are, whether we use gestures or not, speak loudly or softly or talk slowly or quickly. Accepting that we are not our behavior will result in a greater freedom of movement and expand our repertoire when interacting with others. "Change" and "Effective Communication" go hand in hand.

One trainee complained that a colleague at work never talked to him and he didn't know how he could mirror his behavior if the person didn't talk. We suggested that he pay attention to his office mate's breathing, and not say anything, just mirror him when he was nearby. The trainee came back the following month to tell us that it worked so well that now he can't get his office mate to stop talking. So be careful what you wish for. Getting rapport can have its downside. Some people feel very connected to you because you are mirroring. So if you discover you are getting too much rapport, remember that you can always mismatch.

Mirroring will work "face to face," on the phone or when video conferencing. For many sales people, their business relies on client calls, and often "cold calls," which are calls to prospective clients. When you begin speaking on the phone, pay attention to the other person's voice and start mirroring. You can do the same when leaving a voice message. There are formal messages and funny ones. You are not expected to be as formal or as funny, but you can approximate their style. When we receive a marketing call, it is rare that the person changes his/her voice to match ours. He/she could be talking to anyone. However, when he/she does match, it feels like he/she is talking directly to us. That does not necessarily mean we will buy the product he/she is selling, but it may engage us and open the door to communication.

Many countries have different regions where people of the region speak in a particular way. In the United States, people in the northeast will speak quite fast compared to people in the south. Our students will practice slowing down or speeding up depending upon where their clients live. One southern banker told us that the northeastern bankers equated his slowness with stupidity, so he was aware of taking advantage of that stereotype when he negotiated with them. He didn't mirror them, but he was aware of what they thought his slowness meant and used it to his advantage.

Sometimes people go to extremes with mirroring. There was a story we heard about an American company preparing their managers to go to Japan and were told to avoid eye contact because the Japanese managers would not maintain eye contact. The Japanese managers prepared to meet the managers from the U.S. and were told to make eye contact. You can imagine the confusion at the first meeting. Pay attention to what is happening at the time, be subtle, and be authentic. And respect the other person's model of the world.

Does Mirroring Really Matter?

Mirroring someone's form is one of many variables to get rapport. It is our goal to give you many simple techniques to help you find ways to communicate more effectively with yourself and others. In this chapter we have emphasized how to build rapport by mirroring others with form.

You might wonder, "Will mirroring be enough? Is that all I need to do?" The answer is "probably not." But although it may not be sufficient, it is necessary. While mirroring involves matching what people do, deeper rapport requires knowing how people think and feel as well as what they want and need. But only by breaking these skills down and mastering each one individually will we become master craftspeople in the area of interpersonal communication.

Rapport Exercise

Here is a "rapport exercise" for you to practice that will help you learn to establish, build and maintain rapport.

Three Persons (Person A-Person B-Person C)

There are three rounds to this exercise and you will remain the same letter for each part of the exercise. So if you are an A, remain an A until the end of the entire exercise. The same is true for B and C.

Round #1; A will be the first interviewer and it is A's job to get rapport with B. C will be the observer.

B goes out of the room and comes back to the room prepared to talk about his/her ideal job.

While B is out of the room, A is told that he/she will have to build rapport by matching B's facial expressions, gestures and posture. (It is not mimicking). A and C plan a signal, so that A can match for two minutes, then mismatch for two minutes and then match for the last two minutes. The rationale for matching and mismatching is to remind yourself that rapport is a process and if you lose it, you can get it back again.

When B comes back into the room, A and B have a conversation. C is observing. C is to be left out of the conversation. C is the observer.

After the six-minute conversation, B is asked, "What was your experience of rapport?" After a brief discussion A and C may share their observations, and tell B about A's assignment.

Round #2: Switch roles. Keep the same letters. Now B is the interviewer, the one to establish and build rapport. C is the interviewee, and A is the observer.

C goes out of the room and comes back to the room prepared to talk about his/her ideal vacation.

While C is out of the room, B is told that he/she will have to build rapport by matching C's voice quality, which includes, volume, tempo, rhythm, and tone. B and A plan a signal, so that B can match for two minutes, then mismatch for two minutes and then match for the last two minutes. This must be a conversation since B has to calibrate C's voice quality in order to match it.

When C comes back into the room, B and C have a conversation. A is observing.

After the six-minute conversation, C is asked, "What was your experience of rapport?" After a brief discussion B and A may share their observations, and then tell C about B's assignment.

Round #3: Switch roles. Now C is the interviewer, A is the interviewee and B is the observer.

A goes out of the room and comes back to the room prepared to talk about his/her ideal home.

While A is out of the room, C is told that he/she will practice ultimate rapport. This means that he/she will match all forms including Part #1, Part #2 and adding A's representational system (Visual, Auditory or Kinesthetic). There will be no mismatching. B is observing and will make sure that C matches. If he/she doesn't match B will give a signal to remind him/her to match.

After the six-minute conversation, A is asked, "What was your experience of rapport?" After a brief discussion C and B may share their observations, and then tell A about C's assignment.

Discuss within your group the entire rapport exercise. Identify people within your personal and professional life with whom you want to build better rapport.

This exercise can be fun, with a tremendous potential for new learning.

NLP Momentary Practice

Take yourself to some place where you can interact with someone whom you don't know. For example, go to a grocery store or restaurant. When you speak to the cashier or server, pay attention to their response and then verbally mirror their style. You can also practice with someone you know. Pay attention to how he/she is sitting and at some point mirror their posture. Remember you are not mimicking or mocking. Notice the responses you get.

CHAPTER 14

The We Generation: Being Self and Other Oriented

"Do NLP with others not to them!"
-Steven and Rachel

Ed Koch, a former mayor of New York City, was talking about himself at great length. At one point he paused, recognizing that he was doing all the talking and said, "But enough of me. Let's talk about you. What do you think of me?" Have you ever found yourself with someone in the "Koch" mode? Maybe you were the one in it? Perhaps both of you were doing it simultaneously. Being in the "Self" mode is natural, useful and productive. But when it excludes the "Other" it can be isolating, polarizing and heartless. When we are in "Other" mode we are caring and attentive to others' needs. But when we exclude "Self" we neglect our own wants and needs.

There is a term we use to describe the behavior that the Ed Koch story illustrated. It is called "Self Oriented." This pattern is one in which the individual is thinking only of himself/herself, his/her self-interest, his/her wants or needs. When we are being strictly "Self Oriented" we are, at that moment, not including the wants or needs of anyone else. This might fit some people's description of being "selfish." But using the term "selfish" implies judgment. Being "Self Oriented" does not. It simply means that we are attending to our own needs at a particular moment in time. Another common example of this occurs when someone asks, "How are you?" and before you answer, he/she begins talking about his/her day, his/her problems or successes, etc. Of course, attending to our own needs can refer to any of our needs, including survival, control, safety, security, belonging, validation, understanding, sex, success, love, sleep, food, water, recognition, acceptance, and so on.

On the other hand, there is being "Other Oriented" which is what we are doing when we are paying attention to the need of others.

We (S.L. and R.H.) have been together since 1981 so we have had plenty of time to practice the skill of balancing self and other orientation. When we have had a busy day and finally get a chance to connect in the evening, I (R.H.) will often ask, "When is a good time to talk about our day?" I am interested in talking about my day, which is "Self Oriented," but I am also interested in checking in with Steven to find out when it works for him, which is "Other Oriented." He may respond by saying, "This is not a good time. I need some time right now to be alone. How about talking in 20 minutes?" We do our best to each be in touch with each of our wants and needs.

In this scenario we are both being "Other Oriented" as well as "Self Oriented."

While "Other Oriented" is a pattern in which we are attending to the needs or wants of another person, it does not have to mean excluding our own needs. People who know how to recognize and satisfy their own needs are actually in a better position to be more "Other Oriented." These are people who do not think of themselves as "Selfish." They are "taking care of themselves" and know that other people are doing what they can do to satisfy their needs as well. Some people mistakenly think that being "Other Oriented" is being nice, friendly, likeable or pleasing. That is not part of our definition. It is being aware of and responsive to the other person.

If I (R.H.) greeted Steven by launching into the details of my day and he interrupted me by saying, "Leave me alone. I just walked in. I have things I need to take care of," then we would both be "Self Oriented."

Still another scenario could be Rachel talking about her day and I (S.L.) responding, "Sounds like you have some important things to discuss. But before we do, I need take care of some things. How about if we talk in 20 minutes?" This is an example of me being "Self and Other Oriented."

Just because you think you are being other oriented doesn't mean you are._There is a common misunderstanding about what it means to be "Other Oriented". There are some people who seem to always be placing other people's needs ahead of their own. They might think of themselves as being selfless. We might call them "Otherish." It is a pattern in which the individual is responding to his/her perception of what the other person wants or needs, which is not necessarily what they actually want or need. It may come from one's own overriding need to make the other person happy, to be liked or be loved, to be important, to feel safe, to feel connected or not be abandoned or criticized. And it may actually have developed into an amazingly effective way of responding to the actual wants and needs of others. But while it may have the appearance of being Other Oriented, it is not. It is Self-Oriented.

We understand that many people have grown up being taught that any form of Self Orientation is Selfish and bad. They feel criticized and become defensive and guilt-ridden when it is pointed out to them that they are thinking of themselves.

We all know people, or maybe we are the people, who are really good at pleasing other people – knowing what they want and need and "making" them happy. For some people it is their life's work. Sometimes we have difficulty knowing or expressing any of our own needs other than our need to please others. When we do this, we are being Self-Oriented. To care for ourselves, we need to identify and validate our own needs as being significant and worthwhile.

Being Other Oriented requires more than paying attention to words. Let's go back to the original scenario, where Rachel asked Steven if it was a good time to talk. This time Steven responds, "Yes," but as he says it he lifts his shoulder and sighs. When Rachel is being "Other Oriented" she would notice the nonverbal communication and find out what it means. Being "Other Oriented means paying attention to "form" as well as content and requires being in "uptime."

Self Orientation and Uptime

Years ago I (S.L.) climbed Mount Marcy in the Adirondack Mountains. On my way down the mountain I found myself moving at an incredible speed and with amazing dexterity. So I began to think about what I was doing, noticing how I was keenly aware of the ground, the rocks, the soil, the moss, the roots, the changing inclines, the places to hold onto and how my feet and the rest of my body was responding moment to moment as the terrain changed. And then I slipped. At that moment I realized that before I slipped on the ground, I had slipped into downtime. Previously all my attention had been external. I was seeing my surroundings. I was not thinking about it and I was not aware of my feelings. The task at hand required being in uptime so back into uptime I went. Then the thought occurred to me that this would be a great story to illustrate the distinction between being in uptime and being in downtime. And once again I slipped up. Or in this case I slipped down.

Being in uptime can be intense and requires our complete attention. To complement and balance this ability, we also need to make room in our lives for downtime. This includes time for reflection, planning, meditation/trance and sitting quietly.

Being "Other Oriented" requires uptime. Being "Self Oriented" does not.

Manipulation Vs. Influence

When you mention NLP to someone with some prior experience of NLP, you will find two distinct and diametrically opposed responses. On one hand are the people who have experienced NLP in the hands of people doing NLP *with* them (i.e. being "Other Oriented") and on the other hand are people who have encountered NLP being done *to* them (i.e. being 'Self Oriented'). As a result, NLP has, for some, been an empowering and healing experience while for others it has been one of deception and manipulation.

In relationships, being "Self Oriented" is not a problem. Being "entirely" Self Oriented to the exclusion of the other will create one.

This is why using mirroring techniques in an attempt to get rapport and to get what you want from another person can backfire and be met with resistance. When people think that something is or has been done "to them," they will become mistrustful, combative and/or shut down.

When you are selling an idea, a product or service, are you interested in learning what's important to the buyer? Are you carefully paying attention to their responses? Are you interested in satisfying the customer?

We believe that being genuinely "Other Oriented" will, over time, contribute to developing trust and mutually satisfying relationships. And it is central to how we teach NLP at The NLP Center of New York.

It's not enough to want to be Other Oriented; you must know how.

Once we have established rapport by matching and being "Other Oriented" in both our personal and professional relationships, we will have a deeper connection and understanding and will have built a solid foundation from which to move forward. In our training courses, we train participants to practice shifting between being "Self and Other Oriented," by reenacting real life situations. Suppose there is a colleague at work with whom we are having difficulty making a connection. We role-play ourselves, while someone in the group role-plays our colleague. Then we practice the previously learned skills: matching visual cues (including posture and gestures), matching auditory cues (including tempo and volume), matching predicates (V, A and K), being in uptime and being "Other Oriented." It is an opportunity to develop greater flexibility and learn about the choices we have in our communication.

When is Enough, Enough? Learning to Say, "No."

People need to be "Self Orientated when standing up for themselves and saying "no." In the previous example, we chose a situation in which the person did not have rapport and needed to be "Other Oriented." For some people, this is not a problem. For them, the challenge has to do with saying "no." When learning to build rapport, we suggest focusing on being "Other-Oriented."

When we need to say "No", we suggest learning to be "Self-Oriented." Ultimately, we are seeking to do both at the same time.

When we do not stand up for ourselves, it is usually because we want to be liked or approved of, or are afraid that if we say, "No," we will lose the relationship. We can be "Self Oriented," be clear about what we are willing and not willing to do and still maintain rapport. An example that many people can relate to is dieting. If we decide to stop eating cookies, we are making a "Self Oriented" decision. If we then go to someone's home and they offer us cookies we can continue to take care of ourselves by saying, "No, thank you." But they may push back and say, "Oh come on, you have to eat something." Some of us lose it or give in at this point, while others of us have learned to remain firm and respectful. The reply might be something like, "I appreciate your offer. It was very thoughtful of you, but sticking with my health goal is very important to me." Doing this requires having clear outcomes and healthy boundaries. This will be discussed in detail in Chapter 24.

Taking care of yourself is "Self Oriented." But isn't wanting to be liked, loved, accepted, or validated also "Self Oriented?"

Yes. They are both Self-Oriented. The difficulty that most of us face is that we are looking to get something from the outside (from someone else) that we are not getting from the inside (from ourselves). The challenge is in learning how to feel safe, giving ourselves the love, the support, the respect, the encouragement and the acceptance that we have depended on getting from the outside (others). When we have learned to do that, we can care of ourselves.

One way we practice this in the training room is by forming small groups where each student makes a statement, first being "Self Oriented" and then being "Other Oriented." The other students in the group will then give feedback as to how each statement came across. For example, the statement can be, "I'm sorry." The first time they say it, they focus on how guilty they feel (Self) and the second time focusing on how the other person must be feeling (Other).

At this point the group gives feedback as to which one they perceived as being "Self" and which one they perceived as being "Other." When the feedback matches the speaker's intention, they move on. But if not, it is up to the speaker to readjust his/her communication. Remember that the NLP model defines the meaning of your communication as the response you get. If you think you are being "Other Oriented" but you are perceived as being "Self," then it is your responsibility to communicate differently. It is at this point that people begin to discuss what they do internally in order to make the shift. Even though there my be a tendency to lean forward when being "Other Oriented," just leaning forward may not be enough. I (S.L.) have described my experience this way, "When I find that I am 'Self Oriented' I have a bubble around me and I am only aware of what's inside the bubble. And when I am 'Other Oriented' the bubble expands to include the other person. While I am still aware of sensations in my body, I am also focusing on and listening to the other person in the bubble)." I (R.H.) describe my experience this way, "When I find that I am 'Self Oriented,' I feel the back of my spine holding me in place. When I am 'Other Oriented,' I feel my heart open and connecting." Each person will have his/her own way of doing it.

In the training, after determining which orientation is more challenging, each student picks a context and through role-playing, practices that way of orienting.

NLP Momentary Practice

Find someone to practice with. Tell him/her you are doing a communication exercise and ask if he/she would be willing to participate in a role-play. Then ask him/her if he/she would like to go for a meal. Once he/she responds, start out being purely "Self Oriented." Make statements about what you want to eat and where you want to go. Really get in touch with your preferences. Be in downtime. Now pause and tell them that you are going to start the exercise over. And ask once again if they would like to go for a meal. This time become purely "Other Oriented." Become interested in them. Find out what they like to eat. Ask about their food choices and restaurant preferences. Be in Uptime. Now stop and ask him/her how he/she experienced each of your responses.

For a third round, be both Self and Other and find out how he/she experiences it differently from the first two rounds.

CHAPTER 15

Motivation and Influence: Criteria and Key Words

"We are what we repeatedly do. Excellence, therefore, is not an act,
but a habit."
-Aristotle

As a couple, we have had many experiences where one (not always the same one) of us wants to do something, like watch a movie or go to a museum or travel and the other is not particularly interested. While courting and then in marriage, whenever there was a movie decision, we actually took turns. One movie would be an action film and then the next film would be a romantic comedy. Can you guess who preferred the action and who preferred the romantic comedy? Sometimes we do fit into the stereotypes. Our negotiations regarding which movie to see or what activity to do was based on which of our criteria was motivating us to compromise. At first our criteria was *fairness*, each one of us wanted a turn. As our relationship has matured our criteria have changed. We no longer know whose turn it is (we have lost count). Now when we choose a movie or a television show, *togetherness* is a highly valued criterion. For years, I (S.L.) had watched horror movies and TV shows alone, but recently I was pleasantly surprised to find that Rachel wanted to watch "American Horror Story" with me. Even though she periodically closes her eyes, we are still sitting *together*. Then there are the times when one of us wants to be *together* and one of us wants to be *alone*. And so it goes on – finding creative ways to satisfy our own criteria while respecting those of the other. In this chapter, we will be exploring ways of identifying and utilizing criteria.

Diving Into Criteria

I (S.L.) have always wanted to know what lies beneath the surface. So in 1980, I immersed myself in two such endeavors, first enrolling in an NLP Practitioner certification training and second, becoming a certified SCUBA diver. After completing the pool work at the Prospect Park YMCA in Park Slope, Brooklyn, followed by my shore dive at a Rockaway beach, I was ready for my open water dive certification exam. I travelled from Brooklyn to the Jersey shore and boarded a boat along with other students, the captain and my dive instructor. As I got suited up, I rehearsed all the instructions that had been provided during the course to prepare me for this moment. I was the first to gear up, place the snorkel in my mouth and do my back flip into the water. Then I was swimming to the bow of the boat intent on reaching the anchor line where I would pull myself hand over hand into the murky waters of the Atlantic Ocean, down to a shipwreck some 60 feet below the surface. I swam and I swam and I swam. "What was taking so long? Too long!" By the time I finally reached the anchor line, I was exhausted.

Putting the regulator into my mouth, I realized I was breathing quite heavily. Hyperventilating to be more exact. As hard as I tried, I could not catch my breath and finally gave up and somehow managed to get back to the ladder placed at the stern. Arriving back on deck, I ripped off whatever equipment I could and collapsed on the deck, out of breath, defeated and deflated. Once everyone was in the water, the instructor came over to me and asked me why I didn't use the rope that they had tied to the side of the boat to get to the anchor line. It turns out that while I was rehearsing the previous instructions in my head the instructor had revised the dive plan. Downtime strikes again. Because of the extremely strong current, he had attached a rope along the side of the boat so that we would not tire ourselves out while swimming to the anchor line.

As far as I was concerned I failed the test. I had not yet learned that there was no such thing as failure. There was absolutely no way that I was going to get back in the water. I made my intentions clear. The instructor, looked down at me lying sprawled on the deck and said, "You came to *challenge* yourself. Are you telling me that you are really going to give up now and miss out on this *adventure* of a lifetime?"

Immediately, I felt a surge of energy rise up. Something deep inside of me was activated. Without saying a word, I rose, geared up and reentered the water, this time using the rope to pull myself along the side of the boat until I reached the anchor line. Breathing comfortably, I pulled myself down the anchor line going deeper and deeper until I reached my destination. Although I could not see much, with a visibility of about 3 feet, I was exhilarated. I had met the *challenge* and I was looking ahead to some great *adventures*, imagining myself diving in the clear blue waters of the Caribbean.

Whether or not the instructor consciously knew what he was doing or what he did, he effectively used two key (criteria) words, *challenge* and *adventure,* that stirred something powerful inside of me and got me going again.

Now, over thirty years later, these criteria are still two of the most powerful criteria that motivate me to do the things I do.

The Power of Using Criteria Words

For coaches, therapists, educators and other professionals whose primary responsibility is to help, heal, educate and empower others, identifying and using clients', patients' or students' criteria words will help them do their job more effectively and efficiently. And for anyone vested in the wellbeing of family, friends and colleagues, the power of words can make all the difference in the world.

If you were to motivate someone who values *friendship* you might ask if he/she would treat a "friend" the way he/she is treating himself and ask him/her what it would mean to treat himself/herself as he would treat a close *friend*. Whereas if you knew he/she values *fairness*, you might instead ask if he/she is treating himself *fairly*. Finally if you knew he/she places a high value on *being effective* and *producing results*, you might ask if the way he/she is speaking to himself/herself is effective in producing the results he/she wants. Then ask him/her to think of a more effective way of motivating himself/herself.

Of course there are always Self Oriented people who would use words to influence people in ways that are not necessarily in the other person's best interest.

Can you identify the criteria in the following two lines?

Before: Unemployment, hopelessness, desolation, strikes, lockouts
Today: Work, Joy, Discipline, Camaraderie

These are the first two lines of a 1936 German propaganda poster.

The third line from the poster was, "Give the Führer your vote!"

Adolph Hitler and his regime knew how to use language. He once said, "Great liars are also great magicians." In recognizing the power of words, we must also be aware of their potential for deception and manipulation.

Albert Einstein once said, "A little knowledge is a dangerous thing. So is a lot." But our lack of knowledge can also be dangerous. It can render us powerless where others seek to manipulate us. As Sir Francis Bacon said, "Knowledge is power." Therefore we advocate, not dictate, that people, including you the reader, use what we teach to empower others as well as yourself (Being Both Self and Other Oriented) rather than use it in ways that seek power over others, to control them, to take advantage of them and pull the wool over their eyes. We believe in developing mutually empowering relationships. At the same time, we also encourage people to pay close attention to politicians, marketers and anyone for that matter whose self-interests are not in your best interests, so you can protect yourself and "won't get fooled again."

If criteria words themselves were not powerful enough, there are ways to combine them to get an even more potent response. One way is to use a hendiatris, a figure of speech that emphasizes and expresses one unified idea by combining three criteria words. For example, "Liberté, égalité, fraternité" (Liberty, Equality and Brotherhood) which was first used during the French Revolution. Then there was the Nazi slogan, "Ein Volk! Ein Reich! Ein Führer!" One people! One state! One leader! What about "Wine, Women and Song" which has existed in many languages for many centuries to advocate pleasure seeking? Or the updated version of the sixties,

"Sex, Drugs and Rock Roll." One hendiatris that we came up with to express the goals of The NLP Center of New York is, "Healing the Past, Living the Present and Shaping the Future."

Our point is that criteria words, whether used alone, in pairs or triads have been used to motivate individuals and influence the masses for quite some time. Some of us are learning about language so that we may become better communicators. Others are studying to be better healers. Some want to be better warriors. Others seek to be better lovers. We are each driven by our criteria.

Many clients come to us because they want to change a habit – to stop drinking, smoking, procrastinating, or getting into abusive relationships. Or they want to begin exercising, writing a book or learning a new language. A question we ask ourselves when we think about changing is, "What's important (to me) about changing?" Or "Why change?" Many clients who want to stop smoking have said that what is important to them is being *healthy*. "*Health*" is another example of a criteria word. Another meaningful question is, "What's important about not changing?" Two common answers are "Smoking is *relaxing*" or "Without it I feel out of *control.*"

Criteria can be defined as standards or values by which we make decisions, even when our decisions and the criteria that determine them are unconscious. All of our decisions, habits and behaviors are driven by criteria, be it our desire for safety, success, power, intimacy, acknowledgment, having fun or being loved. Or we can be motivated by an avoidance of pain, insecurity, failure, loneliness or boredom. We move towards or away from our criteria (e.g. seeking something positive or avoiding something negative).

If an employee is motivated by rewards, and you know exactly what criteria he/she moves towards, you can offer him/her greater *success*, greater *recognition*, more *responsibility*, *praise* or a raise for *contributing* to the company. If an employee is motivated by avoiding pain and discomfort he/she is more likely to change if he/she knows his/her job *security* is being threatened or he/she will risk a *pay cut*. Most of us know it as "the carrot and the stick."

Criteria usually operate unconsciously, but there are ways to bring them into conscious awareness? One way is to ask questions. Here are a few.

What is important to you about life?
What is important to you about work?
What is important to you about relationships?
What is meaningful about achieving your goal?
What makes life worth living?

A short quiz: Can you find the criteria words contained in the following quotes?

It's all for nothing if you don't have freedom.
-William Wallace, from the movie "Braveheart"

People rarely succeed unless they have fun in what they are doing.
-Dale Carnegie

Honesty is the best policy.
-Benjamin Franklin

Knowledge will give you power, but character respect.
-Bruce Lee

Answers: *freedom, success, fun and honesty, knowledge, power, character, respect.*

In order to learn our trainees' criteria, we ask them why they chose the NLP training. Some of the criteria they have shared include: *effectiveness, efficiency, improved communication, self-improvement, better health, having more choices* and *being empowered.* While you are reading this chapter, ask yourself what is important to you about reading this book and what criteria are being satisfied.

We can utilize our own criteria to influence ourselves. To learn how to motivate yourself, pick an activity that you do regularly. Both of us like to exercise. We exercise every day, either by attending a Bikram yoga class, swimming, biking, running, walking or working out with an exercise DVD. We have recognized that the criteria being satisfied when we exercise are *health, flexibility, fitness, aliveness and longevity.* And it also has to be both *fun* and *challenging.* And when we do yoga together, we satisfy our *"togetherness,"* criteria.

In our training sessions, we begin this topic by asking trainees what are the activities they like to do and activities they don't like to do. Responses we have gotten from the "like to do" list include salsa dancing, gardening, watching sports, shopping and cooking. And responses from the "don't like to do" list have been salsa dancing, gardening, watching sports, shopping and cooking. People don't like the same things. In asking the questions, we are seeking to identify those participants who have opposing interests. We do this intentionally to prepare for the following demonstration that we use to identify and utilize criteria words.

Unlocking Personal Passcodes

Step I Select Two People

We begin the demonstration by selecting two trainees who have agreed that neither one has any interest in doing the activity that other person likes. For example, one trainee, Pardeep, liked watching cricket and another trainee, Sandra, liked going to musicals. Pardeep had no desire to go to a musical, nor would Sandra watch or play cricket. A perfect match.

Step II Identifying Criteria Words

Next we begin to learn about their criteria – their *personal pass code*. We do this by listening to them explain why they do what they do. We tell them to be self-oriented – to think about what they like about the activity. We say, "Just be Joe Smith on the street without any NLP knowledge, telling us why we should like cricket." Pardeep describes how watching cricket is *exciting* and *invigorating*. And he likes to watch the game with friends so he feels *connected*. The criteria words are *exciting, invigorating* and *connected.*

Now we listen to Sandra who says that she goes to musicals because it lets her get *absorbed* in another world, the *beauty* of the spectacle and the *joy* she feels.

Her criteria words are *absorbed, beauty* and *joy.*

Step III Utilizing Criteria Words

Now we speak to Pardeep about going to musicals using his criteria words, describing the *excitement* that happens on stage and in the audience, being *invigorated* listening to the songs, watching the dance movements and feeling the *connection* when sharing the experience with friends before, during and after the show. Basically we have entered into his system and offered him something that would satisfy his criteria. Then we speak to Sandra about watching cricket, describing what it's like to become *absorbed* by the *beauty* of the game and the *joy* of watching such an amazing spectacle.

Each participant was surprised at how he/she felt an internal shift, becoming more curious about and attracted to doing the activity he/she said he/she would not do. Using criteria words are like having access to a person's motivational passcode.

Using people's criteria words are important in getting access to their motivational code, but they are not always sufficient. What if my (S.L.) response to the dive instructor was "I don't feel safe?" That would mean that safety was another highly valued criteria that had to be addressed. Either the instructor might agree that there are always risks and say, "Just follow the rules and everything will be fine." Or he might ask, "Are you going to play it *safe* and miss out on some excellent *adventures* and *challenges?*"

Some people simply resist because they are being told what to do. They feel like they are not being given a *choice*. When choice or freedom is a criterion, it is usually wise to back off trying to convince and make it clear that "it's entirely up to you." But we do remain curious and seek to understand his/her positive intention or purpose. This is discussed in Reframing (Chapter 23).

When we do this exercise, trainees catch on quickly and although they know what we are doing, using their criteria words usually draws them towards the activity that they initially said they didn't like. Basically, we are utilizing their criteria words to influence them. This is an extension of what we described in Chapter 9, where we used people's predicates to determine their language style and establish rapport. Here we are going beyond rapport. We are using their language to lead them, to tap into their internal "password."

This technique will not necessarily convince a person to do what *we* want them to do. It is not designed to convince someone to violate his/her own highly valued criteria. For example, we would not want to convince someone to go Scuba diving by telling them that it is completely safe when it isn't. And if people are risk averse, it is not ethical to sell them on a risky investment.

Using Criteria and Key Words and Phrases To Motivate

Gathering Information

A attempts to convince B to do something that A enjoys but B has not done.

B listens, but does not respond verbally.

C writes down A's key words and phrases.

B attempts to convince A to do something that B enjoys but A has not done.

A listens, but does not respond verbally.

D writes down B's key words and phrases.

Using The Information

C uses A's own key words and phrases to convince A to do what B originally spoke about.

D uses B's own key words and phrases to convince B to do what A originally spoke about.

A and B now switch roles with C and D and repeat the steps.

Some examples might be:

Going to a rock concert
Learning an instrument
Cleaning the house
Watching a horror movie
Skiing
Going horseback riding
Reading an NLP book
Going to a hot yoga class

While you are being asked to convince your partner to do something, it is important to understand that the point of the exercise is really not about actually convincing him/her. The purpose of the exercise is to become more aware of criteria and the impact they have and practice identifying and utilizing criteria words. Keep in mind that when you encounter someone's resistance to being convinced, there are always additional criteria waiting to be discovered. They will not be convinced if doing the activity violates a criterion such as *safety, security, family* or *health*. Remain curious and you will discover what it is.

NLP Momentary Practice

Think of something that you want to do and haven't done yet. Now think of something that you do regularly and easily. Ask yourself what is important to you about doing this activity that you do regularly and effortlessly. Identify the criteria and key words or phrases. See what happens when you apply those criteria, key words and phrases to the activity that you haven't been doing and want to do.

CHAPTER 16

The Eyes Have It: How To Know How Someone's Thinking.

"When I am getting ready to reason with a man, I spend one-third of my time thinking about myself and what I am going to say and two-thirds about him and what he is going to say."
-Abraham Lincoln

Our brain is a great big thinking muscle. While we have not yet developed the ability to copy the exact content of what someone is thinking and paste it into our consciousness, we do have many cues and clues for detecting what and how a person is thinking. Eye movements are one source for making this determination.

You may have noticed that when people are thinking, their eyes move. According to Richard Bandler and John Grinder, early NLP developers, by observing eye movements you can tell not what, but how a person is thinking. These eye movements are referred to as "eye accessing cues." We like to refer to them as eye accessing clues because you are getting a clue about how someone is thinking. By paying attention to where the eyes go, we can know when someone is thinking in images (visual), in inner dialogue and other sounds (auditory) or in emotions and sensations (kinesthetic). We can also determine whether the images and sounds are remembered or created.

Type "eye accessing cues" in most search engines and you will find many images of the patterns we are about to describe. If you are facing someone and his/her eyes go up and to his/her left (your right), then he/she is remembering something he/she has already seen. When his/her eyes go up to his/her right (your left), he/she is constructing a new image. When his/her eyes go horizontally to his/her left (your right), he/she is remembering something he/she has heard and when his/her eyes go horizontally to his/her right (your left), he/she is creating new sounds that may include spoken words. Looking down and to his/her left (your right) he/she is accessing internal dialogue or self-talk. And looking down and to his/her right (your left) he/she is accessing feelings. Have you ever watched someone look straight at you with eyes defocused and glazed over? That is another clue for visualization. The defocused straight ahead look is common when we are daydreaming, lost in an imaginary (visual) world. When someone is deeply absorbed in his/her internal imagery, we can wave our hand in front of his/her face and he/she will show no sign of being disturbed, like a child (or some adults) watching TV. Have you ever spoke to someone who is lost in thought (eyes down to their left), talking to himself/herself, remembering a conversation or rehearsing what he/she is going to say, without hearing a word you said?

The above description is based on what Bandler and Grinder observed in most right-handed people. For most left-handed people the cues are reversed. Going up to his/her left is "visual construct" and up to his/her right is "visual remembered." The same is true with auditory. Lateral eye movements to the his/her left is "auditory construct," and lateral eye movement to his/her right is "auditory remembered." When he/she looks down to his/her right he/she is engaging in internal dialogue or self-talk. And looking down to his/her left is where he/she accesses feelings. As with everything presented in this book, we suggest checking this out in your own experience. Bandler and Grinder also claim that people from the Basque region in Spain have a different way of processing.

When we begin an NLP training we are often asked, "Will you teach the eye thing?" Once when I (R.H.) was teaching a seminar for the American Management Association (AMA), a trainer from another course asked me if I taught the "eye thing." He then proceeded to tell me a story about a meeting where he was negotiating with an individual while his team looked on. As he asked his questions he watched the other person's eyes movements. Then from his observations, he was able to determine when the person was thinking in visual, auditory or kinesthetic terms and responded in kind. He claimed that he and the person with whom he was negotiating were getting along so well that his team said to him, "you are doing such a good job, we are going to leave the two of you to work this out." The trainer said it was his observation of the eye movements that led to a successful negotiation.

Some people have never noticed eye movements before. Firstly, the eye movements are very fast. This is because our brain is processing very fast, taking in and processing a lot of information in a very short period of time. Typically, it is easier to observe eye movements when you ask a question that the person does not have immediate access to and needs a moment to retrieve the information. For example if you ask me (R.H.), "What are the color of Steven's eyes?" I do not have to do a search for the information. I know it immediately. However, if you ask me the name of the book I was reading 9 months ago, I would need some time (which of course can be a few seconds) to search for the information. That is when you can watch my eye movements as I search for the information to determine if it is stored in a visual, auditory or kinesthetic location.

If a person does not immediately know the answer to the question, he/she must search for the answer. And when he/she is searching, we have a chance to observe the direction of his/her eye movements. When someone says, "Let me think about that," we can take the time to watch him/her think. The eyes are connected to the brain and the direction of the eyes show whether a person is thinking with images, sounds (internal dialogue) or feelings.

As you might remember, one definition of NLP is "the study of subjective experience." Our subjective experience is made up of our sensory system. We are thinking based on our senses; visual, auditory, kinesthetic, olfactory and gustatory. We have previously discussed how paying attention to the predicates a person uses will help you identify what system the person is using. The words indicate the person's "primary representational system." The eye movements indicate the "lead system."

Here is an example to differentiate between the two. A person experiencing jealousy may say "I *feel* jealous," but his/her feelings may be the result of constructed pictures (eyes up and to his right) that he/she is making of his/her lover making love with someone else. The lead system (indicated by our eye movements) is usually out of our conscious awareness (unconscious) while the representational system (indicated by the words we use) is usually in the person's conscious awareness.

Asking questions that require some thought like, "How do you spell the word chrysanthemum?" or "How much is 1937 plus 185?" can help you learn to track the movements. In a training environment, we invite a few trainees to come to the front of the room and we ask them questions, while the rest of the training group observes their eye movements. As they silently answer a question like, "When you think about your childhood bedroom, what do you see?" the group looks to see if the eyes go up to his/her left in the visual remembered direction. At the end of this chapter, we will give you some questions that you can use to detect visual, auditory and kinesthetic eye accessing.

Learn to Look for Clues in Eye Movements

Paying attention to someone's eye movements and predicates give us access to how he/she thinks and it is therefore an essential part of becoming an adept communicator. Using the information is one more way to establish rapport. We have already mentioned how matching people's predicates is one way to do this, but using the two together can be even more powerful. Suppose you ask someone what he/she wants and he/she responds, "I want to feel confident" and he/she looks up and to his/her right (visual construct). Using this information you could say, "As you imagine [raising your left hand in the direction of his/her eyes moving up to his/her right] seeing what you are seeing when you are being confident, what are the feelings you are feeling (now gesturing down and to his/her right)." This is one statement that matches both the lead and representational systems. Can you think of others?

Having accessed both visual and kinesthetic, you can now use your words and hand movements to lead the other person to the auditory modality. Accessing all three modalities is something that we frequently do to fully engage the explorer and motivate him/her in pursuing his/her dreams. To do this you might ask, "As you *step* into that image of what it is like to feel confidence (gesturing down and to his/her right) and really feel what it feels like to be there, what are you hearing?" You can accompany the last statement by moving your hand to your left corresponding with their auditory construct. At this point we are no longer just matching or pacing the other person's experience. Now we are leading (into a third modality). (Pacing and Leading will be discussed in Chapter 17).

Let's look at another example. Suppose you see someone whose eyes are moving back and forth between down left and down right. Based on the eye accessing cues, he/she is talking to himself/herself and having feelings. Whether he/she is talking to himself/herself about how he/she feels, having feeling about what he/she is saying or both we do not know. We can ask, "What are you saying to yourself?" and "How do you feel about that?" Or we can ask, "How are you feeling?" and "What do you think about that? If, at this point, you wanted to lead to a third modality you could ask him/her to ask himself/herself, "If I were having the feelings that I want to have, what would I look like?" As you do this, you would be raising your left hand up to their right.

Many of the skills we have been presenting so far in the book – matching predicates, matching posture, matching voice tone, tempo and posture and matching criteria words and now matching eye movements – can be used not only to "pace" another's experience to get into sync and establish rapport, but to "lead" him/her as well.

Eye Movements for Your Self and Applications in Education and Business

Although most people want to know about their own eye movements, attempting to track your own eye movement can be a bit confusing and make you overly self-conscious. So it is usually best to begin by observing others and eventually you will catch yourself thinking. Or you can teach a friend how to read your eye movements and report what they find. One more thing you can do is think of an old visual memory, like the face of a grade school teacher or an auditory memory such as a song a parent or grandparent sang to you when you were young or a kinesthetic memory of how it felt to hold a snowball in your hand. And while doing this move your eyes in various directions, left and right, up and down, noticing which locations make it easier to access the information. It might be useful to note that some people may need to access one modality to get to another, such as making a picture of an event in order to remember the words spoken or remembering a feeling in order to remember the scene.

We heard a story on the radio that described a writing program for children where the teacher took them outside, asked them to look up and write about what they saw in the sky. Apparently their literacy rate increased. We wonder if what also helped their literacy rate was the suggestion to "look up." When you learn about eye movement cues, you learn that not only can you match your language to where someone is looking, but you can also expand their thinking.

Imagine that you are leading a business meeting (virtual or real time) and you want to inspire your team. At the meeting, many people may be looking at you, some will be looking down, taking notes, and some will be lost in thought. To be most effective you can lead their eyes by gesturing in the visual field, moving your hands up while suggesting that the team envision where the company is going and come up with a "vision" statement. You can also lead them with gestures and words to the auditory modality as you ask them how they would put that vision into words and explain it to others. And finally, you could gesture to the kinesthetic direction asking them to step into the vision and experience how it will feel. In these examples you are leading the person to open other areas of experience. Taking your own eyes to different locations will also stimulate brainstorming or finding new possibilities when you are getting stuck.

If someone who is looking down tells you, "I can't imagine what I am going to do," ask, "If you could imagine it (raising your left hand to their visual construct direction) what does it look like?"

Consider the elementary school teacher who says to one of his/her students who he/she catches staring at the ceiling, "Pay attention to me. The answers are not on the ceiling." Well, maybe they are.

A student in our training had a pattern with her husband where she would be talking to him and his eyes would glaze over. As she continued to speak, his eyes remained defocused and he would give her no verbal response. Then, out of frustration, she would either become angry or walk away. The day she learned about eye accessing, she decided to do an experiment. That evening, when his eye glazed over, she paused, stopped talking and just looked at him. After about 20 long seconds his eyes refocused and he looked at her and said, "Hmm. I was just imagining what you were describing. I think it's a very good idea."

When eye-accessing clues were first presented, Grinder and Bandler based their findings on their observation of many workshop participants they encountered. However, they did state that when they had met left-handed people, that the left-handed person's remembered and created sides were the reverse of the right-handed person. They also claimed that people from the Basque region in Spain had a different way of processing information. See each person as a unique individual and ask questions to help determine how he/she specifically processes information.

People need time to think. So when we are in a conversation and ask a question, it is predictable that other person will be moving his/her eyes to retrieve the information. When we ask a question, we remember to look at the eye movements to formulate our response. Our response may be to backtrack what they are saying, to give our opinion, or to ask a follow-up question for clarification all based on where the eyes went to seek information.

Sequencing of Modalities

Following the sequence of the eye movements (the lead system) and the words (the representational system) can inform us of how the brain is processing. We will be using the movements described for most right-handed people. Good spellers, for example, when asked to spell a word will typically look up their right (see the word) then briefly go up to their left to see their stored image of the word. When the two images match they get a good feeling (eyes down right) and when they don't, they get a bad feeling (also eyes down right). The good feeling might show up as a smile, while the bad feeling might be indicated by a grimace. This is an example of a strategy. Learning how to elicit and utilize strategies will be explored in Chapter 28.

Questions To Ask

Here are some questions to ask questions to determine people's lead systems. The questions are set up for each of the six eye-accessing locations. When asking, have the responder answer silently.

Keep in mind that if you ask a person to imagine the Manhattan skyline, it will most likely be a remembered image, whether it was a direct experience or a photograph. But if you ask a person what he/she looked like in the past, it might be a "remembered" image based on a photograph he/she has seen, but it might also be a "created" image of how he/she imagines he/she appeared from an outsider's perspective. Please note that although the questions are written with a specific lead system in mind, the response may not fit your expectations. So if asked to remember a conversation, an individual eyes might first go up left to remember what he/she saw before looking to the left to hear the conversation. We suggest writing down where the eyes moved with each question. Then afterwards when you learn what he/she was actually thinking at the time the question was asked, you will get to correlate the eye movements with the thought patterns. Remember to pay attention to people who have it reversed.

Questions for visual remembered, eyes go up left
What did you look like when you were a teenager?
What did your first boss look like?

Questions for visual construct, eyes go up right
How do you want to look in 20 years?
What will you look like when you have accomplished your goal?

Questions for auditory remembered, eyes go laterally to the left side
Remember something that you were told as a child.
Think of a piece of music that inspired you when you were younger.

Questions for auditory construct, eyes go laterally to the right
What do you want to sound like 20 years from now?
What is something you would like to hear from your significant other that you have never heard before?

Questions for kinesthetic, eyes go down right
What do you feel when you have done a good job at work?
How do you feel when you are appreciated?

Questions for auditory digital, eyes go down left
What do you tell yourself when you have made a mistake?
What do you tell yourself when you have done a good job?

After finishing, we suggest asking, "What did you do?" "Where did you go?" or "What were you thinking?" in response to each question, and compare it to what you observed. And as they answer these questions, again watch their eyes.

(For more information on Eye Accessing Cues go to http://nlptraining.com/articles/let-me-look-into-your-eyes-eye-accessing-cues/ to read the article, Let Me Look Into Your Eyes)

NLP Momentary Exercise

Invite a friend to participate in a communication exercise with you. Ask him/her the sample questions we listed and watch where his/her eyes move. After each question, ask him/her how he/she arrived at his/her answer, watch his/her eyes again as he/she answers your question. After observing where his/her eyes go, respond with the corresponding visual, auditory or kinesthetic language, and notice how he/she responds both verbally and nonverbally, with his/her eyes. As you do this, you are leaning to be a keen observer.

CHAPTER 17

Pacing and Leading: Skills for Listening, Changing and Influencing

"So, I warn all of you, don't ever when you are listening... think you understand... because you're listening with your ears and thinking with your vocabulary. The [other's] vocabulary is something entirely different."
-Milton H. Erickson

When we discussed building rapport, we encouraged you to become more of a matcher. By matching you are building rapport. And once having established rapport, you are in a position to bring about change.

Facilitating change utilizes both pacing and leading. We have already discussed pacing in the form of matching, mirroring, and being Other Oriented. Pacing is meeting the other person where he/she is at the moment – not attempting to change, convince or motivate. We are taking in and reflecting back what we are seeing and hearing. Too often, people attempt to lead (to change, convince or motivate another person) without sufficient pacing.

Many people want to jump immediately into "help mode." There is nothing wrong with knowing where you are going. The problem is often that we do not pay enough attention to where the other person is right now. It's like an infielder in baseball thinking about throwing the ball before he catches it or a soccer player thinking about where he wants to send the ball before having control of it.

Backtracking and Pacing-Improve Your Listening Skills

Before we proceed, there is one additional skill that is essential to effective pacing. It is called, "backtracking." This is not the kind of backtracking where people take back or change what they have previously said. Backtracking in this context is part of active listening or paraphrasing. It is the type of listening we use when we are being given directions. It is where we seek to confirm that we got it correctly. We might say, "What you are saying is …" or "If I understand you correctly, you are suggesting…" We usually do this because we do not want to misunderstand. By backtracking, we can avoid misunderstandings that could cost valuable time, money or a significant relationship. Backtracking is the way to make sure you stay on track.

An Example of Backtracking

A client says, "Over the past 12 months I have been trying to lose weight and I see myself getting nowhere. I have joined a support group. I have read several diet books. I have counted calories. I have changed my eating habits several times. I have tried exercising. I have done everything. But something always happens. I lose my motivation and revert back to my old ways. So whatever weight I lose, I put back on again. It has been quite frustrating.

The guide backtracks, "It must be incredibly frustrating to have worked so hard doing all those things and still not getting the results you are looking for."

An example of attempting to lead without backtracking would be to ask:

"What's important about losing weight?" or "How do you lose your motivation?

Not that there is anything "wrong" with asking these questions. But what's missing is the backtracking of the client's experience before asking questions designed to lead to a solution.

So if we were to backtrack ourselves, we would say, "So what we are saying is that before leading, we must first pace. And to effectively pace we need to use backtracking as well as the other pacing skills: matching predicates, mirroring, being Other Oriented and using key words and phrases."

In backtracking, we are not parroting or mimicking the person. We are not repeating word for word exactly what the other person said. These things can, in fact, lose rapport. We are instead offering more of a synopsis or summary of what the person has said, capturing the main points.

If you inaccurately backtrack what was said, you will get feedback from the other person. Usually they will verbally correct you or exhibit a facial expression that lets you know they weren't understood. Experienced communicators are used to this and do not take it personally. When you discover that you have incorrectly backtracked, just incorporate the feedback and backtrack again until you get some affirmation that it matches the other's experience. To do this, you must learn to be able to reveal that you have misheard or misunderstood and be okay with it. The alternative is to appear to have understood when in fact, you have not. And this doesn't usually turn out very well in the long run.

And sometimes when your backtracking is accurate, the individual, upon hearing his/her own words, recognizes that there is something missing and wants to supply additional information.

I (S.L.) recently worked with a client who responded quite negatively to my "misunderstanding." Being and feeling misunderstood was a pattern of his, dating back to childhood. So we explored what being misunderstood meant to him and I learned that being consistently misunderstood meant to him that there was something wrong with him. Once I "understood" this, I let him know. He smiled and felt understood.

But I continued to let him know that while I misunderstand people all the time and people misunderstand me, nothing is wrong. I also let him know that although he can expect that I will be misunderstanding him from time to time, the misunderstandings are just temporary and it is only a matter of time until he will feel understood again.

Keep in mind that despite accurate backtracking which has to do with the content/words, mismatching the form of your communication, which includes the tone, tempo and volume, posture, breathing, gestures, etc., will most likely lose rapport. To prove this, here is an experiment that you can do.

A. Backtrack accurately while purposely mismatching the form.

B. Then purposely backtrack inaccurately while matching the form.

Now compare the responses you got (meaning of your communication).

This is an experiment best done with fellow NLPers in a practice group, so it can be a valuable learning for everyone in the group.

Example:

Someone tells you that he is *frustrated* and *angry* about not getting a raise.

Backtrack using his keywords *frustrated* and *angry* but mismatch the voice tone, tempo and volume as well as posture and gestures.

Backtrack replacing the words " *frustrated* and *angry*" with the words "*sad* and *disappointed*." And while you are speaking, be in uptime, Other Oriented, match voice tone, tempo and volume as well as breathing, posture and gestures.

In the book, <u>Getting to Yes</u>, the authors, Roger Fisher and William L. Ury, claim that the best concession you can make when negotiating is to at least have the person feel heard. When backtracking, even if it takes a few backtracks to get there, you are letting the person know that he/she was heard. And remember, you are looking to communicate understanding, not agreement. Practicing backtracking is very important in developing effective listening skills that build rapport and enhance the relationship.

If you do not usually backtrack, you may find it to be unfamiliar and uncomfortable at first. It might seem awkward, unnecessary or just plain silly. But once mastered, you will not want to leave home without it, because the responses you get will be more satisfying.

Leading-Moving On

Now that you have sufficiently paced, you are ready to lead people to other possibilities. When leading, as in pacing, we will be using form as well as questions related to sensory experience.

Let's use the example of a man saying, "I am feeling stuck in my job." In this example he is indicating a "kinesthetic emotion" and our goal will be to lead him to his other senses (auditory or visual).

To do this we can ask, "When you are *feeling* stuck, what do you *say* to yourself?" This pace and lead goes from kinesthetic to auditory. We could use our own eye movements and gestures to lead his eyes as well. Our goal is to expand his awareness opening up other "doors" of perception. Leading to the visual mode, we might ask, "When you are *feeling* stuck, how do you *see* yourself?" Having moved him to the visual system, we could stay visual by asking, "And how would you like to *appear* instead." After getting the answer, we could lead him back into kinesthetic by saying, "As you *imagine* yourself *looking* the way you want to *appear, step* into this *image* and notice how you *feel.*" You can then ask, "And what kinds of things are you *saying* to yourself, now?" The purpose of these "pacing and leading" questions is not to tell them what to do, but to engage all three representational systems. Our goal is not to give advice. It is begin a process of exploring new possibilities.

Pacing and leading may be used in daily conversations and can be especially useful in tense and intense situations. The formula is to pace, (match, mirror), and then begin to overlap or lead to another way of thinking, acting or being. Many times people complain that someone is talking too loudly or too quickly. When you practice pacing and leading you will also have the opportunity to change the volume or tempo of another person. (Later on we will look at how to change our own emotional response.)

A trainee described his business partner as someone who frequently raises his volume and speaks with harsh tones. And he noticed that whenever he spoke softly and calmly to try to get his partner to relax and calm down, his partner seemed to get even more agitated. After having learned about pacing and leading he was determined to try a new approach. So when he found himself in a restaurant sitting across from his partner listening to his loud and harsh voice, he decided to pace by backtracking and speaking equally as loud and harsh. After matching his partner's volume and tone for about a minute, he began very gradually and imperceptibly, to soften his tone while reducing his volume. He was pleasantly surprised to find that his business partner followed suit and began lowering his voice and softening his tone as well. People at nearby tables also had a better dining experience.

This can be used quite effectively when someone is angry (e.g. speaking fast, loud and harsh). You start out mirroring and matching the form, not the content. If he/she says, "You are a S.O.B," we do not suggest matching by telling him/her, "And you are a A-hole." We are saying to initially use the intense volume, tone and tempo of the other's voice, while backtracking what they have been saying. For example the content could be, "I know you are hurt and pissed as hell and blame me for what has happened and you want me to know just how upset you are. I get it. I get it now, where do we go from here? What do you need? Is there something more that you want me to understand?" By the time you get to the questions, your volume is lower, your tone is softer and your tempo is slower. By then the person will usually have calmed down and you can begin to have a conversation that focuses on solutions.

If it is not working as we have described, we suggest spending a little more time pacing and then leading even more gradually than before. When you are able to lead someone, then you know you have deep rapport. The NLP style is to listen, backtrack and respond, by pacing and then by leading. It is not always necessary to lead. On occasion, pacing in and of itself can bring about an awareness in which the person discovers where he/she wants to go. When it doesn't, be prepared to take the lead.

NLP Momentary Practice

Pick someone you know and pace his/her language (V, A or K) and then lead to another representational system. After you pace and lead with his/her language, pace and lead with form (e.g. breathing). Compare what happened in both practices. Now ask him/her to do it with you and discuss your learning.

CHAPTER 18

Chunking: What Planet Are You From?

"To exist is to change, to change is to mature, to mature is to go on creating oneself endlessly."
-Henri Bergson

"Honey, I'm home," was a familiar phrase that Ricky Ricardo shouted to Lucy upon entering their apartment door in the 1950s TV show, "I Love Lucy." What often followed was Lucy's immediate unloading of all the details of her latest schemes and misadventures of the day. As she would describe the specific, you could see Desi's eyes began to glaze over. She was giving him more details than he wanted. In our present day culture we often say, "too much information," or "TMI."

In our own household the scenario is similar. I (R.H.) come home from work and I want to tell Steven about my day. I like to give the details. For the moment, he just wants to know the bigger picture. Fortunately, before his eyes glaze over, I give an overview to help him remain connected. In another context, the running of our NLP Center, I (S.L.) will want to give Rachel details about the business including any website updates, Google analytics data and new messages, and Rachel will begin getting lost in the small bits of information. So I start with the overview.

Keep in mind, that this is also a form of pacing the other person. Eventually, both of us will find a way to lead the other to the details.

Of course the opposite also occurs, when one person speaks in vague generalities that could mean almost anything, as in a political speech. And while the listener gets the big picture, he/she may want to know specific details.

We have previously explored the distinctions between someone in the visual mode vs. someone in the auditory mode. And we have made the distinction between someone with a fast tempo vs. someone with a slow tempo. Now we are introducing another significant distinction in interpersonal communication patterns – someone who is chunking small vs. someone who is chunking large.

Why Chunk? The Benefits of Chunking

To have more "flexibility and choice."
To have one more tool for "establishing rapport."
To become a more "effective communicator."
To help others to "improve their relationships."

On one hand there is the pattern called "chunking small." On that hand, we see all the details. As you look at that hand you see each line, each wrinkle, each hair, each vein, each bump, each nail, the pores, any dirt, bruises or discoloration and the unique shape of the hand. And it is composed of fingers (thumb, index, middle, ring and pinky), flesh, bone, blood, blood vessels, nerves and tendons. And of course, is it left or right?

On the other hand, it is part of our *anatomy*, a part of the *human body*, part of an *organism*, which is part of *life*. Now we are "chunking large."

"Chunking small" is the ability to observe the finer details with precision and exactness. When we are chunking small, we are being specific. When we chunk small we are being meticulous, rigorous, thorough and paying close attention to distinct parts and minute details.

"Chunking large" is the ability to see the bigger picture. When we are chunking large we have an overview of the situation; we see the larger whole; we are making generalizations and conceptualizing.

When describing a wine, someone who is chunking small might refer to the country it comes from (Italy), the region (Tuscany), the type of wine (Brunello di Montalcino) and so on. They can also go into the finer distinctions of its qualities: its sweetness, its acidity, its tannins, its fruitiness and its body. While someone chunking large will say it was "red," "delicious," "satisfying," "imported," or will just give it a "thumbs up or thumbs down."

Mismatching may occur between someone who chunks small and someone who chunks large. When chunking small, we are speaking in incredible detail, offering specific descriptions of what we see, hear or feel, while when chunking large we are being global, speaking in generalities, using vague, fuzzy, nebulous, amorphous language without any reference to the specifics.

The typical responses towards someone whom is always chunking small is, "So get to the point" or "Why are you telling me this?" While people who chunk large often hear, "I have been listening for almost 15 minutes and I have absolutely no idea what the hell you are talking about." Do these examples remind you of anyone you know?

If someone tells you, "I have difficulty communicating," he/she is chunking large. If instead he/she says, "Since John and I moved in together five and a half months ago, I have been scared to tell him how angry I get when he leaves his red Calvin Klein briefs on the bathroom floor next to the toilet," then he/she is chunking small.

Of course, one can always chunk larger or smaller. The first statement "I have difficulty communicating" could be "Life is difficult." And the second statement could add even more details, for example, "I scare myself by imagining telling him 'I am angry' right to his face. And I focus on his eyes staring right back at me. I see him standing over me with a scowl on his face while his voice gets louder and louder taking on a harsh critical tone while I shrink back and feel small and insignificant."

So if someone says, "I love life," he/she is chunking large. If he/she says, "I love animals," he/she is chunking smaller. And if he/she says, "I love German Shepherd puppies," he/she is chunking even smaller.

If someone asks, "How are you?" and you say, "OK" or "Not bad" you are chunking large. But if you go into detail describing your feelings and emotions then you are chunking small.

Who among you chunks large? And who chunks small? And who has learned to be comfortable moving back and forth between these two worlds. Neither style is right or wrong. The ability to be flexible, to have choice, will not only set you free, but will help you become more understanding of people who do not know that they are getting stuck in one of the two patterns.

Different Styles of Information Exchange

We gave you the gustatory example of the difference between chunking large and small when it comes to describing wine. But the topic could just have easily been communication. In NLP we "chunk down" to the different styles of communication that indicate different ways of thinking – visual, auditory or kinesthetic. But we can chunk down even further, by specifying the submodality structure. In Chapter 6, we discussed how the submodalities allowed us to identify finer distinctions, letting us know exactly *how* the visual person is seeing (panorama or framed, still or moving, 2D or 3 D), *how* the auditory person is hearing (tone, tempo, volume, location) and *how* the kinesthetic person is feeling (cold or warm, light or heavy, tense or relaxed).

Chunking Up, Down and Laterally

To understand chunking, let's start with a word that represents an object.

For example, let's use, "automobile."

Chunking Up

To do this we ask, "What category is 'automobile' a member of?" In other words, "What is a larger set to which 'automobile' is a subset?"

Depending on how you think, the answer will vary. Two possible *larger* chunks are vehicles or machines.

Chunking Laterally

If you think of an automobile as a vehicle, then other examples of vehicles would include buses, bicycles and boats. These are *lateral* chunks.

But if you think of an automobile as a machine, then other examples of machines could be robots, clocks and vacuum. In this case, "automobiles, robots, clocks and vacuums" would be the *lateral* chunks.

Chunking Down

If you were to "chunk down" further from "automobile" your answer might be "a sports car" or "motor."

If you are thinking of a "sports car" then you are chunking by types of automobiles.

If you are thinking of a "motor" then you are chunking by parts of automobiles.

What other ways that you can chunk up or down from "automobile?"

The more knowledgeable you are in any specific field, the more you understand the larger picture as well as the details. This would be true whether you are a wine connoisseur, a physicist, a car salesman, or an NLP Practitioner.

Where an experienced car salesman can break down (pun intended) the automobile into its component parts, an experienced NLP Practitioner knows about the finer distinctions in how people experience themselves, others and the world around them. When someone has an "experience," it can be chunked down to the five senses: visual, auditory, kinesthetic, olfactory and gustatory. And each of the senses can be further broken down to internal or external. The visual external is what you are seeing with your eyes (sometimes referred to as the real world) while the visual internal is what you are seeing with you "inner" eyes (sometimes referred to as "just" your imagination). The auditory external is what you are hearing with your ears, while the auditory internal includes what we silently say to ourselves as well as the music in our head. And while kinesthetic external would include body movement or someone's touch, kinesthetic internal would include being moved by a painting or touched by someone's kindness. And so on.

Shifting Gears

When we are feeling out of control, it can make all the difference in the world whether we are seeing (an image of) ourselves or seeing the event through our own physical eyes. Knowing this distinction along with the other finer visual submodality distinctions empower us to find the "difference that will make a difference." And when the difference is not found in the visual internal submodalities, we can look to the visual external submodalities or to the auditory or kinesthetic submodalities.

So just as changing a tire or shifting gears will change your driving experience, changing your perspective or shifting your focus (the smaller chunks) will transform the way you experience your world (the larger chunk). To continue the metaphor, many of us are driving an automatic. NLP allows us to shift manually and have more control.

Giving Feedback

Another application of chunking is giving feedback. Often people give us feedback in large chunks, such as, "You need to be more aggressive," or "You are not listening," or "You need to be more supportive."

To provide high quality feedback, you need to chunk down. If someone tells you, "You are not in rapport," they are chunking large. But if he/she tells you that you have been speaking faster and louder than your partner, that you are using auditory predicates when your partner is using visual predicates, then he/she is chunking down.

Many of our trainees have spoken about taking courses with the Landmark Education organization. They have asked about the difference between Landmark and NLP. One difference we have found is in how we each chunk. When I (R.H.) attended Landmark in 2000, I heard the words "possibility" and "declaration" used when describing some action that participants were going to take. These two words, "possibility" and "declaration," are examples of large chunks. Other examples are, "responsibility," "commitment," "resistance," and "languaging." In NLP, when people use these words we chunk them down. We ask, "What, specifically, is possible?" "How is it possible?" "What, exactly, are you resisting?"

and "How specifically, are you resisting?" In the next chapter, you will learn about the Meta Model and the questions we ask to get a deeper understanding.

As you will see in Chapter 19, NLP offers a specific and systematic set of linguistic tools that gets directly at the structure of our subjective experience. In NLP, we are committed to learning what people actually mean. So we ask questions like, "What, specifically, are you committing to?" and "How, exactly, are you committed?" Or, "What do you mean by commitment?" If someone is overwhelmed, we ask, "What, specifically, are you overwhelmed about?" and "How exactly is it overwhelming you?" This precision, built into the model, is one of NLP's distinguishing features.

The Chunking Game

This is a game that will help you think in different chunk sizes.

In a small group, the first person picks an object or an idea and asks the person next to him/her to chunk either down, up or laterally. Once he/she answers, he/she passes to the next person and asks that he/she chunk down, up or laterally. This continues around the circle.

For example:

Person "A" picks the word, "Computer" and asks "B" to chunk down. "B" responds with "Apple" and asks person "C" to chunk laterally. Person "C" then replies, "Pear" (Person "C" is using "Fruit" as his/her larger chunk and no longer needs to include the previous word, computer, in his/her thinking.) Then person "C" tells person "D" to chunk down from "Pear". "D" responds, "Shoes" (Since the words are spoken, "D" thought "Pair" instead of "Pear.") Then "D" asks "E" to chunk down again and ""E" responds with "Horseshoe". "E" proceeds to ask "F" to chunk up and "F" says, "Iron." Then "F" asks "G" to chunk laterally and "G" responds, "Krypton" and asks "H" to chunk down and "H" responds, "Vulcan." Finally, "H" asks "I" to chunk up and "I" responds, "Humanoid."

At any point along the way if it does not make sense to you, you can "challenge" the answer by asking for an explanation.

Here are the explanations for the last two examples. A horseshoe is made of iron, so iron is a larger chunk. Iron (Fe) and Krypton (Kr) are both elements, so they are lateral chunks. Krypton and Vulcan are both imaginary planets (from DC Comics and Star Trek, respectively) and are therefore lateral chunks. Also, a Vulcan is a humanoid and shares the same name as the planet. The more you play this game, the more you will learn about how other people think and what you have or don't have in common with them.

NLP Momentary Practice

When your day is done, find someone to talk to. Ask him/her about his/her day. As he/she responds, determine if he/she is chunking large or small. First match his/her chunk style by backtracking. Then if he/she is chunking large, lead him/her to the smaller chunks. For example, if he/she says, "My day was terrible." Ask them "What specifically, was terrible?" or "How was it terrible?" And if he/she is giving you many small details, get him/her to chunk up by identifying a theme or pattern. You can ask questions like, "What do you think it all means?" or "What are these all examples of?" Notice the responses you get.

CHAPTER 19

The Meta Model: A Linguistic Tool

"The art and science of asking questions is the source of all knowledge. "
-Thomas Berger

A man entered the studio of Pablo Picasso and asked the artist to show him a painting he recently completed of his (the man's) wife. Upon seeing the painting, the man became visibly upset and complained, "This is not what my wife looks like." Amused by the man's reaction, Picasso inquired, "Well then. What does she look like?" The man reached into his back pocket for his wallet removed from it a photograph and handed it to Picasso and triumphantly declared, "This is my wife." Pausing to look at the photograph, Picasso responded, "This is your wife? 7 cm high, 5 cm wide, 0 depth, only a head, no body and only black and white?"

Being in rapport and understanding are not the same. You can be in rapport, yet have no real understanding. And you can understand and still be out of rapport. That is, you can match someone's form-tempo, tone and volume, breathing, gestures predicates, chunk size, criteria and key words while backtracking and making your best attempt to be other oriented and still have no idea what the other person is talking about. Similarly, you can understand him/her yet unconsciously be mismatching the form. You can understand someone, even when he/she feels misunderstood. And he/she may feel understood even when you are not being understanding. Understand?

To truly understand another person, you must first be willing to acknowledge your ignorance. You must stop telling people what "the truth is" and start listening for what is "true for them." A radical idea! You must recognize that truth is not singular; that there is more than one truth. Misunderstanding is often the result of interpreting based on your own map. Alfred Korzybski, founder of General Semantics and author of *Science and Sanity*, was the first to use the phrase, "The map is not the territory." People, who are convinced that their map is the territory, are fundamentalists. Where there exists only one truth that you or a select group of people with a specific ideology believe and you find yourself starting your sentences with, "The truth is..." or "The fact of the matter is..." or "The point is..." or "At the end of the day, when all is said and done... then you too are exhibiting symptoms of fundamentalism." We (S.L and R.H.) see this pattern when we hear people frequently using the pronouns "you," "one" or the collective "we" when they are actually referring to their personal experience.

Compare the following statements.

"When you lose rapport, it is difficult to get it back."
"When we lose rapport, it is difficult to get it back."
"When I lose rapport, I have difficulty getting it back."

The first two statements are statements of universal truth. The third is a statement of one's personal experience. It is the goal of this chapter to offer ways to get back to your experience and assist others in getting back to theirs.

We have responded to people making the first statement, "When you lose rapport, it is difficult to get it back" by asking "Are you saying that when 'I' lose rapport, that 'I' have difficulty getting it back?"

Some people will respond, "No. I mean when I lose rapport, I have difficulty getting it back." Other people defend their universal truths either by reiterating what they have already said or claiming that it is most people's experience. And with some people, if you tell them, "Would you like to learn an easy way to reestablish rapport after it has been broken?" they will continue to argue that it isn't easy.

Perhaps the most elegant way of offering a counterexample is by giving them an actual experience – by actually breaking rapport with them, mismatching their form (not content) and once having lost rapport, reestablish it again by matching. Once you have accomplished this feat, tell them what you did. In this way, instead of using words alone to "prove" your point, you are giving them an experience that runs counter to their "truth." They may insist that "believing is seeing" and not acknowledge any evidence that contradicts their map.

I (S.L.) have heard people protest, "It's not *just* me" even when nobody is suggesting that it is (*only* their map). I believe that many people do not make statements using the personal pronoun "I" because they feel that to be valid, it must be a shared map. Hence some people tend to spend their time with people who have the same map.

There is a story about a man who awakes one morning and tells his wife that he has become a zombie. She argues with him, trying in vain to convince him otherwise. So she takes him to a psychiatrist. The psychiatrist, after hearing him explain that he is a zombie, asks him, "Do zombies bleed?" The man responds, "No, they do not." At this point, the psychiatrist takes out a needle and pricks the man's finger. The man looks down at his finger, seeing a drop of blood. As his facial expression goes from shock to astonishment, he says, "I cannot believe it, zombies do bleed."

The Meta Model: Our Map of Reality

The Meta Model is a linguistic tool based on in transformational grammar that was first introduced by Richard Bandler and John Grinder in their book, <u>The Structure of Magic</u>. Its basic underlying principle is that people do not directly experience the world. We filter the world through our senses forming a map (or model) of the world based on generalizations, distortions and deletions. When we learn about the generalizations a person is making, how he/she is distorting reality and what he/she is noticing and not noticing, we are discovering how he/she thinks. And so does he/she.

Generalization

We are using the word "generalize" to refer to the process of chunking up from small chunks. So if you were unfamiliar with crossword puzzles and asked to solve a few crossword puzzles from the Saturday New York Times, you might come to any number of different conclusions. One might be "New York Times crossword puzzles are difficult." Another might be "I am not very good at crossword puzzles." A third might be "I'm stupid." Each of these is a generalization. (By the way, the Saturday New York Times crossword puzzle is considered to be the most difficult puzzle of the week. Monday is the easiest. And as the week goes on it gets more and more difficult.) Other examples of generalizations are "Dogs are dangerous," "People can't be trusted" and "I am resilient."

We make generalizations about men and women, different professions, cultures, religions, etc. which give us the illusion of *knowing*. But as we shall see, while generalizations can be useful, they can also be quite limiting. When you are driving and approach a green light, you may have the generalization that pedestrians, cyclists and other automobiles will stop at the red light. I (S.L.) have found this generalization to be quite reliable in Switzerland, but not in New York City where pedestrians, cyclists and some drivers seem to have other ideas. In New York it is a good idea to rely on your senses. But even when I have been in Switzerland, I am on alert. You never know when a tourist from New York might be crossing the street.

Distortion

By "distortion" we are referring to how we form and transform what we experience. Experiences stored in our brain that are coded using submodalities are distortions. Change a submodality and we alter our perception of reality. Whether it is words, a photo, a Picasso or a picture in our head, it is not the thing it is represents. It is a "distortion" of reality. Whether we hear the word "dog," see the word "dog," visualize a "dog," or are looking at a photo of a "dog," it is not a dog. And even if we are looking at an actual dog with our own eyes, we are still seeing it from one perspective at one moment in time and not seeing exactly what we or someone else would be seeing if we were looking from a different angle or in a different light, at a different time or a different species. And it may be "colored" by our stored memories of dogs. We do not have a direct experience of "dog." We only have our subjective experience.

Have you ever played the game "telephone" as a kid, where you sit in a circle and one person starts by whispering something into his/her neighbor's ear, then that person whispers what he/she heard into the next person's ear and so on? By the time it gets to the last person, it no longer resembles the original statement. The game "telephone," like gossip and the rumor mill, is an example of distortion.

Distortion is a wonderful ability that has its limitations. The way we view the past is but one version. Both planning for the future and worrying about it are distortions of reality. And when we watch the same event, we each come away with a unique version of what "really happened."

Deletion

"Deletion" means leaving stuff out. As you are reading this, you are probably not noticing your breathing – until now. And now that your attention has shifted to your breathing, you are probably not aware of your lips. When we get a paper cut on our finger, we are probably not sensing our toes. And when we stub our toe, we are usually not aware of our nose. There is always a lot of stuff being left out of our conscious awareness. The conscious mind can only be aware of 7 plus or minus 2 chunks of information. The rest is unconscious (consciously deleted). By deleting aspects of our experience, we don't become overloaded with extraneous information. Imagine visiting New York City and taking in "everything" around you; the deletion process maintains a balance of what you can take in without becoming overwhelmed. And when we believe something to be true, we often delete the information that does not fit that belief.

The Map is Not The Territory Revisited

It is these three modeling processes that result in the formation of our map. Maps serve us well; they can be quite useful in helping us navigate the territory. But they can also limit our perceptions of what exists and what is possible.

So what we are about to explore is not "objective truth." We are about to explore what is true for us, what is true for you and how we know what we know.

The story of the three blind men and the elephant is an excellent example of maps.

Many years ago in a small village, there lived three blind men, who believed that if they were to "experience" the essence of an elephant, they would learn the meaning of life. As it happened, one day an elephant arrived in town. The three blind men in their search for the meaning of life, asked to be taken to the animal. The first blind man was led to the animal's leg. As he felt the leg, it reminded him of the bark of a tree. The second blind man was led to the elephant's trunk, which reminded him of a snake. And the third blind man, who was led to the elephant's ear, was reminded of a huge fan.

Later that day, the three blind men discussed their experience. The first blind man said, "Now I know the essence of elephant. It is like a tree. A tree is firm and rooted and will remain strong. Now I know the meaning of life." The second blind man said, "You are mistaken. The essence of elephant is like a snake. It is a presence that is fast, yet deliberate, and has a power that can frighten others. Now I know the meaning of life." The third blind man said, "You are both mistaken. The essence of elephant is like a fan. It can cool us off and keep us calm. Now I alone know the meaning of life." And they are continuing to argue on into the night.

The Meta Model Language Patterns: Getting Specific and Gaining Understanding

There are nine Meta-model language patterns. The names of the patterns come from transformational linguistics. We will present each pattern by giving some examples of the pattern followed by a description of the pattern. Then we will provide the questions to ask in response to each statement followed by the purpose for asking each question.

The examples that we will be using for each category are called "surface structure" statements. The "surface structure" is a bare bones statement that does not go into depth or detail. The Meta Model questions that we ask are designed to get at the "deep structure," a more detailed description of the persons map.

Surface Structure vs. Deep Structure Examples

Surface Structure: "I am worried about an upcoming event."

Deep structure: "I am visualizing myself doing a presentation of the Meta Model in front of 100 people and forgetting what I planned to say. It is a colorful, panoramic image of the auditorium in which I see myself standing silently and I feel myself sweating in discomfort while I watch people fidgeting uncomfortably in their seats thinking, 'Has this guy ever presented before?'"

The "Deletion" Category: Patterns I-IV

These questions are asked when information is missing or vague and requires greater specificity. The large category for when information is missing is called Deletion. Underneath this Deletion category there are four subcategories: Deletion, Lack of Referential Index, Unspecified Verbs and Nominalizations.

I. Deletion

a. I was surprised.
b. He is confused
c. She is upset.

Each sentence has something inherently missing. In the first sentence, we know that there is something that surprised the speaker, but we do not know what it is. In the second sentence, we know that he is confused about something, but again, we do not know what it is. And in the third sentence something or someone is upsetting her, but we do not know what or who it is.

Questions To Ask:

a. What surprised you?
b. Confused about what?
c. What is she upset about? Upset with whom?

We ask the questions to get the deleted material. Although asking this question may seem to be the obvious question to ask, it is not necessarily the question asked.

When the speaker does not provide this information and the listener does not ask for it, the listener is left to make up the answer. This is one way miscommunication happens. By using the Meta Model, when someone says, "I am incredibly angry!" we ask, "Angry about what?" or "Angry at whom?" without assuming we know the object of the anger.

People tend to use "Why" questions. The Meta Model questions are "What," "Who" and "How." "Why" questions direct us away from our experience, away from our senses, our bodies and into our "heads." "Why" questions can be extremely useful when we are looking for a cognitive understanding, an explanation, a justification or a reason. Often, asking "why" questions will elicit a defensive response, as in the question, "Why did you hurt me?" But if you are looking to know what the other person is experiencing or how they are experiencing it, it is not the question to ask. We invite you to experiment by asking both questions to learn how the responses differ.

II. Lack of Referential Index

a. *It* is not working.
b. *This* is what I am talking about.
c. I have a difficult time expressing *feelings*.

In each sentence, there is one word, a noun or pronoun (*in italics*). These words are vague. They are stand-ins for something more specific that is not known to the listener. Just as with the first pattern, people quickly assume they know what the word means, so they do not ask. Your job is to "not know" and ask.

Questions To Ask:

a. What, specifically, is not working?
b. What, exactly, are you talking about?
c. What feelings do you have a hard time expressing?

Although it is not necessary to use the words, "specifically," "exactly," or "precisely" here, it is important to know that the purpose of asking the question is to chunk down and get the details. So a person might says, "*Things* are difficult" and you ask, "What *things* are difficult?" The response you get may be, "You know, *work, relationships, people.*" While you now have smaller chunks, you still have a ways to go, if you are going to understand his/her experience. So you can ask, "What about work (or relationships) is difficult?" Or ask, "Who are you having difficulty with?"

How often have you heard someone say, "**It** doesn't matter," and not asked what exactly is **it** that does not matter?

Many years ago, we heard that someone told comedian Gracie Allen, "I like your zany character." Her response was, "I like him too. That's why I married him," (referring to her husband, George Burns.) Comedians often use this pattern to switch to a meaning that is different from the one people are expecting.

III. Unspecified Verbs

a. My boss is abusive.
b. I am preparing to give a presentation on NLP.
c. She is resisting me.

Just as with the previous pattern, the words are not specified. Here the words are verbs, action words that describe "how" someone is thinking, feeling or acting.

Questions to Ask:

a. How, specifically, is he abusing you?
b. How, specifically, are you preparing?
c. How, exactly, is she resisting?

The purpose of asking the question is to "specify the verb." When we say, "specify" we want to know how the person is "seeing," "hearing" and "feeling." So if you ask, "How is he abusing you?" and the answer you get is, "He is bothering me," or "He is disturbing me," you are getting lateral chunks, not smaller chunks and nothing more specific. To these questions, you can ask, "How, specifically, is he bothering you?" or "How, specifically, is he disturbing you?" When the other person is not filling in the details, you can always, chunk down yourself by making something up. For example, "Is he touching you?" "Is he criticizing you?" or "Is he picking his nose?" It does not matter if you are accurate, since it usually gets the person to chunk down. And once you get a response like, "He criticized me," you can proceed chunking down with questions like, "How, specifically, does he criticize you?" "What does he say?" And "How does he say it?"

It is important to remember that Meta Model questions "lead" from large chunks to small chunks, so it is essential to do sufficient "pacing," establishing rapport and being Other Oriented, especially when encountering resistance.

Warning: Pay attention for possible loss of rapport and if that happens, stop asking the questions and do more pacing before proceeding.

IV. Nominalizations

a. I want some *acknowledgement*.
b. My colleagues are not giving me *support*.
c. There is a *disconnection* between the two of us.

Nominalizations are nouns formed from verbs. For example, "decision" comes from the verb, "to decide." "Perception" comes from "to perceive." And "recognition" comes from "to recognize." Verbs are action words where there is ongoing movement of thinking, doing and feeling. When it is changed to a nominalization, it becomes inanimate. Being afraid becomes "fear." Being loving becomes "love." And being free becomes "freedom." It becomes a thing you have (e.g. I have mixed feelings) or an abstract concept (e.g. ambiguity).

Questions to Ask:

How, specifically, do you want to be acknowledged?
How, precisely, do you want to be supported?
How, exactly, are you disconnected?

What you are doing when you ask these questions is first transforming the noun back into a verb and then asking the "unspecified verb" question.

So if a person is speaking of "recognition" as an abstract concept, you transform the word "recognition" back to the verb form "to be recognized" and ask, "How do you want to be recognized?" You want to find out how he/she wants to be seen and/or heard.

An interesting consequence of asking these questions is that the speaker will usually become more engaged, more animated, more alive, more in touch with what they see, hear and feel. So while you are learning about them, they are learning to reconnect with their experiences. And while this can be a wonderful thing, some people have locked away their feelings and emotions because they are afraid to experience them or do not know how to deal with them. So unless you are a coach, counselor or psychotherapist, you might consider backing off. And even if you are not touching sensitive material, you want to respect people's boundaries so that you are not "probing" into private territory.

In the special case of public figures, asking these questions will probably lead to more vague answers. In September 2012, according to the New York Times, one of Mitt Romney's campaign advisors said, "Campaigns that are about specifics, particularly in today's environment, get tripped up." I wonder what campaign, specifically, was he referring to?

If you want to learn more about nominalizations there is a wonderful article that was published in July 2012 in the New York Times entitled, "Zombie Nouns." You can find it at http://opinionator.blogs.nytimes.com/2012/07/23/zombie-nouns.

NLP Momentary Practice
Grab a book. Open to any page. Look at a sentence and find the

deletions, lack of referential index, unspecified verbs and nominalizations.

The "Generalization" Category: Patterns V and VI

In this category, people are making all-embracing statements and describing a set of rules about what is possible and necessary. These next patterns are referred to as limitations of the speaker's model. They include Universal Quantifiers and Modal Operators.

V. Universal Quantifiers

a. *Nobody* Cares.
b. You *never* listen to me.
c. I am *always* forgetting.

Universal quantifiers include the following:

All, always, never, every, none, everyone, no one, everything, nothing, whenever, whoever

Questions to Ask:

a. Nobody? Not anybody? Has there ever been a time when someone did care?
b. Never? Not once? Has there ever been a time that you remember me listening to you?
c. Always? Are there times when you do not forget?

Universal quantifiers are "almost" always generalizations that have counterexamples. The purpose of asking the question is to get counterexamples.

When we work with a client who says, "I have been depressed 'all' my life," We will seek out the counterexamples by asking for examples in his/her life when he/she was not depressed. We do this by asking, "*All* your life?" placing the emphasis on the word "all." Or we ask, "When in your life (or recently) have you not been depressed?" Or "What is it like when you are not depressed?" Once we get the counterexamples, we can contrast how his/her world is different when he/she is not depressed and discover how he/she thinks, acts and feels differently at these times and use the information to manage his/her emotional state.

If we mistake a statement of someone's map (I have been depressed all my life) as the territory, then you will be drawn into his/her map. When you recognize that his/her words are actually a description of his/her map, not the territory, then you can question, explore and modify his/her map.

In the exploration, we may discover just how attached we have become to a map. We can become quite possessive, calling it "our" map. But be careful if you suggest to someone that it is "only" a map or "just" a map. It is a map. And even though it may limit him/her, the map has helped him/her successfully get through life. It has been and still is "his/her" reality. Not respecting his/her map will create resistance.

We have worked with many couples accusing each other of many things using this pattern. "You never listen to me." "You are always complaining." We have found that it is not "always" a good idea to use this Meta Model question. In this instance, rather than say, "Never?" or "Has there ever been a time when I have listened to you?" we suggest something like, "Yes it's true. There have been many times when I am not listening and I know when I get distracted it upsets you. Now I am listening and want to hear what you have to say; you have my full attention." If done sincerely and not defensively, the interaction will usually to move forward in a positive way. However, it won't "always" work, which brings us to the next pattern.

VI. Modal Operators

a. The Meta Model *won't* work with him.
b. I *can't* help.
c. I *should* learn this.

There are different types of modal operators.

Some are modal operators of necessity. They are "have to, should, must, must, ought to, need to, be obliged to, be required to, to be compelled to..." as well as "shouldn't, must not, ought not...

There are also modal operators of possibility. They are "can't, won't, to be unable, to be impossible, to be unattainable, to be unachievable, unthinkable, unimaginable..."

We also include words such as "want to, intend to and try to."

Questions to Ask:

a. What will/would happen if it does/didn't work? What will/would happen if it doesn't/didn't work?
b. What stops (or prevents) you? What is stopping (or preventing) you?
c. What will happen when you do learn this? What is stopping you from learning this? Or how are you stopping yourself from learning this?

Some of the above questions such as "What stops or is stopping you?" are being asked to determine what is getting in the way (a belief, a fear, an imagined negative consequence...) Other questions like "What will/would happen if/when you did or didn't?" will give you what the person imagines the consequences of each scenario to be.

If we ask, "What do you imagine will prevent the Meta Model from working with him?" you might get, "He is always resisting." Then we can continue using the Meta Model and ask, "Have there been times when he has not resisted? (Universal Quantifier) Or "What is he resisting?" (Deletion) Or "How is he resisting?" (Unspecified Verb) It is not a matter of asking one question. It is a process. These questions become part of the repertoire of the NLP Practitioner. With these language skills, we will not only be able to understand and be understood, but we will learn to update and transform our maps.

Asking, "What will happen if/when the Meta Model does work with him?" will take you in still another direction. Depending on the situation, we decide whether it is more appropriate to use "if" or "when."

We would also like to point out that sometimes when a person says, "I can't do it," what he/she is really saying is "I do not know how to do it." When we suspect that this is the case we will ask if he/she "can't" or if he/she does not know "how." When we are working with someone who says, "I can't stop feeling this way" and it really means, "I do not know how to stop feeling this way" then we will ask him/her if he/she would like to learn how to do it. If he/she says, "Yes," then we will help him/her learn how to do it. Sometimes a person (or some part of him/her) is really saying, "No. I won't let go of these feelings." And that calls for a different response that we will address in the chapter on reframing.

The question, "What stops you?" appears to be assuming that there is something "outside" his/her control that is stopping him/her (e.g. "not enough time," "lack of confidence," "procrastination" or "self sabotage".) But the purpose of asking the question is to identify how the person is actually preventing himself/herself from getting what he/she wants. By becoming aware of "how" he/she is (unconsciously) creating the "block" in the first place, he/she can learn how to "unlearn it," to create a different result.

NLP Momentary Practice

Identify something that you want to do, but are not doing. Describe why you are not doing this with different modal operators (e.g. "I can't do it," "I have to do it," "I should do it," "I need to do it.") Then ask yourself, "What's stopping me?" "How am I stopping myself?" "What will happen when I am doing it?" and "What will it be like to have done it?"

Notice how each question sends you in different directions where you access different information.

The "Distortion" Category: Patterns VII-IX

The final set of language patterns are related to the Distortion category. We are now exploring the limitations of someone's semantic model. There are three patterns in this category. They are Mind Reading, Cause-Effect and Lost Performative. (In my

(R.H.) work with the business community I changed the label Lost Performative to The Judgment Factor.)

VII. Mind Reading

a. You are not listening to me.
b. He doesn't love me anymore.
c. She cares about me.

Mind reading occurs when someone is claiming to know what someone else is thinking or feeling. It is also referred to in NLP as "hallucinating."

Questions to Ask:

There is basically one question that is asked for this pattern.

It is, "How do you know?"
a. *How do you know* I am not listening?
b. How do you know he doesn't love you anymore?
c. *How do you know* she cares?

One thing that we have not mentioned so far is that the answers to the Meta Model questions may not be conscious. As a matter of fact, they are often unconscious. So in addition to being "Other Oriented" and in rapport, you must be curious and patient. And what will happen if you don't? Don't ask! Warning: Impatience can erode curiosity. So if you ask the question and you get the answer, "I don't know," we suggest asking "If you did know, what do you think it might it be?" in a most curious voice. Getting the person to be curious and feel safe is essential. If either of you become critical, frustrated, impatient or defensive, the answer will remain elusive. It is quite common for people to not know how they know. We assume the answer exists and is knowable, so we are creating an environment along with specific questions to find the answers. It is also important to understand that we are not questioning whether his/her "mind reading" is accurate or not. We are only attempting to learn how he/she knows what he/she knows.

The purpose of asking, "How do you know?" is to get what we refer to as the "complex equivalence." Learning about someone's "complex equivalence," is another way of talking about someone's map. We have within us a way (our map) of determining if someone is listening, if someone cares, or if someone is angry. So when we look and listen to someone, we have a map that lets us know what is happening. So a certain tone, facial expression or posture means, "caring." Another tone may mean "impatience" while another means "mistrust."

When someone says, "You don't care," we can ask, "How do you know that I don't care?" We are not agreeing that we do not care and we are not disagreeing. We are attempting to learn how the person arrived at that conclusion. In other words, we want to know his/her map, his/her "complex equivalence" for "caring."

We can also ask, "How do you know when someone cares?" When asking this question, we are looking for sensory specific information. Assuming that we do in fact care, it is with this information that we can adjust our behavior to give him/her what he/she needs- to be cared for." That is, we can successfully communicate our caring. If his/her complex equivalence includes, "buying flowers once/week," "greeting him/her when he/she arrives home with a kiss," and texting 'I love you' each day, then we know how to show him/her we care. By making it quantifiable, it can be tested. When providing all aspects of the person's complex equivalence, you will demonstrate caring. If you do it all and the person still does not feel cared for, then there is a missing ingredient that the person still needs to identify. So back you go to the person being curious and wondering out loud what this missing ingredient might be. It is also important to assume that it exists and is retrievable.

The same is true when someone says, "You are not listening." We then learn what the person needs. Is it is eye contact, frequent head nods, a smile or occasional backtracking to know that we are listening? We are learning their "complex equivalence" for "listening" and so is he/she.

Sometimes we think we are listening (according to our own map) but the other person doesn't think so (according to his/her map). Rather than spending hours arguing and not getting anywhere, we ask about his/her "complex equivalence" and demonstrate it.

"Complex equivalence" also shows up with nominalizations. If someone says, "I need your *support*," we ask, "How do you need to be *supported*?" This will not only specify the verb, it will also provide us with the "complex equivalence" of *support* that we can then utilize to show our support.

Too often we *support* other people according to our own "complex equivalence." If for us *support* means offering suggestions, then we offer suggestions. But for the other person, if support means silently nodding, saying, "Wow" or "Oh" or "That must have hurt" then that is how we need to communicate it if we want the other person to experience it. When we learn people's complex equivalences, we not only begin to understand their map, but we can begin to communicate more effectively with them.

VIII. Cause Effect

a. You *make* me angry.
b. They *forced* me to do it.
c. She *did not allow* me to express myself.
d. He *inspires* me.

"Cause Effect" occurs when someone claims that his thoughts, feelings or behaviors are caused by specific external stimulus.

Questions to Ask:

a. How, specifically, did I make you angry?
b. How, specifically, did they force you to do it?
c. How, specifically, did she not allow you to express yourself?
d. How, specifically, does he inspire you?

Often, the cause effect pattern is accompanied by the assigning of blame and fault.

For the NLP Practitioner, cause effect is a stimulus-response phenomenon. And he/she is interested in learning how the phenomenon occurs. When blame, fault and guilt do show up they can be addressed as nominalizations in the manner previously described.

The same stimulus will elicit different reactions from different people, depending upon their map. The same joke can leave one person feeling offended and outraged while another person is shaking with uncontrollable laughter. So for one person the cause-effect statement might be "You are insulting." Or "You insulted me." While for another person the statement might be, "You are funny" or "You crack me up." The NLP practitioner is interested in a person's subjective reality. If someone has a phobia of dogs, "Dogs make me afraid," we want to learn "how a dog causes fear" and teach him/her (not the dog), "how" to respond differently.

IX. Lost Performative (The Judgment Factor)

a. NLP is amazing.
b. PBS is a national treasure.
c. Groucho Marx was the funniest comedian of his time.

Questions To Ask:

According to whom?
Who says?
Who's Groucho? (No, this is not a Meta Model Question. But if you do not know, please Google him.)

With this pattern, the source of the statement is being omitted. Although sometimes the answer to the question may be a friend, colleague, family member or a blogger, it is often the speaker himself/herself.

When people say, "the point is" or "the truth is" it is their "point" of view or their personal "truth." And that's the point of NLP. We confuse "the truth" with "our truth," intentionally or unintentionally.

The Meta Model is not in and of itself a technique for change. It is a tool for learning about our maps and will be an integral part of everything that follows.

NLP Momentary Practice

Review the 9 patterns and create your own statements that include each of the patterns. How many patterns can you fit into one sentence?

174 NLP A Changing Perspective

When learning the Meta Model, it is easy to become obnoxious by continuously asking for more and more information. Sometimes when we ask a person for information, he/she can feel like we are putting him/her on trial. This is a sure way to lose rapport. Even when we want to really understand someone, before asking him/her questions, we need to pace (mirror, match). By practicing the Meta Model, we learn how to ask these questions judiciously. The Meta Model is an essential linguistic tool of the NLP practitioner. It is a means, not an end. But it is important to know to what ends we are using it. This means that before we "chunk down," we must "chunk up" to know our purpose or our outcome for doing what we are doing. This is the topic of our next chapter.

Here are some statements you are probably already familiar with. See how many Meta Model patterns you can find in each of the following slogans?

1. Think different
2. Things go better with Coke
3. Just do it
4. Change you can believe in
5. Yes we can
6. Be all that you can be
7. We do it all for you
8. Fair and balanced

CHAPTER 20

Outcomes and Present States: What Do We Really Want? How Are We Stopping Ourselves from Getting It?

"We must walk consciously only part way toward our goals and then leap in the dark to our success."
-Henry David Thoreau

Many of our clients start their sessions by describing *feelings* that they want to stop feeling (e.g. anxiety, stress or anger), thoughts that they want to stop thinking (e.g. worrying or negative self-talk) or *behaviors* that they want to stop doing (e.g. cigarette smoking, overeating, watching porn on the internet). Often, it is a combination of feelings, thinking and behaving.

After listening to them describe their "problem," we will ask them how they want to be different. If they are anxious about making presentations, we will ask them, "How do you want to feel before, during and after a presentation?" If they worry about their career, we ask, "Instead of worrying, how do you want to think about your career?" And if they are obsessively watching porn on the Internet, we ask them, "How will you be spending your time, instead?"

While this is just the beginning, it is a way to shift their focus from what they don't want (which we will refer to as the present state) to what they do want (their outcome). We do not want to focus on not thinking of a *pink elephant*. What occurs to you when you read, "Don't think of a pink elephant?" You think of a pink elephant. It's like the "Do Not Smoke" sign that pictures a cigarette in a red circle with a red diagonal line across it. You are still seeing a cigarette. When someone says, "I don't want to *be anxious*," he or she is hearing *"Be anxious."* Instead of describing where they are in terms of where they have been, we want our students and clients to place their attention on where they want to go – perhaps a "green giraffe," "clear lungs" or "lasting confidence."

Goals and Outcomes

Many people attending our NLP Coach Practitioner Training often come to the training with specific personal and professional goals. Some want to have a successful business or make a career change. Others want to live a healthier lifestyle or find a partner to share their life. As empowering as an NLP session may be, clients will not walk out of the session with more business, a different career, a changed lifestyle or with their soul mate. But they can leave the session with an updated map, a new set of skills, and a different way of thinking, feeling and acting. This begs the question, "How do you want to be different?" which will lead to identifying an "outcome."

We differentiate between "goals" and "outcomes." Goals require time and will not be achieved during the session. But outcomes can. For someone with a phobia of birds, an outcome might be to hold a parrot on his/her finger while being relaxed and comfortable. This is an example of a program change that can be accomplished and tested out during an NLP session, although the testing with an actual bird may not occur until sometime after the session when the bird is available. And it is something that does not require additional time, practicing or rehearsing.

For someone who is shy, an outcome might be to comfortably approach someone he/she does not know and confidently start up a conversation. For someone who procrastinates, an outcome might be to make a list of specific things that he/she wants to do and follow through. And for someone who thinks he/she is incapable of attaining his/her goals, an outcome would be to believe he/she can and will achieve his/her goal.

Even when we ask people directly, "What do you want?" they still often describe what they don't want, i.e. " I don't want to be nervous when I do presentations," or they tell us what they think is getting in the way, i.e. " I have a lot of negative self-talk and sabotage myself." In fact, it is quite common for people to describe what they think is wrong instead of what they actually want. Many people spend hours talking about their problems and dwelling on the past. Of course, this is actually part of what has been keeping them stuck.

When someone says, "I get anxious when I think about going up to an attractive woman/man on the street and starting a conversation," he/she is describing his/her "present state." This person is describing what has happened in the past when he/she considered approaching a woman/man. The statement also assumes that this is an ongoing pattern that will continue. We respond by backtracking, "So in the past, whenever you thought about going up to a woman/man you became anxious." If there are counterexamples, we will explore them to learn more. We will also follow it up with, "How do you want to feel when approaching an attractive woman/man?" This question shifts the focus from the current unwanted pattern to a description of how he/she actually wants to be instead. This is just the beginning of a series of questions that we ask to determine the outcome.

When we get in a taxi outside the NLP Center of New York in Manhattan, we do not tell the cabbie, "I don't want to be in Union Square." We tell him/her we are going to Brooklyn or the Lower East Side. And we chunk down to the specific cross street. When planning a route using a Global Positioning System, the GPS will determine where we are, but it is up to us to input exactly where we want to go.

As an NLP Coach Practitioner, to be an effective guide, we will need to know both where a person wants to be (Outcome) as well as where he/she currently is (Present State). The following are ways to gather this information.

The Five Conditions for Well-Formed Outcomes

Consider the following statements a coaching client might say in response to the question, "What do you want?"

I want to stop feeling sorry for myself.
I want my partner to show me respect.

I want to be more assertive.
I want to get rid of my negative self-talk.

Before guiding a person, the NLP Coach Practitioner establishes a "Well-Formed Outcome." None of the above responses are "well-formed."

Condition #1 The Outcome must be stated in the positives.

Stated in terms of what we want, not in terms of what we don't want.

The first statement, "I want to stop feeling sorry for myself," is not stated in the positives. Other examples of this pattern are, "I want to be free of anxiety," "I don't want to be overweight," and "I want to stop taking things so personally." One way to satisfy condition #1 is to say, "I understand that you do not want to feel sorry for yourself. What I'd like to know is how do you want to feel towards yourself?" For some people, this may be the first time they have been asked the question, so the answer may not be immediate. There might be a pause. So just wait as they process it. What you are looking for is a response such as, "I want to be encouraging and loving" And if at first you do not succeed, keep varying your behavior and questions until you get them to describe it in the positives.

Condition #2 Within Our Control

Refers to changing our own thoughts, feelings and behaviors.

The second statement, "I want my partner to show me respect," does not fit the condition of being within our control. Other examples of this pattern are, "I want to be liked," "I want to be perfect," and "I want to be taken more seriously." One way to satisfy condition #2 is to say, "I understand that your partner has been behaving in a way that shows a lack of respect. When he/she does this, how have you responded?" Once you get the answer, ask, "How do you want to be able to respond the next time he/she acts that way?" If you get the answer, "I want to feel centered and balanced and connected to my core self," then you have a statement that satisfies both conditions #1 and #2. Another approach would be to ask, "When he/she is showing you respect how do you feel?" If the answer is "I feel significant and important," you can then ask, "Do you want to feel significant and important, even when someone is not showing you respect?" Holding onto an outcome that is not within our control and insisting that it is the other person who needs to change is disempowering, reinforces feeling like a victim and guarantees perpetuating the problem. When we encounter people whose behavior reminds us of the way we had been mistreated when we were younger (e.g. being dismissive, critical or neglectful), we often regress and blame the other person, insisting that he/she be the one to change and we resist taking responsibility. When this happens, the outcome might turn out to be "intrapersonal" instead of "interpersonal" (e.g. Our adult self being attentive, accepting and validating of the younger self).

Condition #3 Contextualized

Where, when and with whom do we want to have this outcome?

The third statement, "I want to be more assertive" does not satisfy this condition in that it does not indicate any particular context or specific situation. Other examples of this pattern are, "I want to be more playful," "I want to be less impulsive," and "I want to feel safe." All of these statements, whether stated in the positives or not, imply that there are already situations where the speaker is "not assertive", "not playful", "impulsive" or "feels safe." We follow this statement by asking, "When do you want to assert yourself? Where do you want to assert yourself?" And "With whom, specifically, do you want to assert yourself?"

We are looking for a statement such as, "I want to be assertive when I am eating in a restaurant and I am not satisfied with the food I ordered."

Condition #4 Measurable and Testable

How will we know that we have arrived at our outcome? What will be the evidence?

The third statement, "I want to be more assertive" in addition to not satisfying condition #3, does not satisfy condition #4 in that it does not specify "how" he/she will know when he/she has accomplished it. The examples we just used that did not satisfy condition #3 also do not satisfy condition #4. Some questions we use to get a statement satisfying this condition are, "How specifically, will you be asserting yourself? What exactly will you do? What will you be saying? How will you be saying it? How will you be thinking? How will you be feeling? How will you know that you are being assertive?" You can also ask him/her to "act as if" he/she is asserting himself/herself and demonstrate it right in front of you, so you get to see and hear it. Another method for getting the answer is to say, "Imagine we have just done an NLP technique that has worked. And you now know how to be assertive. How will you know it has worked? What will be the evidence (sensory based) that will convince you that you have in fact achieved the outcome?"

Condition #5 Ecological

This refers to an outcome that could potentially be psychologically or physically harmful or detrimental to us or to people around us. This is another way of saying, "Be careful what you wish for."

The statement, "I want to get rid of my negative self-talk," is potentially not ecological because we have no idea what purpose the self-talk serves or what, if any, negative consequence may result by eliminating it. It is also not stated in the positives. Some other examples of statements that "may" not be ecological are, "I want to stop worrying," "I want to be honest and tell people exactly what I think of them," "I want to function on three hours of sleep," and "I want to feel confident all the time."

When we are determining if an outcome is ecological or not, we are looking for any positive intentions for the current behavior or unintended negative consequences that the change may cause. Sometimes people ignore or do not consider the possible negative consequences, because their present state feels so bad and they are flooded by a sense of urgency. But if we only focus on getting ourselves "out of the frying pan," we could end up "in the fire." Perhaps we need to get out of the kitchen completely, leave the house and travel to a beautiful tropical island. Just remember to bring suntan lotion with a high SPF that protects against UVA and UVB radiation. What we are saying is that any outcome could have unintended negative results, so making changes require awareness of potential risks. Can you think of any negative consequences for eliminating negative self-talk? Never worrying? Telling everyone exactly what we think? Limiting our sleep to 3 hours? Always being confident?

Some questions we ask to address ecology are, "How will having this outcome affect your life, your health, or other people? What price, if any, will you have to pay to get this outcome? What will you be giving up? How does not having this outcome serve you?"

The last question is related to the NLP presupposition, "Every behavior has or has had a positive intention (or purpose)." In the case of negative self-talk, we would be learning about the purpose of the self-talk. The positive intention might be to motivate, even if it feels bad or is not effective. Knowing the positive intention can help to reformulate the outcome into something like, "I want to talk to myself in a way that empowers, encourages and inspires me."

Contextualizing can also address ecological concerns. So if the outcome is, "I want to tell people what I think," you might ask, "Everyone?" "All the time?" or "Everywhere?" By asking these Meta-model questions, we distinguish between contexts that would be ecological from those that would not. And in the above example, in order to do a thorough ecological check we would also need to use the Meta Model to find out which people or what person you want to express what thoughts and how exactly you want to express them. As a NLP Practitioner, you want to think twice before encouraging and helping someone "express exactly what he/she is thinking" if it will likely result in abusive, offensive or disrespectful behavior or getting oneself fired, injured or killed. Without checking for ecology we can easily solve one problem only to create another. Often our present state is the result of a non-ecological solution to a previous problem.

Present State: Finding Your Current Location

In order for a Global Positioning System (GPS) to determine how to get you to your destination, it must first know your current location. And that is what we need to learn once we have established the outcome. After determining the well-formed outcome we ask, "Where are you now?" We are not asking about your physical location or what you are experiencing this very moment. We want to learn how you are currently programmed to think, act and feel in the specific context in which you want the change to take place.

So if the outcome is "To remain calm and centered when speaking with my boss," we ask, "What do you experience in his/her presence?" or "What has happened when you speak with your boss," or "What stops you from being calm and centered?"

When we get an answer like, "I become anxious and overwhelmed. I lose control and I start lashing out," we chunk down using some of the following Meta-Model questions.

What do you get anxious about?
Overwhelmed with what?
How do you become anxious?
How do you become overwhelmed?
What do you lose control of?
What are you attempting to control?
How do you attempt to control it?
How do you lose control of it?
How do you lash out? At whom do you lash out?

Of course we do not rapid fire all of these questions at once. But they are all part of our repertoire.

Basically, we are leaning how they do what they do and often ask, "If I were to be you for a day, how would I do it? Teach me how to think, feel and act, so that I can do it exactly as you do it."

Most of what we do, we do unconsciously. That is, we do not consciously know how we do what we do. The information is stored in the unconscious; so we need to retrieve it from the unconscious. When we learn how people are doing what they are doing, we are finding the present "location" of the "internal map," i.e. their "present state." And although they may be framing it as problem, we see it as an accomplishment. And we want to learn how they accomplish it.

To help break it down, we might ask, "How do you know when to start becoming anxious and overwhelmed?" By asking this question, we are looking for the "trigger." We want to know what initiates the program.

This question is not always easy to answer and sometimes it is helpful to have the client take some time to focus inward and recall a specific time when he/she became angry. This is where Ericksonian Hypnosis plays an important role. Triggers are usually external triggers, whether it is someone's facial expression, a specific word, or a voice quality, although occasionally it happens internally, perhaps an image or an internalized voice. In this case it could happen when his/her boss tells him/her what to do in an authoritative tone, or his/her boss rolls his/her eyes while the client is talking.

After learning how it begins, we want to know what happens after that. We want to learn the entire sequence of steps, what he/she is thinking, feeling and doing. To draw out the information we ask questions about his/her thoughts, feelings and behaviors. We want to know exactly what he/she is paying attention to.

Questions We Ask To Find The Present State

Is he/she visualizing? If so, what is he/she seeing and how is he/she seeing it?
Is he/she looking at something? How is he/she seeing it?
Is he/she talking to himself/herself? What is he/she saying and how is he/she saying it?
Is he/she listening to something? How is he/she hearing it?
Is he/she feeling? If so, what is he/she feeling and how is he/she feeling it?

We also want to know what he/she is actually doing? And how he/she is doing it?
How is he/she moving? How is he/she speaking?

If the situation involves other people, we also want to know, what he/she sees and hears them doing and how they are doing it.

As we are gathering information, we find it useful to break down the information into "Behaviors," "Feelings," and "Thoughts." And in any interaction between *two* individuals there are *two* sets of behavior, *two* sets of feeling and *two* sets of thinking.

Imagine yourself interacting with another individual. And picture two Pies or Circles. One for your "Self" and one for the "Other." And each circle is divided into three subcategories, behaviors, thoughts and feelings. The Self Circle indicates your own thoughts, feelings and behaviors. The Other Circle indicates what you think the other person is thinking, what you feel the other is feeling and what you see and hear the other person doing and saying.

Read the following statements and identify which of the six categories they each fit into.

Client Statements

I feel my stomach tighten.
He is probably thinking that I am not trying hard enough.
I say to myself, "No one talks to me this way."
I am angry.
I see myself getting angry.
He is upset.
He is rolling his eyes.
I find myself walking back and forth.

Answers:

I feel my stomach tighten. (Self/Feeling)
He is probably thinking that I am not trying hard enough. (Other/Thoughts)
I say to myself, "No one talks to me this way." (Self/Thought)
I am angry. (Self/Feeling)
I see myself getting angry. (Self/Thought)
He is upset. (Other/Feeling)
He is rolling his eyes. (Other/Behavior)
I find myself pacing back and forth. (Self/Behavior)

The following statements show different patterns.

Statement 1: "When he grits his teeth, it makes me angry."
Other/Behavior and Self/Feeling.

Statement2: "Whenever I ask her for advice, she tells me she doesn't have time."
Self/Behavior and Other/Behavior

Statement 3: "I am always thinking of him. He never thinks of me."
Self/Thought and Other/Thought

Statement 4: I think he is too sensitive. He is always getting upset and then he tells me that it is my fault.
Self/Thought, Other/Feeling and Other/Behavior

Our goal as coach or therapist is to expand awareness. As we notice that there is a certain pattern emerging, we ask questions to fill in the missing sections of the circle. People get stuck in certain sections of the Awareness Circles and do not recognize what is going on in the other sections. These are our blind spots.

So in the last statement, we ask, "How do you feel when he/she gets upset?" (Self/Feelings) "What do you say or do when he/she blames you?" (Self/Behavior).

Back to the Outcome Frame

After identifying the present state it is important to revisit the outcome. The original outcome statement is a work in progress, so it can be quite enlightening and revealing to return to the outcome questions and discover that the outcome has changed in light of the new information. Also, when people come to us deeply ensconced in their present state, we often start with present state questions before moving to the outcome questions.

So once we know how someone is thinking, feeling and acting (Present State), we can ask, "How do you want to think, feel and act *instead*?" (Desired State/Outcome)

Additional Questions

"How do you want to feel when he/she gets upset?"
"What do you want to do differently when he/she blames you?"
"How do you want to be thinking differently?"
"How do you imagine he/she needs you to respond when he/she

gets upset? Do you want to give him/her what he/she wants? "
"What do you need or want (from him/her)? How might you get
it?"

As we have indicated that as much as we say we would like to be
somewhere other than where we are, it is important to recognize
that there is a reason we got here in the first place and recognize if
any attachments still exist. We did not get here by mistake. And
"the self" that does not want to be here may need to reconcile with
"the self" that got us here.

Do you remember the NLP presupposition, "Every behavior has or
has had a positive intention?" We developed the present behaviors
for a purpose. And whatever purpose it serves, it is incumbent
upon us to find out what it is so that we can move on.

Questions To Determine The Positive Purpose

How is the present state serving us?
What is the positive intention of the present state?
What is the positive byproduct or secondary gain of the present
state?
What are our present behaviors, thoughts and feelings doing or
trying to do for us?

Possible purposes might be motivation, protection, preparation
and avoidance of pain.

These are present state question, but the answers frequently
provide information that needs to be incorporated into the
outcome.

Once you learn that becoming anxious and overwhelmed came
from a part of you wanting to control the situation in order to feel
safe, the initial outcome of "being calm and centered when
speaking to my father," could change to, "being calm, centered *and
feeling safe.*"

Or we may learn that when he starts "lashing out," he feels more
powerful. So *being empowered* might need to be included along
with being calm, centered and feeling safe."

Attempting to change while ignoring the positive intention can
lead to resistance to changing, which in turn can lead to

frustration, disappointment and a sense of failure. To successfully and ecologically change, incorporating all positive intentions is absolutely necessary.

Throughout the present state elicitation we are not trying to fix anything. Firstly, we do not see the person as being broken. Secondly, we are seeking to learn about their map. Modifying the map comes later.

With NLP, everything we do with others we can eventually do with ourselves, but learning theses NLP skills requires practice. Practicing with others and having others practice with us is essential. In a training program everyone takes turns at being coach or client. Ultimately, we get to be both, at the same time.

Eliciting the outcome and present states are skills for understanding where you want to be and what is stopping you from getting there. Eliciting this information gives you both the bigger picture and the finer details. It can be helpful to frequently backtrack the changing description of where they are and where they want to be. And once you have a complete picture, draw a line segment and write down the present state on the far left side and the desired state on the far right side.

At this point we choose an NLP technique. These techniques will be discussed in the following chapters.

NLP Momentary Practice

In this moment, what is it that you want? Pick something that you believe you could change today. Ask yourself the 5 outcome questions and the 6 present state questions. Then ask yourself, "What is the next step that will move you towards your outcome?"

Outcome Questions

1. Is my outcome stated in the positive?
2. Where and when do I want this outcome?
3. Is this outcome within my control?
4. How will I measure and test this outcome?
5. Is this outcome ecological for me?

Present State Questions

1. What is stopping me?
2. What is the trigger?
3. What is the purpose or positive intention of the behavior, thought or symptom?
4. How am I thinking about this? (Self and Other)
5. What am I seeing? (Self and Other)
6. What am I feeling? (Self and Other)

To increase self-awareness and identify your triggers, the next time you "suddenly" find yourself in a "negative state," ask yourself about what you were seeing and hearing immediately before the state change.

CHAPTER 21

Ericksonian Hypnosis: Preparing for a Change

"You use hypnosis not as a cure but as a means of establishing a favorable climate to learn."
-Milton H. Erickson, M.D.

At this point in our NLP Level I Coach Practitioner training, we segue from pattern identification to pattern utilization. Our focus will shift from how we communicate with others (the interpersonal), to how we communicate with ourselves (the intrapersonal.) But before embarking on learning techniques for personal transformation, we will explore some further distinctions that are essential for mastering these NLP change techniques.

Are you "In" or "Out?"

We begin with *Association* and *Disassociation*. Disassociation is not to be confused with "dissociation" a term used to describe a psychological disorder in which a person detaches from reality to cope with stress or trauma. Disassociation is the ability to view a situation from an outside perspective. To teach association and disassociation we sometimes ask our students to think of a roller coaster ride at an amusement park. Over the years we have discovered that just saying the words "roller coaster," strong feelings (both positive and negative) come up. That is, people immediately associate to memories of either liking or disliking roller coasters. If the feelings are extremely negative we suggest choosing a different ride. This is, after all, supposed to be for your amusement.

Association: Stepping into Your Own Shoes

Think about an amusement park and select a ride that you have enjoyed being on. Remember what it was like prior to getting on the ride. See what you are seeing, hear what you are hearing and feel what you are feeling. Perhaps you remember buying the tickets, getting on line for the ride, finding a seat, and fastening your seat belt. Maybe there is a bar to hold onto. Are there any familiar smells? As you wait for the ride to begin, you can look around, hearing sounds and music and taking in the surroundings. You might remember feeling the air along with feelings of anticipation. And as the ride begins, you can feel the sensation of movement, the vibrations and accompanying sounds of the ride in motion, the gradual shift in your perspective and the position of your body along with the accompanying feelings. And you may also be aware of different emotional sensations. Becoming aware of the changing scenery together with the change in speed and direction and the other senses will take you deeper and deeper into the experience. And you can continue to see what you are seeing, hear what you are hearing and feel what you are feeling, as you explore both inner and outer awareness in this shifting environment.

As the ride is coming to its final destination, notice what you are experiencing. And when the ride comes to an end, you can prepare to disembark. Feel yourself getting up and walking to the exit.

The practice that you just completed was in the associated state. When you are associated into an experience, you are experiencing everything from your own eyes, ears and body sensations.

As you were reading the previous paragraph, did you associate into the experience? If you at some point found yourself watching yourself, then you were not fully associated. It might make a difference to ask someone to read it to you while you sit with your eyes closed.

Disassociation: Stepping Out of Your Own Shoes

We now invite you to go through the experience again, but this time from a difference perspective. Consider what it would be like to be an observer. To do this you will need to pick a location from which to observe. We usually suggest a convenient vantage point, such as a park bench facing the ride. Or you might prefer to sit at a cafe. Once you have selected your spot, imagine "seeing yourself" prior to getting on the ride, buying the ticket, getting on line for the ride, arriving at your seat. You can feel the park bench or café seat below you and your feet (as an observer) on the ground. As you watch yourself in the distance, you can also enjoy taking in the sounds and sights of the amusement park from that observer perspective. As you see yourself waiting for the ride to begin, notice his/her facial expression and body movements, both the background and the foreground, the color of the sky and other rides in the park. As the ride begins, take it all in, continuing to see yourself, the movements of your body. And as you continue to watch yourself on the ride, you can remind yourself of your perspective by zooming in (just seeing yourself) and zooming out (getting a panoramic view). And when you do this, be sure to include both sights and sounds while remaining in the observer position, with the only physical sensations being those of you the observer. Once the ride has ended, see yourself getting off the ride.

Being in a disassociated state means you are the observer of the event. If you would prefer to have someone read it to you with your eyes closed, please do so.

Now that you have an experience of both association and disassociation, take a moment to compare the two. How are they different? Which one was easier for you to do? Did you find yourself being pulled into the associated experience or pulled out of it? Did you have a preference? What do you see as the potential benefits of each position? Typically our students will say that in the associated state they felt more alive and more real. If someone selected a ride that was quite intense, they would once again feel the thrill and rush of excitement in their body. By comparison, the disassociated exercise gave them an outside perspective, seeing and hearing things that they had not seen nor heard before with different or more neutral feelings and emotions.

Think of something that you did yesterday. Are you associated or disassociated?

Now think of something you are planning to do tomorrow. Associated or disassociated?

For some people, past memories are associated while future representations are disassociated. For others it is the other way around. Still others have them both associated or both disassociated. How do you do it? However you do it, see what happens when you do the reverse. Please go ahead, we'll wait.

Did you have any difficulty? Was it unfamiliar? Association and disassociation are learnable ways of thinking. Once you know how to shift from one to the other, it becomes natural and effortless. Hint: Some people "step into" and "step out of" the experience. Others "float" in and out. Some do not even move. They stay put while watching the image of themselves move in and out. Still others have themselves "beamed" in and out with Star Trek-like technology. One client who felt stuck in a negative association imagined a friend capturing the moment on his iPhone, and then fast-forwarded to the following week as he sat in front of his computer watching the video that his friend had taken the previous week. This helped him get out of his stuck state because he went from associated to disassociated, from being in the experience to observing it.

Association and disassociation are not limited to memories of the past or the future.

As you are reading the text, looking through your own eyes, seeing the page and the words, hearing external sounds through your own ears, feeling feelings in your body and feeling the tactile sensations of holding the book or e-book device, then you are associated in the present moment.

If you were to observe yourself reading this book by seeing your body from a distance (close or far) and a specific perspective (front, profile, ¾, back or above) hearing any sounds from the distance and letting all feelings stay in his/her body, then you are disassociated in the present moment. When we took you through the Stuck-Meta-Resource exercise, from the Meta position we directed you to speak in the third person using the word "he" or "she" when describing the Self in the stuck state. This is how you describe yourself when you are disassociated.

When would it be useful to be associated? And when would it be more practical to be disassociated?

In general, it is empowering to associate into resourceful states such as calm, centeredness, compassion, curiosity or playfulness. It can be equally empowering to disassociate from unpleasant states such as rage, guilt, blame, overwhelmed or upset to get a different perspective. By viewing ourselves from the outside, we are in a position where we can think more clearly about what to do next. Disassociation is especially useful when working through traumas, phobias and overwhelming memories.

Association and disassociation are critical skills will play a major role in many of the upcoming NLP techniques.

Ericksonian Hypnosis, Hypnotic Language and Unconscious Communication: The Milton Model

The foundation of NLP is to a great extent built upon the work of Milton Erickson, M.D. Much of what Erickson did unconsciously, Richard Bandler and John Grinder made conscious. That is, Bandler and Grinder identified the underlying beliefs and language patterns used by Erickson to communicate with the unconscious. Erickson's interest in communicating with the unconscious was to facilitate problem solving and therapeutic change. Hypnotherapists, charismatic leaders and storytellers use trance language. Suggesting that a listener "go deeply into trance, now," when using a convincing gaze accompanied by an engaging tone, tempo, volume and inflection with emphasis placed on particular words can elicit the trance phenomena. Hypnosis also requires "safety" and "trust," particularly trust in our own ability to connect with a deeper self and listen carefully. But the language of the unconscious is not words. The unconscious "speaks" in symbols and through the body.

You do want to become more adept at communicating with the unconscious, don't you? And isn't it nice to know that you will soon be learning the language patterns used by Milton Erickson, even if it is just the tip of the iceberg. And you will discover how these learnings will complement the Meta Model that you read about in Chapter 19.

In the hands of an experienced psychotherapist, counselor or coach, these skills can be used for healing the past, creating a compelling future or enhancing and enjoying being in the moment. In the hands of someone motivated by a self-serving agenda, these skills can be deceptive and manipulative.

With the knowledge of hypnosis and its language patterns, we can learn to heal ourselves, live the life we want to have, be more present and enhance the enjoyment of our interactions with others. At the same time this knowledge can protect us from self-serving advertisers, leaders, pundits, salespeople and others. Learning about hypnosis will make you a better listener, a more informed customer and a not so naïve reader or audience member.

For those of you interested in going deeper into the field of hypnosis we suggest taking an Ericksonian Hypnosis training where you can listen to and watch hypnosis being demonstrated and have a direct experience of being both hypnotist and hypnotic subject. You will discover not only how the following verbal patterns are being used, but also how the accompanying form (voice, facial expressions, body movements, etc.) makes all the difference in the world. Typically, the form is slow and rhythmic, soft and deep, with emphasis on the action verbs.

Here are some of the hypnotic patterns of Milton Erickson. In honor of Dr. Milton Erickson, the following language patterns are referred to as the Milton Model Language Patterns. For each pattern, we will offer you specific ways to apply the patterns in hypnotherapy, in coaching, in advertising/sales, in business, and with family members and friends.

I. Presuppositions (Pre-existing beliefs and/or expectations)

This pattern is called Presuppositions. We have used this term before when talking about the NLP presuppositions and when presenting the Problem Frame vs. Outcome Frame. All statements contain presuppositions. Erickson used presuppositions to direct his patient's awareness, indirectly.

Instead of telling them to "close your eyes," he might say, "When you at some point feel your eyelids getting heavy, you can let them close." He is presupposing that his patient's eyelids will eventually become heavy and will close. Consider the following statement. "How surprised will you be when the symptoms you described will have long been gone by the end of the session?" This statement presupposes that the patient's symptoms will be gone by the end of the session, but it is not said directly. The patient could say that they will be "very" surprised, "a little" surprised, or "not" surprised at all. In any case, by focusing on the degree of surprise, the client is not conscious of the indirect suggestion.

There are many ways to embed presuppositions in language. For example, by starting a sentence with, "Before you..." or "After you..." or "When you ..." the message that follows is being presupposed.

Here are some examples of using this pattern.

After reading the next few examples, you can make up your own statement in which you presuppose that you will be successful.

Before finishing this chapter...

When you practice these language patterns...

These three statements presuppose that you will read the next few examples, finish the chapter and practice the patterns.

Does it mean that you will do it? That you must do it? That you have to do it? No. They are hypnotic suggestions. They are ideas that you can now consider. It's all up to you.

Yet some people incorrectly interpret them as commands and react by rebelling against them because they do not wish to be told what to do. They are waiting to be told what to do, so that they can assert their independence by resisting. Who are we to tell people what to do? We are not in the business of giving advice. We are in the business of teaching people how to connect with a place within that will facilitate creative problem solving.

Question: What presuppositions will you be using to become a more successful communicator?

196 NLP A Changing Perspective

How many presuppositions can you find in the previous question?

It presupposes (1) that you will be using presuppositions, (2) that you are already a successful communicator and (3) using certain presuppositions will make you even more successful.

Here are some examples of statements and/or questions containing "Presuppositions."

In Hypnotherapy: You can continue to go deeper into trance.
In Coaching: What's it like to step into the experience of having already accomplished your goal?
In Advertising/Sales: What do you like best about this product?
In Business: When can we meet to discuss how we are going to meet our target goals?
With Family and Friends: Do you realize how much I love you?

NLP Momentary Practice

What are some ideas that are important for you to communicate in your personal or professional relationships? Create five sentences that use presuppositions to communicate these ideas.

II. Mind-Reading: (claiming to know what someone else is thinking or feeling)

You might remember mind reading from the Meta Model. We will be revisiting some of the same Meta Model patterns, but instead of using them to chunk down to learn how the person is thinking and feeling, we will use them to chunk up to direct thoughts and feelings.

Here are some examples of statements and/or questions containing "Mind Reading."

In Hypnotherapy: You may be wondering how hypnosis will work for you as you continue to think about going into trance, experiencing sensations in your body and becoming aware of new ideas and possibilities.
In Coaching: You have certain ideas of what is important to you, what you want to achieve and how you are going to make it happen.
In Advertising/Sales: After learning about this product, we know how much you are going to appreciate this unique opportunity.

In Business: You just might be curious how we are going to get the job done on time and under budget.
With Family and Friends: You do know how much I love you.

III. Nominalizations/Unspecified Verbs (labels for things and actions)

Here are two more patterns also found in the Meta Model. While the purpose of the Meta model was to ask questions to get specific details, here with the Milton Model we are using artfully vague language on purpose to make indirect suggestions and create ambiguity.

Examples of Nominalizations: Awareness, Experiences, Thoughts, Sensations, Safety, Comfort, Solution, Integration, Balance, Knowledge, Discovery and Empowerment

Examples of Unspecified Verbs: To be aware, to think, to sense, to be safe, to solve, to integrate, to know, to discover, to empower

Here are some examples of statements and/or questions containing "Nominalizations and Unspecified Verbs."

In Hypnotherapy: What inner resources will you need to access to successfully transform your experience and discover the power that resides within?
In Coaching: What skills, gifts and abilities will you be implementing in the pursuit of realizing your dreams?
In Advertising/Sales: When elected, I will provide this country with the strong leadership necessary for peace, freedom and national security.
In Business: We are now in the process of consolidating our resources to build a solid foundation and create an environment to maximize our profitability and lead the way to future success.
With Family and Friends: I appreciate the support you have shown and your commitment to our relationship.

IV. Linkage (joining unrelated ideas)

Often Erickson's trances were one long run-on sentence. Although he was presenting unique and distinct ideas that did not necessarily have anything to do with one another, like, "You are listening to the sound of my voice *and* you are becoming relaxed," each one was linked together either using the simple conjunction "and" or other linkage phrases such as "as you ..." or "when you ..." or "before you ..." or "while you ..." as in the sentence, "*As you* read this paragraph, *you will* notice the patterns themselves being used *and* your ability to recognize these patterns *will have* you learn *and* integrate them in a way in which *you will* easily *and* effortlessly utilize the language patterns automatically *and* unconsciously discovering that practicing the patterns *will* inevitably *result* in deep trance for the speaker *and* listener (or writer *and* reader) depending upon the medium being used to communicate a hypnotic suggestion such as 'The more you read (or listen), the deeper you will go into trance' *and the more* you allow yourself to comfortably enter into a state of amused confusion, *the more* open you will be to playfully *and* spontaneously using these patterns over *and* over again."

For the linear conscious mind, here is another way of expressing it.

A. Simple Conjunction (And)

You are feeling the temperature in the room *and* you are relaxing.

B. Implied Causatives

As you ... you will ...
E.g. *As you* read this chapter, *you will* be learning to go into trance.

While you ... you can ...
E.g. *While you* read this sentence, *you can* come up with more examples.

Before ... why not ...
E.g. *Before* continuing to the next pattern, *why not* take a deep breath?

The more ... the more ...
E.g. *The more* familiar you become with the hypnotic patterns of Milton Erickson, *the more* flexibility you will have in communicating ideas.

After ... you will ...
E.g. *After* completing an NLP course, *you will* become an even more skillful communicator.

C. Cause Effect

x will make you y
E.g. Leaning Hypnosis *will make* learning NLP even more fun.

x will cause you to y
E.g. Closing your eyes and listening to the sound of my voice *will cause* you to go into a deep trance.

x will force you to y
E.g. Maintaining silence *will force* you to become more aware of your body.

x will allow you to y
E.g. Developing these skills *will allow you* reach your full potential.

Here are some examples of statements and/or questions containing "Linkage."

In Hypnotherapy: Closing your eyes *will allow you* to go into a deep trance.
In Coaching: Taking just 15 minutes every day to write down your goals and visualizing yourself actively engaged the things you need to do *will result in* living the life you dream of having.
In Advertising/Sales: *If* you can see it in your mind, *then* you can see it in your driveway.
In Business: *The more* we focus our attention on getting the job done, *the more* effective we are going to be in achieving our goals.
With Family and Friends: As I reflect on our journey together, *I realize* just how much my love for you has grown.

V. Factive Predicates (presupposes the truth of the clause that follows)

Are you aware that you are...?
Did you know...?
Do you realize...?
How surprised will you be when...?

Here are some examples of questions containing "Factive Predicates."

In Hypnotherapy: *Do you realize* that you are already in trance?
In Coaching: *Are you aware* that you are well on your way to

making your dreams come true?

In Advertising/Sales: *Are you aware* that by purchasing this product your sales will skyrocket?

In Business: *Did you know* what a valued member of this team you are?

With Family and Friends: *Have you noticed* that I have been listening more attentively to you since we spoke about it last week?

VI. Lack of Referential Index (the sentence is vague about who is acting or about the action itself)

Here are some examples of statements containing "Lack of Referential Index."

In Hypnotherapy: *People* can go deeply into trance.
In Coaching: *Shit* happens.
In Advertising/Sales: *Things* go better with Coke.
In Business: *It* is important that we take *bold steps*.
With Family and Friends: *It* really makes a difference to me.

VII. Deletion (something is being left out)

Here are some examples of statements and/or questions containing "Deletion."

In Hypnotherapy: And you can explore and learn.
In Coaching: Be prepared and pay attention.
In Advertising/Sales: Think different. (Apple)
In Business: We must each be responsible and accountable.
With Family and Friends: I would like to be supportive and attentive.

In each of the previous examples, the speaker is making a statement in which some information is being left out, so the listener is being presented with an idea that can be interpreted in various ways. In the first example, the hypnotist is not specifying what it is the trance subject is to be exploring or learning. It is open ended to allow the subject to fill in the meaning. This pattern is used when your intention is to create ambiguity for the listener. Do not use this pattern if you have a specific idea that you want to directly and clearly communicate.

VIII. Temporal Predicate (shifting of past, present and future tense verbs that can create disorientation in time)

Here are some examples of statements and/or questions containing "Temporal Predicates."

In Hypnotherapy: When you *think back* on that resourceful memory, *remember* how that feeling can and *will be* experienced right *now* in the *present moment*.
In Coaching: What *will* it be like when you *are* saying to yourself, "I *did* it?"
In Advertising/Sales The *future is now*.
In Business: People who purchase this product *will be looking back* and wondering, "How *did* we ever get along without it?"
With Family and Friends: When I *look into the future*, *remembering* what you just *said*, I *am* feeling confident that you *will be* pleased.

IX. Embedded Question (a statement which is actually a question containing presuppositions)

Here are some examples of statements containing "Embedded Questions."

In Hypnotherapy: I am curious whether or not *you will be experiencing trance sooner or later*.
In Coaching: I don't know if *you realize the potential power of the words you are using*.
In Advertising/Sales: We are wondering *what features of the new phone you like best*.
In Business: I do not know if any of *you notice the improvements in customer service*.
With Family and Friends: Isn't it nice to know that *we can work together to discover mutually satisfying solutions*.

X. Embedded Command (an indirect suggestion disguised as commentary)

Here are some examples of statements and/or questions containing "Embedded Commands." The embedded commands are indicated in *italics*.

In Hypnotherapy: Some people in our courses spontaneously *remember a lost forgotten pleasurable childhood memory.*
In Coaching: Successful people *feel confident and persevere.*
In Advertising/Sales: You may want to *recommend this book to three special friends.*
In Business: Excellent managers will *communicate clearly and effectively.*
With Family and Friends I know it is not necessary to remind you to *buy flowers today for our anniversary.*

XI. Quotes (another person is cited as an authority)

For example if you want to tell someone to keep moving, instead of telling them directly that they have to keep moving, you can quote Albert Einstein and say, "Albert Einstein once said, 'Life is like riding a bicycle. To keep your balance, you must keep moving'."

Here are some examples of statements containing "Quotes."

In Hypnotherapy: Milton Erickson used to say things like, "Feel both feet on the ground, rest your hand lightly on the lap and allow your eyelids to slowly close. That's right."
In Coaching: And as Rabbi Hillel once said, "If not now, when."
In Advertising/Sales: As the Nike commercial says, "Just do it."
In Business: Bikram Choudhury said, "If you can, you must."
With Family and Friends: As James Taylor said, "You've got a friend."

XII. Analogical Marking (a specific message is contained within the sentence and marked out with gestures or voice, etc.)

When writing a book we can use "quotes", bold lettering, different fonts, different size fonts etc., to emphasize a specific word or passage, but when we are speaking we need to use our voice or gestures to mark the words or passages that we want to stand out. To do this we might change our tempo, tone, volume or inflection or offer an accompanying gesture, facial expression or body movement.

Analogical markings are often used when giving embedded commands and using quotes. Here are some previous Milton Model examples taken from the last two categories of "Embedded commands" and "Quotes." Read them out loud using a different tone, tempo, volume and/or inflection when reciting the words in bold. Notice how things change.

In Hypnotherapy: Some people in our courses spontaneously *remember a lost forgotten pleasurable childhood memory.*
In Coaching: And as Rabbi Hillel once said, *"If not now, when?"*
In Advertising/Sales: You may want to *recommend this book to three special friends.*
In Business: Bikram Choudhury said, *"If you can, you must."*
With Family and Friends: I know it is not necessary for me to remind you to *buy flowers today for our anniversary.*

XIII. Tag Question (an apparent mismatch actually reinforces the point)

In Hypnotherapy: You are learning, *aren't you?*
In Coaching: You will do it, *won't you?*
In Advertising/Sales: This is amazing, *isn't it?*
In Business: You will have the assignment ready for me on Monday, *won't you?*
With Family and Friends: You know how much you mean to me, *don't you?*

NLP Momentary Practice:

Isn't it nice to know that there are several patterns that you are already familiar with because you learned them when you learned the Meta Model? Ask someone to assist you by picking a resourceful state that he/she would like to have right now. The resourceful state can be relaxation, calm, being peaceful, being centered, etc. Then select no more than seven patterns and practice leading that person into that state (associated). Become aware of using words that will associate your partner into the experience rather than have him/her just think "about" the experience. As you use these patterns, watch your partner as he/she becomes more and more resourceful. Then do the same with the remaining six patterns. You can also practice using language that will put him/her into the observer position, disassociating him/her from the experience. Remember to use a rhythmic voice, with soft volume, slow tempo and take pauses. As

Stephen Gilligan, a soulful Ericksonian hypnotherapist, says, "90% of hypnosis is musicality."

CHAPTER 22

Anchoring: Recapturing Our Life

"You have so many different learnings and most of them you have forgotten about, so I am not asking you to learn a new skill, I'm only asking you to be willing to utilize the skills you already have, but have forgotten."
-Milton Erickson

Having practiced association, disassociation and the Milton Model language patterns, we are now ready to begin learning the NLP techniques. Many of these NLP techniques will involve stored memories. All that has happened (past memories) and all we have imagined that is going to happen (future memories) is stored and organized in the unconscious. Memories are potential resources that can serve us now and in the future. And we can learn to utilize these resourceful memories by bringing them to the present moment and building a bridge that will take them the future. Whether we have 20 years, 40 years or 60 years of stored memories, not to mention our collective unconscious, we can learn to become more proficient in harvesting specific resource states associated with different times in our life and have them readily available when we need them.

You may be wondering, "What about times in the past when I was not so resourceful in handling difficult situations and could have actually used some inner resources that were not available at the time?" We will be addressing this very issue in a later chapter. For now, we will limit ourselves to remembering only resourceful experiences.

The process that we will be using to retrieve these inner resources is known as "anchoring." Anchoring is based on the cause-effect (stimulus response) phenomenon. Have you ever happened to hear a song that you had not heard in a long time and it brought back old memories? Do you remember seeing a look on someone's face and found yourself getting upset? Is there a certain tone of voice that makes you feel encouraged? Is there an internal voice that makes you feel angry? An anchor can be any external or internal image, sound or voice that automatically and instantaneously results in a strong feeling, either pleasant or unpleasant. It could also be a specific touch, smell or taste.

When I (S.L.) first met Rachel's grandmother, during the time we began dating in 1982, she prepared a traditionally Ashkenazi Jewish, albeit very unhealthy, dish known as "Schmaltz and Gribenes" which consisted primarily of chicken fat and salt, served on rye bread. It was something that I had not tasted since I was a little boy visiting my grandparents in the Bronx. But upon tasting it, I was "transported" back in time, recalling not only smells and tastes, but also faces and voices of deceased relatives being very much alive. No, I was not imagining a zombie apocalypse. I was remembering leaning on the windowsill with my grandmother overlooking a busy thoroughfare, picking at the decaying cracked paint and counting passing cars with all of the accompanying emotions of being a six year old. Now that's an anchor. For someone who had never tasted anything like it before, it would not be an anchor. Schmaltz itself has no intrinsic power. It is the power of the connection that our neurology makes between the stimulus and the associated experience.

As you read about anchoring, perhaps there are there some special memories that come to mind? Of course, the intensity of the experience will depend greatly upon whether the memory is associated or disassociated as well as the submodality structure. If it is a flat, still, disassociated memory it will not be much of an anchor. But if it is conjures up a bright, panoramic, colorful, three dimensional, moving, associated image with surround sound, texture and feeling, then you have got quite an anchor. It is also important to know that anchors may evoke a range of pure emotions including being happy, sad, angry, compassionate, scared, safe and curious with no conscious awareness of anything. That is, images and sounds remain unconscious, while the physical and emotional reactions are strong and unmistakable. Have you ever found yourself saying, "I do not know why I am laughing? Or crying? Or getting upset?"

This might remind you of the stimulus response experiment developed by Pavlov who would ring a bell and give a dog a treat. Eventually the ringing of the bell would cause the dog to salivate. We teach anchoring to our clients and students to awaken positive resourceful memories that will be readily available anytime they are needed. We also teach people how to neutralize existing "negative" anchors to create equanimity and presence of mind.

Find Memories that Boost Your Self Esteem

Each of us has stories about our self and our life experiences. Our self-concept is built upon these collected memories. In this chapter we will be locating experiences that will contribute to building and reinforcing a positive self-concept. Often these experiences come from events in which we were confronted with a difficult choice or chose to take on a major challenge. As a result of these experiences, we discover inner resources such as "confidence," "resiliency," "perseverance," "focus," "commitment," "playfulness," "passion," etc.

As we look back over our life, there are certain resourceful moments that come to mind. When we created the NLP Center of New York in 1986, I (S.L.) had recently resigned from teaching for the New York City Board of Education and I (R.H.) made a transition from being a dance/movement therapist. The decisions required "confidence," and "trust" in our abilities and each other. As time went on we found ourselves developing "resilience" when things did not go as expected, "focus" when we had a deadline, renewed "motivation and persistence" whenever activities became routine, humor when we found ourselves being too serious and "playfulness" when we needed a break. Through anchoring, these resources do not remain buried in the past. They are all very much alive and available when and where we need them.

NLP Momentary Practice

An easy way to begin collecting evidence about our life is to divide our age into decades. This is something we learned from Jack

Canfield, a leader in the self-esteem movement. We both studied with him, Steven in the 1970s and Rachel in the 1990s. By dividing our life in this way we can look for specific activities, learning experiences, and life events that occurred during that time that demonstrated a variety of resources.

For example, we might think about how in our early childhood we learned to read, write, ride a bike, make friends, become independent, etc. In our later years, we can recall jobs, relationships, travel experiences, life transitions, etc. Each time we remember an event, we can ask, "What resource did I acquire during that time?" It is useful to write these resources down with a brief description of how old we were and what was happening to us at that particular time. You might not have even recognized it or labeled it as being a resource state when it originally took place.

Find a place to record these resources, now, so you can refer back to them later in the chapter when we ask you to practice anchoring.

Identifying Anchors in Every Day Life

An anchor can also be thought of as a trigger. The trigger or anchor is the stimulus that creates a response, the cause that has an effect, the person that pushes our buttons or the muse that inspires us. When we speak of triggers, we often speak of blame. We attribute fault. "It is his fault that I am feeling angry." "It is my fault that I am depressed." "It is their fault I am sad." Only when joking would we say, "It is his fault I am so happy," or "It is your fault I am feeling safe." But we do say, "You make me so happy" or "You make me feel safe." In either case, we experience being at the effect, not the cause. We can feel like a victim to people and circumstance. But what about rescuing ourselves by rewiring our "buttons" so that even when people try to push our buttons, they do not have the same effect? What about no longer being victims of circumstance? How about empowering our selves (being both cause and effect)?

We are not trying to say that there are no victims. When we began writing this chapter, Hurricane Sandy was wreaking havoc here, all along the eastern seaboard of the United States. There are many victims whose homes in the region have been flooded or burned to the ground, with no power, gas or water. There is certainly no shortage of victims in need of help who are suffering from physical and emotional abuse as well as deadly forces of nature. Yet as with all disasters, natural and manmade, whatever assistance we eventually receive, connecting to our inner resources will ultimately be what helps us move on.

If we accept our "buttons" as given, and not within our control, then we are resigning ourselves to unnecessary ongoing suffering. And that leaves us in the painful position of being a victim, giving away our power and helplessly looking to blame.

Obviously, the early NLP developers did not invent anchoring. Anchors have always existed and have been part of our programming. But it is by becoming aware of our anchors/triggers, that we can do something about them. We can eliminate the anchors that do not serve us, create ones that do and use them to transfer resources from one context to another. But before we go into some specific anchoring techniques, let's examine the various types of anchors. Just as we have five senses, we have five potential sources of anchors. Let's explore each one.

Visual Anchors

Every day we get to experience a multitude of visual stimuli that we respond to either consciously or unconsciously. It may be a smile, a wink, rolling eyes or a hand gesture. If we are walking down the street and see someone who looks like someone we know, we might react with a warm feeling (if they remind us of someone we like) or a cold feeling (if they remind us of someone we dislike). The visual trigger could also be a company's logo, a gesture or a religious symbol. Our reaction will depend largely upon our previous associations. People have screen savers that evoke particular feelings, such as the images of Jesus, Elvis, their children or the Starship Enterprise.

Take a moment and think about something you have seen during the past week that triggered a particular pleasant emotional state.

Auditory Anchors

Many people have songs as triggers. I (S.L.) remember the first time I heard "Sgt. Peppers Lonely Hearts Club Band" on the radio.

The songs in the album still evoke the uplifting mood of the 1960's, as does the album cover itself. We love the music of Bruce Springsteen, whose voice, lyrics and melodies combine to transport us to various times and places. We even decided to have our first child at a Bruce Springsteen concert in New Jersey. We just made the decision there. We had also used John Lennon's song, "Grow Old Along with Me" at our wedding ceremony. It was already a positive anchor; using it at our wedding only intensified its strength.

Just before heading to the closing of the sale of my (S.L) parents' apartment in Queens, I returned for one last visit. Before leaving, I decided to create an anchor so I would have a strong positive memory of my experience of saying goodbye. I looked through the songs on my iPod (the iPhone had not yet been invented) and selected the Cat Stevens song, "If You Want To Sing Out, Sing Out" and listened to it while dancing throughout the apartment and recalling many moments at different stages of my life. The song had already been a positive anchor. Now when I hear that specific song or think about that time, I have an uplifting, loving memory of closing a chapter in my life that held so many rich memories of growing up.

Perhaps you have already selected meaningful songs to use for special people on your smartphone when they call. Music is only one type of auditory anchor. If you have travelled in Europe, you may have noticed that the police sirens are quite different from those in the United Sates. When I (R.H.) was 16 years old, I visited France for the first time. And hearing the sirens triggered feelings of sadness and fear, because they were associated with air raid sounds I had heard in World War II movies.

Auditory anchors can include voices, animal sounds, certain phrases and combinations of particular tones, tempos volumes and inflections.

Kinesthetic Anchors

Take a moment and think about what type of handshake you like. The sense of touch is very powerful. I (R.H.) had a grandfather who always squeezed my hand when he wanted to prove his physical strength. It was quite a strong grip and made my hand feel like it was in a vice. Nowadays when I shake hands with someone with a strong handshake I get triggered to the memory of my grandfather. Although it was often a bit too strong, the overall experience was positive, and I actually think about my grandfather and feel more positive towards the person shaking my hand with a tight strong grip. Think about various fabrics and the way they feel against your skin. Do you have any particular associations with them? We can be associated to all types of touch: hugs, kisses and pats on the back.

When I (S.L.) began my NLP training, one of my teachers gave me feedback that I became more animated and self-assured when I wrote on the chalkboard. Yes, that is what we used to use before whiteboards, and power point presentations. I had not realized that writing was an anchor for "teaching excellence" until she pointed it out. So when I worked with a training group I used writing on the board as a way of getting into a state of excellence. Any unique movements or gestures can be a kinesthetic anchor as well. This would include placing our hands together (in prayer), touching our fingertips together (in contemplation), clapping, raising our hands, biting one's lip, shaking or nodding one's head or sitting in lotus position.

Olfactory Anchors

What are the smells that create connections for you? The hindbrain is the ancient brain and is related to smells. Many students describe certain perfumes or colognes as powerful anchors. I (R.H.) remember smelling my mother's perfume, Shalimar. She always wore it when I was young, and then later on in my life, someone would be walking down the street and the whiff of Shalimar would immediately remind me of my mom and I would have a positive feeling. Some department stores use scents to trigger customers to linger longer while shopping. The aromatherapy profession also capitalizes on scents as positive healing scents and associations. Lavender oil, for example, can be a stimulus for relaxation. Food smells are very powerful and many real estate agents have recommended putting apple cider on the stove or baking cookies in the oven when selling a home in order to create an association with a warm, cozy, loving domicile.

Gustatory Anchors

What tastes bring back memories to you? One of our training assistants told us that he loved eggplant parmigiana. Whenever someone said, "Would you like to have eggplant parmigiana?" he would get in a good mood, and then again when he would eat it, he would have very positive feelings, happy memories of being a child. There are so many potential recipes for anchors. In Marcel Proust's classic book, <u>Swann's Way</u>, he described eating a madeleine cookie and that bite of cookie, 10 pages later, brought the reader to the protagonist's first memories of when he was ill and was taken care of by his mother. This is a great example of a gustatory anchor. Is there some food that you had as a child, but have not had for a long time that just thinking about it brings up certain memories? These types of anchors can become anchors not so much for specific moments in time, but for specific time periods.

NLP Momentary Practice

Take each category – visual, auditory, kinesthetic, olfactory and gustatory – and make a column for each one. Identify at least one of your triggers for each category.

Create Your Own Anchors

Having just finished a full day of downhill skiing, I (R.H.) am now relaxing in a restaurant in Zermatt, Switzerland, writing this chapter on anchoring. The sun above is shining brightly. A chill is in the air, as I gaze up at the Matterhorn rising above me 12,000 feet above sea level. I am feeling the awe and power of the moment. At the same time I am feeling safe, protected and secure. The convergence of all these elements is incredibly inspiring. So I want to anchor the moment. I take it all in, the clear blue sky, the white capped mountains, the bare tree tops, the voices speaking French, English, Italian and German, the red and white Swiss flag blowing in the crisp thin mountain air, are all part of my experience. I close my eyes and feel the intensity of the moment and still see the image of the Matterhorn in my mind's eye. I bring my hands together and press them close to my chest and experience this moment of inspiration. I don't know when and I don't know where in the future I will once again access "inspiration in this way," but now I have an anchor to do it.

Before I finish, I want to confirm that I have in fact created an anchor. So I open my eyes and "shake it out." I distract myself with some irrelevant thoughts and once again close my eyes and press my hands together close to my chest in exactly the same way. And I am once again filled with inspiration. Now I know I have an anchor. The touch is my self-anchor. And so is the image of the Matterhorn (visual anchor).

Whereas most anchors happen by chance, here I am creating it consciously and deliberately. Anchoring is something we can do any time we, or someone we are with, is in a resourceful state that we want to be able to easily activate again in the future. And when we want to anchor a state that we are not currently experiencing, we need to identify and label it and "bring" it into the present moment.

We also need to decide what we are going to use as the anchor. It can be auditory (a word or phrase, like "presence" or "peace of mind," spoken out loud or in our head). It might be kinesthetic (a movement and touch like bringing two fingers together). Or it can be visual (a picture in our mind's eye).

As we said, we can only anchor experiences that are happening in the moment. But we can also retrieve a stored memory and anchor it just as long as we are re-experiencing it in the here and now. So if we want to anchor "tranquility," we close our eyes (for most people closing the eyes makes it easier) and ask, "When in my life have I enjoyed a moment of 'tranquility?'" and notice what comes to mind. Some people immediately get a feeling that can be enhanced by slowly expanding and spreading awareness throughout the body, re-experiencing tactile sensations, body movements and the emotional as well as the environmental climate of the time. Others initially get a visual memory that can be enhanced by associating into the experience, gradually bringing things into focus, adding movement, making it panoramic, three dimensional, making it bright and seeing things both close up and in the background. Still others first remember the voices of people speaking or the sounds of the environment, enhancing it by tuning into the surroundings. To get the most powerful experience, we suggest developing awareness of all the senses then enhancing them all by finding the submodalities that increase the intensity.

NLP practitioners are skilled in using the hypnotic language described in the previous chapter to guide people deeply into these altered states of consciousness. If you can guide yourself into a deep state of awareness, then you have no need for assistance. One of the things that can interfere is our rational, linear conscious mind. When the conscious mind is active, it can significantly interfere with our ability to do this. If you only see "words" and are not "transported" to another place and time, then you are in your linear/rational mind, which is not the way to do NLP. You are welcome to "try it again," and this time allow yourself to be absorbed in the experience. One of the skills we teach is eliminating interference by de-potentiating the conscious mind.

The Four Points for Creating An Anchor

There are four criteria that must be satisfied when creating an anchor.

I. Uniqueness of the Anchor

When creating an anchor it is important for it to be unique. For example, if you have a habit of regularly placing your index finger up to your lip, it would not satisfy this criterion. It must be something you never or rarely do. So whether you are creating a self-anchor for yourself or intend to anchor someone else, make sure it is distinctive. And it must be something that you will be able to repeat in the same way. For example, when creating a kinesthetic anchor, it is important to replicate the exact movement, location, pressure and surface area.

II. Intensity of the Experience

Whether you are getting yourself into a resource state, leading someone else or being led, it is essential that the experience be fully associated and intense. If it is not strong and powerful, if it is not deep and profound, then it is not going to be much of an anchor. At best, you will anchor a watered down experience. Using your knowledge of submodalities will help to maximize its potency.

III. Timing of the Anchor

A common mistake is to hold your anchor before or after experiencing the intensity of the state. First pre-plan the anchor you will use, so that you are ready to use it when the intensity of the recalled memory is peaking. Only when the person being anchored is fully associated into the resourceful memory and feeling it strongly do you fire off the anchor. Hold the anchor at the peak of the experience. Then release the anchor, and go to neutral. This is where you would do the "NLP Shake." Some people vary the anchor by slightly increasing the pressure of the touch or slide their hand along the surface of the body as the intensity builds. Always fire off the anchor again to test.

IV. Purity of the Experience

We said earlier that the conscious mind might interfere with fully associating into the resourceful state. Suppose you are associated into a state of "relaxation" and while you are in it, the conscious mind is saying things like, "Is this really going to work?" or "Am I doing this right?" If you attempt to anchor the experience while hearing this inner voice, you will be anchoring doubt along with relaxation. And we doubt if that is what you want. So make sure you are anchoring only the pure state.

When you are testing an anchor and it does not reproduce the resourceful state it means that one or more of the above criteria was not being met. We suggest that you use the following checklist, and systematically go through each criterion to determine which one or ones need to be redone.

1. Is the anchor unique enough? Is it being replicated in exactly the same way?

2. Does the initial experience need to be made more intense by changing submodalities that will increase the potency?

3. Did you time the anchor correctly, firing it off at exactly the same time as the experience?

4. Is there any thought, feeling or belief that is interfering with the purity of the experience?

Once you have satisfied all four criteria, you will have an anchor.

Just as we have learned to be anchored to negative states in specific contexts (e.g. becoming anxious when flying, feeling insecure when meeting new people, getting upset when hearing a certain tone of voice), we can also learn to anchor positive states to specific contexts (e.g. enjoying flying, being comfortable meeting new people, getting curious when hearing that same tone of voice). There is no inherent link between the anchors and the contexts. It is all a matter of programming.

Anchoring A Resource and Transferring It To Another Context

Here's one technique for linking a resource state to a specific context. We suggest that when practicing this technique, you choose a context that does not already have a negative charge. We want to keep this as simple as possible so that you experience success. Some people insist on using a situation that is already a problem for them. Be patient. We will get to that type of situation shortly. If you are anxious meeting new people or making presentations, please wait. If you are impatient when it comes to learning, you will have to wait until later in the chapter.

Now find a context that you want to "enhance" rather than "fix." It could be being more playful with a family member or having greater focus when reading or having compassion towards people suffering.

The situation or context we will use as an example is "interacting with co-workers on a break," and the resource is "playfulness." Feel free to select a different context and resource state. First recall a time in your life when you were being playful. Choose a non-work related context where playfulness happens naturally and effortlessly. Select what you will be using to self-anchor and associate into the experience of playfulness, fully and completely, just the way you like it, and when it has become sufficiently intense, engage the playfulness anchor.

Now do the "NLP shake" and test your anchor. Having verified that the anchor works, think of being with co-workers on a break and fire the anchor seeing what you are seeing, hearing what you are hearing and allowing the resource of playfulness to fill your entire experience.

Think of the anchor as an intermediate step that you are using to bring the resource and the context together. Now imagine being in that context in the future and fire off the anchor. The process of connecting the resource with a time in the future is called "futurepacing."

The final test is to think of being in the situation in the future without using the anchor. When the resource state automatically activates, you are done. The situation itself has now become the anchor, so you no longer need to consciously use the self-anchor, but it still remains available for you to use in other situations.

While this exercise describes how to anchor yourself, the same steps will apply when anchoring another person.

Empower Yourself: Creating your Personal Anchors

Transferring Anchors to Another Context involves locating and anchoring resources from the past and programming our brain to automatically access them in the future. This next section is about de-potentiating our old "negative" anchors, so that we are no longer at the effect of external triggers and instead become the initiator of the states we want to experience. This is a form of state management. People ask us, "How can I manage to not be at the effect of something that has plagued me my entire life?" And "Just how much control do I actually have over my response to those external events?" Let's find out.

Jack Canfield uses the following formula: Event + Response = Outcome.

We all want to respond resourcefully to external events. NLP provides the "know how" to reprogram or install a new sequence into our bio-computer so that nothing further needs to be done, rehearsal is not necessary and the conscious mind is free to attend to other things.

Here are a couple of examples of how I (R.H.) overcame some "negative" anchors.

I remember a time when I was helping my elderly mother with bills. I was in a resourceful state, and then suddenly found myself regressed. I felt like a twelve year old girl resisting my mother. Something triggered my state, but I was not conscious of it until after I became agitated. I asked myself, "What was it that triggered me?" I then realized that my mother's tone of voice, which I interpreted as stubborn and authoritative, was an anchor from when I was a rebellious teenager. Once I realized what happened and identified the trigger, I stopped myself, breathed and asked myself what resource(s) I need at that time. I felt that I needed to be present and mature. Once I identified what I needed, I recalled times where I felt myself most present and mature. I was able to catch the unconscious anchor and manage my resourcefulness with my mother. Our interaction that followed was much more pleasant. I created a new pattern.

When I had breast cancer, I used a rectangular silk eye pillow over my eyes to help me visualize a healing scene while receiving the chemotherapy treatment. I brought this "eye pillow," to all of my treatments. When my chemotherapy treatments were finished, a friend offered to give me a massage for some nice relaxation and celebration for ending the treatments. During the massage my friend placed an "eye pillow" over my eyes and I immediately felt nauseated. Feeling nauseated was the way I had felt after receiving the chemotherapy. (Some people become nauseated just hearing the word "chemotherapy"). The "eye pillow" which helped me through the treatments had now become an anchor for nausea. I took the "eye pillow" off and then enjoyed the massage. At the time our children were eight and ten years old. I told them the "eye pillow," story and both kids started teasing me by saying the word, "eye pillow," and laughing at my sickened response. At first it disturbed me, but the more they said it, the more the situation became funny and playful and eliminated the association to the chemotherapy side effects. Currently, I can comfortably hear the words "eye pillow" as well as see and touch one and only have an association to the story, but not to any upsetting feeling. In this example I was able to eliminate the anchor, by adding joy and humor.

Neutralizing Anchors: How To Dismantle an Existing Anchor

As we previously indicated, attempting to transfer a resource to a context that is already "inhabited" by a negative emotion can produce mixed results. So here is a technique that we can use with a "pre-existing" condition. It can help us with a trigger that "gets us" upset, frustrated, irritated, impatient, annoyed, etc. It is called "Combining Opposite Anchors." It is also known as the "Collapse Anchor Technique." The purpose of this technique is to neutralize an existing trigger of an unwanted feeling. Once the feeling is neutralized, we can then apply the previous technique for "Transferring a Resource to Another Context."

In our training we call the person who is working on him/herself, "the explorer" (aka the client) and the person who is leading the process, "the guide" (aka the coach). Depending upon the nature of the professional relationship, we could be talking about a client and his/her coach, a patient and his/her psychotherapist, a hypnotic subject and a hypnotherapist, etc. To simplify it, we will use the terms, "explorer" and "guide."

Suppose we are working with a person who frequently becomes impatient. Please note that impatience in some contexts may motivate and activate useful behaviors. If we try to eliminate a behavior that is attempting to serve a purpose, we will likely get resistance, which is actually a healthy response. In Chapter 23 we will discuss how to work with such "resistance." Once we have determined that the person wants to change his/her state and he/she has no inner objections, we can proceed with this process.

In previous examples, we have been using self-anchors. Although this technique can be done this way, we will now introduce how one person can anchor another. For this technique we will use kinesthetic (touch) anchors, although visual and auditory anchors can work just as well. When you plan on using kinesthetic anchors professionally with clients, it is important to discuss it with them beforehand and get their permission to touch them in places that are acceptable (usually knuckles, hands and shoulders). If you prefer, you do not have to ever touch someone to anchor them. Recently, we have begun working with people using Skype, so kinesthetic anchors are not an option, but visual (gestures and facial expressions) and auditory (voice) anchors will work just as well. You can also teach the explorer how to self-anchor.

By asking the explorer to think of times he/she became impatient, we determine the common trigger(s). Is it when he/she is waiting on lines, actual or virtual? Is it when someone is driving slowly in the passing lane or taking too much time to answer a question?

Anchoring The Unwanted Feeling (Impatience)

Having the explorer sit with his/her hands on his/her lap and associate into one of these times, we proceed to anchor it by choosing a specific place like the knuckle on the left thumb. The uniqueness of the anchor is extremely important here, so we have to remember exactly "where" and "how" we are touching, including which finger we are using to apply the touch, the specific angle and amount of pressure. We have found that for some people it does not have to be so exact. But for others, it does.

Test your anchor. This is anchor #1.

Anchoring The Opposite State

Now ask the explorer to identify the "opposite," "inverse" or "contrasting feeling" state. In this case, it might be patience, acceptance, tolerance or understanding. We are not looking for the resource state or the state you want to have instead. And we do not tell the client what the opposite state is, even if we have our own idea. We ask "What is it for you?"

Once we have a name for the opposite state, we get the explorer to access the state, associate into it and anchor it on the opposite side. For example, if the first anchor was on the knuckle on the left thumb, we will use the knuckle on the right thumb. For this example, let's use patience as the opposite state of impatience.

Test your anchor. This is anchor #2.

The intensity of anchor #2 must match the intensity of anchor #1. If it doesn't, then have the explorer recall another memory of patience (#2) and anchor it in the same location. This is called stacking anchors.

Now you are ready to proceed.

Asking the explorer to close his/her eyes and think of the situation, we fire off both anchors simultaneously. Continuing to hold the anchors, the explorer will invariably show some shifting in his/her facial expressions, breathing and body movements. The two opposite states will eventually settle down to state of relaxed breathing and stillness- a place of balance and equanimity. When this happens, you can release the anchors.

It is one thing to read about this process and understand the steps. It is quite another to experience it. It is fascinating to experiencing the two energies coming together. Some people experience it as an electrical circuit flowing back and forth between two poles before settling down.

If this does not happen and we have anchored properly, it may be that the intensity of anchor #2 (patience) was not as intense as anchor #1 (impatience), the identified "opposite state" was not actually the opposite state, or the overwhelming feeling is rooted in some memory or memories from the past and needs to be addressed by another NLP technique.

To test our work, we fire off anchor #1. If we get the neutral, balanced state then we have eliminated the anchor. If there is more than one trigger, we might have to do this with each one.

If we are working with someone who comes into the session already in a stuck state, it may be easy to anchor the stuck state, but anchoring the opposite feeling will require that we get the person to fully disassociate before identifying and stepping in to the opposite feeling.

After neutralizing the anchor, the ensuing state of calm or evenness may be all the explorer needs. But if he/she would like to have something more, we can anchor an additional resource and transfer it to that context. In the case of the impatient client, some possible resources might include hope, eagerness, commitment, desire or zeal.

Once we know the steps and have become facile in associating and disassociating, this technique, as most NLP techniques, can be done on our own. Just remember to set up unique anchors, fully associate into the experience, time the anchors properly, keep each experience pure, and identify the actual opposite state.

Chunking Resources Technique

What if you have no memory of a resource?

The Chunking Resource technique is useful when you or someone with whom you are working does not remember ever experiencing a particular resource. For example, a client may want confidence but he/she claims that he/she has never experienced it. Now you can ask him/her how confident is he/she that he/she has never had it before. If he/she confidently answers, "yes," be prepared to anchor it.

Alternatively, we can offer a cooking metaphor. "Imagine that you are preparing a stew. What are the ingredients that you would use to prepare this meal? They might include potatoes, carrots and onions. Find and mix all the ingredients together and you get stew. And while you might have tasted each of the ingredients separately, you might never have tasted them all together."

What are the ingredients that would make up the "confidence" stew? For each of us the ingredients may differ. For example, one of our trainees said that courage, faith and persistence were the ingredients for confidence. Another trainee identified them to be focus, inner strength and commitment. Take a moment now and write down your ingredients for confidence.

For the client who "chunks down" confidence into courage, faith and persistence, we established three kinesthetic self anchors, one for each of the three states. Our goal is to fire them off simultaneously, so physical anchors will be the easiest to use. If you will be creating your own self-anchors, a simple way would be to use your thumb pad and anchor your index finger pad, and then your middle finger pad and then your ring finger pad. Then bringing the three together can be your self-anchor. Often when we work with a client, we will set up the individual anchors and have the client prepare his/her own unique self-anchor that he/she will use once all the resources come together.

One at a time, we anchor all three states "courage," "faith" and "persistence." Once we have them anchored, we fire off all three simultaneously, letting them flow together, combining and eventually becoming one state. Then the explorer creates a self-anchor and futurepaces to specific contexts.

In the previous example, we chunked down from confidence. Another way to chunk resources is to chunk up. In our training groups, we do this as a form of exploration and discovery. It is similar to cooking a stew, but this time we are opening the refrigerator, taking out different ingredients and seeing what creative meal we come up with. We can do the same with resources.

Let's say we select, curiosity, passion and commitment. We anchor each one individually just as we had in the prior example. Then we fire them off simultaneously and discover what we get. At times the resulting state can be quite profound and may require some time to put it into words. Chunking up resources in this way can be a creative and empowering experience.

NLP Momentary Practice

Pick three distinct resource states that you have already experienced. Use the Chunking Resources Technique and see what new resource emerges.

Chaining Technique

What other paths can I take to get to my resource state?

We have already introduced chaining with the Stuck-Meta-Resource technique. In teaching this technique, we often use the metaphor of crossing a stream. Imagine that you are hiking and you come to a small stream. You want to get across, but it's not possible to jump the entire width. So you look and see where there are stepping stones to help you easily get across. When a client is in a state of anger or frustration, he/she may want to feel calm or patient, but it may be too great a leap. As we stated earlier, there are many different ways to achieve a resourceful state, and the chaining technique is one that uses a progression of steps, like "stepping stones." Linear thinking clients may be more comfortable with this technique because it moves in a straight line. For example, a client comes in and says he/she wants to be more understanding, but he/she feels angry towards his/her co-worker. On a piece of paper, write the word "anger" on the far left side and then on the far right sight side, write the word "understanding." Show him/her the paper and indicate that you are about to create a pathway or chain starting with "anger" and ending in "understanding."

Forming the chain may require a combination of brainstorming and making modifications. The important thing is to create a progression that makes it easier to move from "anger" to "understanding." To go directly from "anger" to "understanding"," would be too big a leap, so we look to create an intermediate step, perhaps "sadness." Each step is a momentary stopping point that we will use in traversing the whole path. So now we have "anger" to "sadness," and we are looking for another small step to go from "sadness" to "understanding." And what comes to mind is "compassion." So we now have "anger" to "sadness" to "compassion" to "understanding." It is essential that we work closely with the client to come up with a sequence that makes sense for him/her and flows easily. In this case the final chain we have come up with is:

Anger->Sadness->Compassion->Understanding.

This sequence does not need to make sense for you. But it must make sense to the client. This is why each chain must be tailor made for the individual.

The chaining process is sequential and it can be done with movement, as in the Stuck-Meta-Resource technique, or it can be done anchoring with words, with images or with touch. To anchor the initial negative state (anger), we have the client think of the situation that gets him/her angry. Then we anchor the other states. Next we fire them all off sequentially. We often say the name of each state as we touch each knuckle. When we get to understanding, we remain there a little longer. We don't want the explorer to loop back to the beginning so we interrupt it at the end with the NLP shake. The process is repeated at least three times with the explorer passing through each state, going slowly or quickly depending upon the person's tempo. To test the work we have the explorer think of the situation that used to make him angry. If he/she transitions to the state of understanding and remains in that state, the work is done.

You have in essence created a new neural pathway for the chosen context that will move the explorer out of "anger" and into "understanding."

For all of these techniques, knowledge of the NLP skills previously presented – the rapport skills, pacing and leading, criteria, submodalities, the Meta Model and the Milton Model – will be essential for getting the desired results. By demonstrating and modeling these skills and techniques and providing opportunities for practicing and integrating these skills, our NLP training can be a wonderful learning environment for developing these unconscious competencies.

NLP Momentary Practice

You have been given several anchoring techniques. Select one: "Transferring A Resource To Another Context," "Anchoring Opposites," "Chunking Resources" or "Chaining" and practice with yourself or a colleague.

CHAPTER 23

Reframing: What Isn't the Meaning of Life?

"Life is without meaning. You bring the meaning to it. The meaning of life is whatever you ascribe it to be."
-Joseph Campbell

Reframe #1 After Rachel and I (S.L.) got married, Rachel noticed a behavior of mine that I was already very familiar with since I had already lived alone with me for quite some time. I would occasionally withdraw and not be very communicative. While I knew that it only lasted for a brief time, she didn't. For me, it was a time for me to recharge and replenish my energy, but Rachel initially took it personally. I started feeling badly that a behavior that had never been a problem for me was now becoming a problem for us. I made numerous attempts to explain it with little success. One day Rachel said, "Oh, I get it. It's like you are having your period." Since that day, it has never been a problem. Period.

Reframe #2 Rachel was pregnant with our first child when I (S.L.) traveled to Virginia to take a workshop with Connirae Andreas, who along with her husband, Steve Andreas, were among the early developers of NLP. In the workshop, participants were asked to make a personal belief statement that we felt was limiting. My statement was, "Having a child will severely restrict my personal and spiritual development." To which Connirae replied, "How will having a child actually enhance and promote your personal and spiritual development?" Now, 27 years later, I can probably write a book on how having children enhances personal and spiritual development. I'm confident that there is also someone out there who could write a book on how having children limits the pursuit of self-development. If not for the new frame of mind, who knows? It could have been me.

Reframe #3 A client of mine (S.L.) explained to me that he was going through a "mid-life crisis." When I referred to this period in his life and called it a "mid-life challenge," he began to view it in a very different light.

Reframe #4 Over a decade ago, both of us had life-threatening diseases: Rachel, breast cancer, and Steven, heart disease. When I (R.H.), was diagnosed with breast cancer, one of my friends said, "The illness is like ugly wrapping paper, but what is inside is a beautiful gift that you will be able to use." My friend gave me a new way of thinking about the experience and helped me begin the process of using my diagnosis as a process towards healthy living.

Reframe #5 When I (S.L.), was diagnosed with heart disease, my initial thought was that my body failed me and that the life that I had been enjoying was over. Yet I believed that I had the resources I needed to meet any challenge. But what were these resources? I would have plenty of time to think about it after undergoing quadruple bypass surgery. Emerging from the surgery, I began thinking, "How will having heart disease actually help me live a better, healthier life?" I can now look back and remember how I began applying my NLP skills to eating healthy, changing my work routine, losing and maintaining weight, exercising regularly, reducing stress and increasing relaxation through self-hypnosis. In addition to doing Bikram Yoga four to five times/week, I bike 30 minutes to work from Williamsburg to Union Square, stopping on the way to have a fresh squeezed vegetable juice. Did having heart disease actually help me live a better, healthier life? Or did "believing that heart disease would actually help me live a better, healthier life," help me live a better happier life?

All of these stories have one thing in common. They all involved changing the way we thought about an event. They all involved giving new meaning to an experience. They all involved "reframing" the situation.

Was getting ill the worst thing that could have happened to us or was it a wake-up call to start living a more mindful and healthier life? We made a choice about how to perceive these events.

When something unforeseen and unwanted happens to you, what does it mean? You get to choose.

Creating Multiple Perspectives

This chapter is about reframing. We are always framing. We are always giving meaning to our experience, whether we are aware of it or not. We are not saying that there isn't an "objective" reality out there. What we are saying is that we each have our own "subjective" experience of it. We frame things as being "good or bad," "right or wrong," "positive or negative," "worthless or valuable" etc. Most arguments come down to two people or two groups who are arguing over whose frame is right. To see things as being either "right" or "wrong" is in itself a frame. To see things as being neither "right" nor "wrong," is a frame that we find to be quite valuable and useful in understanding people, resolving conflict and facilitating change. Many of our students, when they learn that we are married, will ask, "What do you both do when you fight?" We explain, "We both know that we are both right."

Am I being selfish or taking care of myself?

Are we being stubborn or firm?

Is it a problem or an opportunity?

Is it failure or feedback?

Is this a mistake or a learning experience?

Am I procrastinating or am I taking time to think things through?

Is this illness a "death sentence" or "a blessing in disguise?"

Not recognizing that there is more than one way to frame our experience is one way of defining a "stuck state." Adhering to or believing in only one frame (one truth) and invalidating all others, is one way of defining fundamentalism. Fundamentalism confuses *a* truth with *the* truth. Sheldon B. Kopp wrote the book, If You Meet the Buddha on the Road, Kill Him. When you find the answer, keep looking. When we speak of flexibility, we are talking about the ability to recognize, step into and choose from among the many possibly frames.

A reframe can be useful when there is a miscommunication or when we are in a "stuck state." This can include feeling powerless, hopeless or worthless. There are two categories of verbal reframing: content reframing, and contextual reframing.

Content Reframing (or Meaning Reframing)

Content reframe happens when we create new meaning for an event, a statement or a situation. For example, when I (R.H.) was on a mountain taking ski lessons, I noticed that there was a sharp drop in the approaching ski run. I asked the teacher, "Is it easy to go down the next slope?" My teacher's reply was, "Are you the nervous type?" I replied, "No, I am very creative, and I can see a lot of possibilities happening." For the ski instructor, "asking the question," meant I was "nervous." I reframed the meaning for her by equating "asking the question" with "being creative." I could have also reframed the ski instructor's statement by saying, "Thanks for being concerned about me."

When you want to do a content reframe, ask yourself how else could this experience be defined or what else could it mean. One of my (R.H.) clients was complaining about her boyfriend who always left socks in the living room. As it turned out, the client and her boyfriend were having a trial separation. The client realized that now that he was no longer in the house, there were no more socks in the living room, but the house was very quiet and she felt lonely. The meaning of the messy house now changed. Instead of being annoyed with him, she was missing him because the absence of socks meant emptiness and loneliness. The client laughed about this, as she recognized the change in the meaning of socks being left on the floor. When they reconciled, I asked her what was it like now that he was back at home. "It's great, and I don't notice his socks anymore."

When Tom Sawyer (in The Adventures of Tom Sawyer by Mark Twain) convinced his friends, who were on their way to go fishing, that they were missing out on a valuable opportunity to whitewash (paint) a fence, he convinced them that it was "fun" not "drudgery" and not only got them to do his job of painting, but got them to pay him to do it, while he went fishing. Now that's reframing.

Humor is filled with content reframing. For example, take the sentence, "A woman's place is in the house." Then add, "and the Senate." This changes the meaning of "house" and gives the sentence a completely new meaning.

Excellent comedians and excellent Therapist/Coaches are skilled in the art of reframing. The comedian sets up the joke and then with one word or phrase changes the frame and gets the laugh. The Therapist/Coach listens for the description of his client's reality and sometimes with one word or phrase changes the frame and initiates healing.

A client of mine (S.L.) once said, "My mother never listens to me. She gets so caught up with herself." I widened the frame by suggesting that perhaps "nobody is listening and nobody is being heard." The next time I saw this client she told me that she and her mother were now listening to each other. She told me that her mother still spoke about herself, but then "she would stop, ask about me and listen." My suggestion made her realize that there was something that she could do that she had not been doing: listening. So she "temporarily" placed her needs and criticisms to the side and actively listened to her mother, giving her mother her complete and undivided attention. And "miraculously" once her mother was heard, she began listening.

Context Reframing

Context reframes occur when we identify a context where a particular comment or behavior would be appropriate. This type of reframe can be used when there is a comparison and someone says something like, "You are too X or too Y." If you are with a child in a museum and he/she is speaking very loudly, the reframe would be, "when we are at a ballgame, we can speak as loudly as we want. Here in the museum we get to use our quiet voice."

Instead of contextualizing a child's behavior, some parents will verbally attack a child, so instead of learning about contextualizing behavior, the child "learns" that the behavior is bad or that he/she is bad.

We had a friend who would annoy people because he would always say something whenever he saw something. After 9/11, nobody complained.

The question to ask is, "Where and when would this behavior be acceptable?" One additional example illustrating this pattern is the situation in which a writer's inner critic is actively criticizing everything he/she is writing as he/she is writing or when thinking about writing. Since our inner critic plays an important role in the writing process, if we were to actually eliminate the critic we might get the article or book completed, but it may not be very good. So instead of struggling with the inner critic, we speak with the inner critic, compliment him/her for his/her contributions and intention to improve the document. Then we ask the inner critic (editor) to wait awhile, say until the end of each chapter, when it will have more material to work with. And when it does resume, to focus on evaluating and improving the manuscript.

Verbal reframing is a very useful life skill. It is essential for dealing with misunderstandings, especially when each person in an argument sees the other as "being wrong." Typically one person verbally attacks the other person by saying something like, "Why are you so lazy?" Rather than reacting defensively, you can respond by reframing the behavior with something like, "It's not about being lazy, it's about knowing how and when to relax and recharge so I can be more productive." Another way to reframe is to respond to what the other person is experiencing. When he says, "Why are you so lazy?" a reframe for him could be, "You have been working hard. And I know you are exhausted and want us to get the job done ASAP. I know you are not simply interested in attacking me. I also want to make sure that both of us are pulling our weight and that you are not doing all the work yourself. There is a lot to be done and I am prepared to work with you and be part of the team, but right now I need a break." When we use reframing we are not making someone wrong. We are redefining the assigned meaning. Verbal reframing is like Aikido, a martial art that takes the energy of the attack and redirects it. We encourage a cooperative interaction that supports each person in the relationship.

Some clients talk about being nagged by their spouse while others are the ones doing the nagging. Apparently nagging is a universal behavior that no one likes. However, many people like to be thought of and cared about. We also understand that the nagger has his/her own outcome and reason for nagging, like wanting fairness or cooperation, being in charge when they are feeling out of control, or feeling important when they are being minimalized. Next time someone is "nagging" you, discover what happens when you reframe the meaning or the context of the message. One response may be, "I appreciate both your knowing what you want and your persistence. You don't give up easily. I can use some of that myself. You are also reminding me just how important it is to avoid tunnel vision where I only see what I want and ignore what's important to you." Another response could be, "You really care about this issue and I appreciate your concern." What other responses can you come up with? Keep in mind that either the nagger or the "naggee" can be the one to reframe. And be authentic.

NLP Momentary Practice

Think about criticisms that you have received. How would you reframe them? It helps to ask yourself, "What is the other person's positive intention in saying that?" Remember it may not be positive for you, but there is a positive intention for them. Also do this when you are being critical and ask, "What is my positive intention in being critical?" and "How else can I express myself to get the response I want?"

The Six-Step Reframing Technique

Updating Your Program – Replace Limiting Old Habits with Healthy New Ones

There are many habits (including addictions) that we say we want to stop, while we continue to do them. These habitual thoughts and behaviors include smoking, drinking, procrastinating, worrying, nail biting, obsessively surfing the Internet, and over eating – to name just a few. These habits can also include negative internal voices or upsetting images. In verbal reframing, we looked at the positive intention behind a statement. Earlier in the book, we introduced the NLP presupposition that every behavior (which includes every habit) has or has had a positive intention or purpose.

When a client tell us that he/she wants to stop smoking because he/she wants to be healthy, it's clear to us that he/she has a positive intention. Yet he/she is still smoking. And as much as he/she has tried to stop, he/she has not done it yet. It is almost as if there is another part of him/her, another self, if you will, taking over at the time he/she lights up. If the smoking client wants to stop smoking, then who is in charge? And what is the positive intention of this other self in charge? Sometime we need to point out to him/her that he/she is not in charge, otherwise why is he/she here in our office seeking help. It is not unusual that people strongly object to the idea that there is a part of them with a "positive" intention, since he/she believes that it is a "negative" behavior. When this happens with a client, we pace his/her experience by pointing out that we understand that the behavior does indeed have some very real negative consequences. We are not disagreeing with that. Then we offer examples of possible positive intentions. For example, cigarette smoking may be or may have been an attempt to relax and calm down, to feel connected with other smokers, or to seek independence and self-expression by rebelling. We make the distinction between "the behavior itself," "the negative consequences" and the "positive intention."

Sometimes we also do a context reframe and recognize the contexts in which that behavior had been or would be useful and appropriate. Then we get unconscious agreement to do that behavior only in those contexts, as in the example of the writer and the critic.

However, we want to eliminate the behavior in other contexts. To accomplish this we first need to identify the positive intention of the part responsible for the behavior. Most people come to us only after unsuccessfully attempting to use their will power to stop the behavior. Using our will power to overcome what we believe is a "negative" behavior without recognizing its purpose usually backfires and creates resistance. And if it does work, the results are only temporarily. But when we reframe a behavior as something that is really designed to help us, rather than harm us, instead of continuing to be at odds with our (other) self, we begin to see this self (or part) as an ally on the same team rather than an enemy to be defeated. Some of you reading this might object and say, "But that's not true." Or, "How do you know it is true?" Our answer is that we are not claiming to know the truth. What we do know is that we see people constantly fighting themselves, hating themselves, blaming themselves, criticizing themselves, imposing unreasonable demands on themselves and being miserable. And when people are willing to "take on" the NLP assumption that all their parts (selves) are fighting for something important, whether it is "safety," "love," "acceptance," "connection," or trying to escape from "loneliness," "danger," "emotional pain," or "physical pain" then positive change happens. All parts may not be fighting for the same thing, but they are fighting for the same person.

It is not an absolute truth, but it is a powerful reframe. And it is at the core of the NLP technique called Six Step Reframing.

Step 1: Identifying the Unwanted Behavior
The first step of the reframing process is to identify the limiting behavior. This means to recognize and label the specific thought, feeling or behavior that the person wants to eliminate.

Step 2: Establishing Communication with the "Part" Responsible for the Unwanted Behavior
A client of mine (R.H.) came in because he wanted to stop drinking alcohol. Having established rapport and gathered information, I asked him to take a moment to focus on his surroundings, becoming aware of what he is seeing, hearing and feeling as I began suggesting that he slowly turn his attention inward, connecting to his breathing in and breathing out, developing a comfortable rhythm, expanding his inner awareness of what he is thinking and feeling, and other sensations in his body, his hands,

his arms, with this awareness continuing to spread throughout the body to both areas of tension as well as areas of relaxation, connecting to a deeper place. Utilizing hypnosis and hypnotic language patterns can help someone move from their conscious rational mind to a body centered, connection with the unconscious. And having established a receptive state of wonder and curiosity, I asked him to locate in his body the part of him (or the younger, though not necessarily young, self) that is responsible for the unwanted behavior and speak directly to that self and ask him to give a signal to affirm a willingness to communicate.

Now this idea of communicating may at first seem strange if you have never done it before. But consider for a moment that there exists another mind, the unconscious mind, that thinks independently of the conscious mind and operates at a deeper level. It is the mind that creates dreams, that has intuitive hunches, that comes up with solutions to problems when your conscious mind stops trying to solve them. It is the mind that thinks in symbols and body sensations. It is intelligent, but not rational. It does not think linearly. And it communicates through body signals. Sometimes these signals show up in the form of unwanted symptoms, such as tiredness, twitches, aches or anxiety. This time, instead of the body initiating the communication, we are. And we patiently wait, listening, sensing, wondering how the body will respond. When we do get a response, we ask the body to increase the signal in some way to confirm that the signal indeed means that "yes, it is willing to communicate." It might be an increase in temperature, in pressure, in heaviness, in discomfort, etc. If is appears that the signal is visual, the increase might be in brightness, in size or in color. And if it sounds like the signal is auditory, it might be a change in volume or location. It is also a good idea to get a separate signal to indicate "no" (e.g. a twitch of the left hand for "yes" and a twitch on the right hand for "no").

A variation can be asking the part to increase the signal for a "yes" and decrease for a "no." This might mean increased tension for "yes" and a decrease in tension (or an increase in relaxation) for a "no." Sometimes the client may simply hear a distinct voice saying "yes" or "no" in his/her mind.

Some people find this step quite easy while others find it difficult. Individuals with prior experience communicating with their unconscious will be able to do this with little or no help from the guide. And the guide who has developed a high level of expertise from his prior experiences working with the unconscious will be more effective in teaching the neophyte how to do it.

When my client asked the part of him responsible for excessive drinking if he/she (the part of him) was willing to communicate, he received a very loud "yes." Yes, men can have female "parts" and women can have male "parts." If the person doesn't get any signal, it usually means we need to deepen the trance or de-potentiate the conscious mind.

Step 3: Identifying the Positive Intention

Having established the connection, I then asked my client, who still had his eyes closed, to ask this part, "What is the purpose of the drinking? Or what is the positive intention?" The answer that came to my client was that the positive intention of the drinking was to keep him connected to his family. The background story is that all the men in his family had worked for a beer company whose logo was a set of intersecting circles. When the part responded and said, "remaining connected to family," the client realized that the connection was like the actual circles of the company's logo. That was a big "aha" moment for him.

Step 4: Getting Alternatives Behaviors to Support the Positive Intention

Once discovering the positive intention of connection, I then asked the client to invite the creative unconscious to explore alternative ways of remaining connected with his family (and heritage) other than drinking. For many years, the drinking was his only way to connect to family. We now needed something to replace it. Without alternatives, drinking will continue to be the way to satisfy the positive intention. The suggestion to "Go to the creative unconscious" is for the unconscious mind to generate alternative behaviors that would still preserve the positive intention.

The suggestion he received from the creative unconscious that was most intriguing was to spend some time each day reliving special memories of being with his family and write about them in his daily journal.

Step 5: Getting Agreement

Once he had received that suggestion, we went back to the original part responsible for drinking and asked if that part would be willing to take responsibility for this new behavior. The essential piece is that you are keeping the positive intention and changing the behavior. Again he received a loud "yes."

Step 6: Addressing Objections?

As an extra check I asked him to speak to all of his parts to determine if there were any objections. I used the metaphor of a meeting place and said, "Imagine that you are having a board meeting with all of your parts. And ask them if there are any objections to taking on this new behavior." If there is an objection, you ask for its positive intention. For example, the part may be worried that by giving up drinking, he will lose the close connection he has with his drinking buddies. If this happens, we thank the part for wanting to make sure that he can still enjoy close connections with people. Then we go to the creative unconscious as we did in step 4 and generate ways that this can be accomplished and proceed to steps 5 and 6. Sometimes we ask the parts to negotiate an agreement. One common objection is a worry that we are replacing an old familiar habit with new untested alternatives. To address this concern we might ask for a two-week trial run or beta test. Then after two weeks, we meet again to determine if there is a need to make any modification. It is important to understand that this is all happening on an unconscious level. When the conscious mind tries to do this on its own, it will not work. Changes require unconscious agreement.

Keep in mind that people do manage to eradicate unwanted behaviors without addressing the positive intention. This often explains why people revert back to their old behavior or suddenly engaging in a completely different set of behaviors that may be just as objectionable as when a person substitutes overeating for smoking. Or a person might stop biting their nails and begin acting snarky. When you look at things this way, you no longer think of yourself as acting irrational. It all starts to make sense.

This technique can be used with any internal or external behavior or with any symptom. The Six Step Reframing Technique establishes channels of communication between a person's unconscious and conscious minds and between parts of the unconscious. It also installs the belief that all parts are allies.

Steps For Six Step Reframing:

1. Identify the limiting behavior.
2. Ask the part responsible for the limiting behavior if it is willing to communicate consciously.
3. Ask the part responsible for the limiting behavior for its positive intention.
4. Ask the creative unconscious to select alternative behaviors that will satisfy the positive intention.
5. Ask the part to agree to take responsibility for replacing the old behavior with the new alternative(s).
6. Check for objections. If there are, cycle back to step 3.

When complete, rehearse for the future (futurepacing).

As with most of the NLP techniques, once you are familiar with the process, have seen it demonstrated, guided someone through it and been guided through it, you will easily be able to do it with yourself.

Many years ago when I (S.L.) was still an NLP novice, I guided myself through the Six Step Reframe with an unlikely behavior. Actually, it wasn't really a behavior. It was a symptom. Warts were growing and spreading along the bottom of my left toe. I wanted to eliminate them.

Having identified the symptom (Step 1), I put myself into a deep trance state using self-hypnosis and established a connection to that "part of me" that was responsible for the warts. (Step 2) When it came time to learn the positive intention, I was quite surprised to get an answer that made sense. The answer was twofold.

The first answer was "to bring my attention to my feet." I was ignoring my feet and was told that they needed my attention. Since the warts started showing up, I began picking at them so they were certainly getting lots of attention. The second answer was that I was too much in my head and needed to be more grounded, more connected to the earth and my body. The warts were acting as "roots." (Step 3) So the alternative that addressed the first positive intention was to gently and firmly hold and stroke my feet each day, especially in the area of my big left toe. The alternative behavior addressing the second positive intention was to feel the earth beneath my feet when I was sitting, standing, walking or running. And especially when I was talking. (Step 4) Both alternatives were enthusiastically received by the part responsible for growing the warts in the first place. (Step 5) And finally I asked if all of me was fine with making these changes. And I got a resounding, "yes." (Step 6)

We strongly advise that before you use this or any other NLP technique when a physical symptom is involved that you get it checked out medically. This is not something to do as an alternative to getting proper medical treatment. At the same time it does not have to be a last resort. We have had continuing success working with symptoms such as migraine headaches, arthritis and lethargy.

Ways to Negotiate with Our Self and Others

"Hello, I must be going."
-Groucho Marx

On the one hand...

There are times in life when we say something that feels so right and absolute. It could be, "I love you" or "This is exactly what I have always wanted" or "This is the perfect gift." It sometimes takes the form of an unqualified, "Yes" or "No." Or from the perspective of the fundamentalist, things are clearly "right or wrong," "good or bad."

For the speaker, it is accompanied by a pleasurable feeling of "knowing." The listener usually experiences this person as charismatic – someone who is clear, certain, confident, and trustworthy. Alternatively, he can be seen as someone completely fooling himself and deceiving others. Some politicians and cult leaders might come to mind.

On the other hand...

Then there are times when we are ambivalent, times when we have doubts or mixed feelings, times when we just can't make up our mind. Perhaps that's because there is not only one mind. Earlier in the chapter we spoke of parts or "selves." We introduced the idea that is more than one of us.

This internal dichotomy is often accompanied by an unpleasant, unresolved feeling. The observer may experience this person as contradicting himself, "wishy-washy," flip-flopping, untrustworthy and/or weak. Or he can be seen as thoughtful, considerate, struggling with difficult issues or grappling with what's the best course of action.

Congruity and Incongruity

The word congruity comes from Latin and its original meaning is, "I meet together, I agree." When we use the term in NLP, we are referring to the phenomena when all of our "parts" are working in cooperation and have a common purpose. Incongruity happens when "parts" do not agree and are not cooperating. We are being congruent when our words, our voice and our body, including facial expressions, gestures and posture are all carrying the same or a compatible message. When we are saying one thing with our words and something completely different with our non-verbal behavior, we are being incongruent. When content and form match, there is congruence. When they don't there is incongruence.

So if we say one thing and do another, we are being incongruent. If we say "yes", but we are shaking our head "no," we are being incongruent. If we shout that we are not angry while we are clenching our fists, we are being incongruent. If we say we are angry while having a huge smile on our face, we are being incongruent. If we are on the phone saying, we must be getting off, but continuing to carry on the conversation, we are being incongruent. And if we are complaining about our job, but continue to work there, we are being incongruent. We are not defining incongruence as something bad, but we are saying that there are parts in conflict. And when there are inner conflicts, we encourage people to learn how to resolve the conflict instead of burying it and hoping it will go away on its own. Hence, whenever the conflicting parts are recognized and discover healthy ways to co-exist as allies, there will be congruence. In addition to being perceived by others as being strong, trustworthy and believable, being congruent usually feels better.

There is a psychoanalytic term known as "introjection" which can be defined as the unconscious adoption of others ideas or attitudes. Gestalt Therapy refers to these "introjections" as undigested attitudes, "shoulds" and "ought tos," that we "swallowed whole" from people making the rules. When this occurs, people can give the appearance of being congruent, but in fact they have not gone through the process of considering different perspectives or "chewing over" and assimilating new ideas. Unquestionably, the congruence demonstrated by people who do not question is quite different from the congruence we are talking about. We are talking about including and embracing contrasting perspectives and seemingly irreconcilable differences while still pursuing harmony, balance and resolution.

Yet human beings spend a considerable amount of time engaged in conflicts. Some of them are interpersonal in nature, while others are intrapersonal. While this chapter will examine how we respond to inner (intrapersonal) conflicts, the same principles apply to the interpersonal.

"Do I stay or do I go? Do I hold on or do I let go? Do I play it safe or do I take my chances?" are all examples of intrapersonal conflicts. These conflicts show up in the form of incongruities. If we are stuck in "either/or" thinking, if our attitude is "damned if I do and damned if I don't," then we have put ourselves in a "double bind", a "no win" scenario. In this mind set, even if some part of us wins, some another part of us loses. When this happens, the solution will require some "out of the cube" thinking. In life we will at times have to choose between Scylla and Charybdis When this time

242 NLP A Changing Perspective

comes, congruence will mean choosing one path and not looking back or second-guessing.

And when these conflicts come up as they always do, how we frame the conflict will determine if we are part of the solution or part of the problem. John Weakland, one of the founders of "brief psychotherapy," once remarked, "When you have a problem, life is the same damn thing over and over. When you no longer have a problem, life is one damn thing after another." So let's learn how to solve these seemingly irreconcilable damn things so we can move on to the next challenge. And while congruence may be our destination, we are looking to make the journey more satisfying and rewarding.

The Six-Step Reframe is a way of addressing a part of us that is expressing itself through an unwanted behavior or symptom. Next we will be examining how to work with two or more parts in conflict. To do this, you will first need some interpersonal tools for detecting and responding to people who communicate incongruently.

Mixed Messages: Let The Buyer Be Aware

You invite someone to work with you on a project and he/she says, "Yes, I would love to work with you on the project," but he/she rolls his/her eyes, giving you the impression that perhaps he/she really doesn't. A friend shouts, "I don't care" while contorting his/her face and furrowing his/her brow indicating that he/she does in fact care about something.

These are two examples of mixed messages, where form and content do not match. These incongruent messages often indicate parts in conflict. In the first example, maybe the person wants to work with you, but does not like the project. Or they like the project, but do not want to work with you. Perhaps they have mixed feelings about either working with you or working on the project. Maybe they do not want to work with you or on the project, but don't want to hurt your feelings. And there is always the possibility that they do want to work with you and they do want to work on the project, but there is something going on in the personal life that might be interfering. We do not know. All we know is that the person is being incongruent. Jumping to any other conclusion is "mind reading." And this is an ideal time to engage in the process of "not knowing" rather than "thinking you know."

There was a communication study done in 1967 titled, "Decoding of Inconsistent Communications," by Dr. Albert Meharabian, which explored the percentages of importance in someone's message based on actions, content and tone. His study determined that people paid 55% of their attention to actions, 38% to tone and 7% to content (words). This study led many people to understand that body language and tone of voice was more important than words. Of course, we all know the cliché, "actions speak louder than words." And here was the study to prove it.

What many people do not realize is that the attention on actions (55%) and tone (38%) occurred when the actions and/or tone did not match the words. If they match, then there is nothing to look for. For example if someone says, "I really want to work with you," and he/she smiles, his/her eyes "light up" and his/her voice is enthusiastic, we will accept the one message. It is through the roll of the eyes, an unusual facial expression or a change in tone, tempo or volume that gives the attentive and observant communicator a hint that the message is mixed and the individual is being incongruent. If we ignore these signs or dismiss them as irrelevant, it may not be until hours, days, weeks, or even years later, that we realize that they were not congruent with their communication.

Take a look at any photo of Bernie Madoff. When you look at his face, notice his compressed lips. According to David Givens, PhD, in an article for Psychology Today, 2012, entitled, "The Body Language of Business, Bosses and Boardrooms" he refers to the "chronic lip inversion" as a protective "non-verbal lockdown. It wasn't even that Madoff was moving his lips when he lied. It had become a permanent fixture." Abraham Lincoln supposedly once said, "You can fool some of the people all of the time and all of the people some of the time, but you cannot fool all of the people all of the time." And Madoff was able to fool many people for quite some time. Part of the NLP training is about training people to observe non-verbal cues, to look and listen, to pay attention to the form and to be in uptime. Let the buyer be aware.

244 NLP A Changing Perspective

Okay. So let's assume that you notice an incongruity. What are your choices? You can notice it and do nothing for the moment. You can take your money and run. Or you can see something, and say something. But what do you say? It all depends upon your outcome. Working as psychotherapists/coaches, one of our outcomes is to resolve conflicts between people as well as within them. So when we detect an incongruity we want to bring it to our client's awareness, so that he/she can eventually learn to become congruent. So here are some of the ways that we respond to accomplish this outcome. As we describe these ways of responding, think about how you can adapt them in your own relationships.

Responding To Mixed Messages

What is the real message being sent? If you ask this question, you are making an assumption that there are both real messages and unreal messages. That's like saying there is false hope and true hope. Hope is hope. And messages are messages. We assume that they are all significant and that each one has a purpose.

Here are five ways to respond to mixed messages. Before attempting to use these methods, it is important to establish rapport and be prepared to re-establish it in the event that you lose it.

I. Being Sensory Based

The words (content): "I'm fine."

The nonverbal-form (tone and body language): Eyes squinting and head slowly shaking.

Response: I hear you say that you are fine and I also see that your eyes are squinting and your head is shaking. (While describing what you see, you can also mirror back with your eyes and head, exactly what you saw.)

An alterative way is using our hands to mark out the parts spatially by extending one hand, palm facing up and saying, "On the one hand you are saying 'I am fine,'" then extending our other hand we continue, "and on the other hand I see your eyes squinting and your head shaking." We are simply describing what we are observing without making interpretations. This is an invitation for the other person to let us know what's on the other hand. So we stop talking and wait for the person's response. They may say, "Well, I know eventually I am going to be fine, but right now I really feel terrible." For some people it is helpful to have a visual of the hands indicating two distinct locations for the parts. And we want to remain objective and curious when describing what we have observed. Since we might be bringing into awareness something that had been hidden, some people might feel criticized and go on the defensive. Of course, if we are indeed being critical while say something like, "You are being incongruent" in a judgmental voice, we can expect to get a defensive response. And telling someone that they are being incongruent can easily be misinterpreted since it is not sensory based. And if they are being defensive, it is usually not a good idea to tell them they are being defensive. The outcome is to "help" the person to separate and acknowledge each part. That is why we say "and" on the other hand" instead of "but" on the other hand. Using "but" negates the previous statement as in the example, "I like you, but..."

You will be on solid ground when you remain sensory based.

II. Playing Polarity

The words (content): "I really have to leave my job."

The nonverbal-form (tone and body language): With a low voice, a deep sigh, head dropping and eyes going down and to the left.

This time you will be addressing the content of the message as true or not true. If you act as if it is true you can say, "I completely agree. And now that you have made up your mind and know what you really have to do, it's time to take action, walk in tomorrow and hand in your letter of resignation." You emphasize your agreement and watch the person's response. If the person congruently says, "Yes, I will," then there is nothing more to do. But if the person says, "Whoa! Not so fast. The job gives me security and community. I can't just walk away right now," you have found the other side of the incongruity. You can also play polarity the other way and say, "Perhaps this is not the right time to do anything. You have job security and community. Don't rock the boat. Stay where you are." Now the person may say, "But I am miserable here. It's so boring. All I do is follow procedures. I need to be challenged. I need to use my creativity." And now you have both sides of the incongruity. And what you have done is separated the conflict into the two distinct parts, one that wants challenge and creativity and the other that wants security and community. And when we identify separately with each part, each will actually look and sound congruent. In essence, what you have done is turned a simultaneous incongruity (where both messages are being communicated at the same time) to a sequential incongruity (having separated the parts so that each one is expressing itself clearly and congruently). When you play polarity you are responding to the content and either agreeing or disagreeing with it.

Playing polarity also occurs unintentionally as is the case when we side with one part and the person in conflict identifies with the other part. It's not that they are being difficult; it's that they are being incongruent. By taking on one side of the conflict, we are actually playing out interpersonally what is going on intrapersonally for that individual without realizing it. The more we try to convince the person to act one way, the more they dig their heels in. They are not really fighting you. They are fighting themselves.

III. Exaggeration

The words (content): "I am not angry."

The nonverbal-form (tone and body language): With a harsh, loud voice, furrowed brow and fingers curled into fists.

This time instead of responding to the content, we are now responding to the form.

Take on the form of the person (harsh loud voice, furrowed eyebrows and tight fists) and exaggerate it while saying, "You are making it abundantly clear that you are not angry." As you can see this one will require rapport, so the person will understand that you are not making fun of them, but in fact giving them a mirror so that they can see themselves more clearly and recognize the meaning of their non-verbal communication.

Or you can take on and exaggerate the opposite form (soft low voice, smooth eyebrows and open palms) and say, "I am glad that you have nothing to be angry about, that you are feeling well and have nothing more to communicate."

A common incongruity involving anger is the conflict between the self that is angry and wants to express himself/herself, to be seen, heard and accepted and the self that does not feel safe expressing anger and holds back. He/she usually assumes the other is overly fragile and fears injuring (emotionally and or physically) the other person. But the fear is actually a fear that the other will retaliate against him/her, reject him/her or withdraw. So on one hand he/she wants to "express himself/herself" and on the other hand he/she wants to be "safe" (not get hurt). In this scenario, one part is hiding and needs to feel safe enough to come out. It is important to recognize that when you are working with parts, creating a safe space is essential.

IV. And...or But

We said earlier that we use "and" instead of "but." But there are times when a statement carries an "implied but." When a person does this, although they do not use the word "but" the words are spoken with a tone that conveys the impression that the next word is a "but." So we say it for him/her.

If he/she says, "I really need to take a vacation..." then we say "but..." with a tone of curiosity allowing him/her to finish the sentence. The person will usually fill in the blank thus revealing the other side of the incongruity. By using the word "but" we are pacing his/her belief that it is an either/or conflict. Eventually we will guide him/her to see it as both/and.

Not noticing or not responding to a mixed message can lead to a problem down the road. Take, for example, the situation where you ask your partner to go out to dinner with friends. And he/she gives an incongruent "yes." Later, as you are about to arrive at the restaurant, your partner becomes irritable and says, "I really did not want to go." Sometime we may want to do something so badly that we ignore the part of the communication that could potentially ruin our plans. Similarly, some times we may want to avoid conflict so badly that we hide the part of us that has an objection, only to find it erupting or exploding at a later time.

V. Silence

And sometimes it is wise to notice the incongruity and realize that it is better to address this issue with the person at a later time.

NLP Momentary Practice

Think of something you are not sure you really want to do. Say the statement incongruently. Then say the same sentence congruently.

Practice the five ways of responding to mixed messages with a friend or colleague.

The Spatial Reframe: Working with Parts in Conflict

The technique that we are about to describe is called the *Spatial Reframe* and was adapted by Anne Linden, an NLP trainer and author, from an earlier NLP technique called the visual squash (to be described later on). Individuals who have had Gestalt training will see the similarity between this and the empty chair technique.

This technique can be used anytime we are ambivalent, conflicted, indecisive, or feeling pulled in different directions. This can include staying or leaving, stopping (a habit) or continuing to do it, wanting something or someone and at the same time not wanting it or them, being free or feeling safe, pleasing others or expressing oneself, holding on or letting go, including or excluding, etc.

The goal of the Spatial Reframe is to create understanding, harmony and cooperation among our parts. The conflict may involve a decision to say "yes" or "no," to commit to a relationship or to leave, to change careers or remain where we are, to change or maintain the status quo, etc. It may be part of an ongoing inner conflict between a part of us that is pushing us to achieve and another part that pushes back and wants to be left alone. We see working through these conflicts as part of our personal development.

The technique you are about to learn is about interrupting intrapersonal adversarial relationships and developing and maintaining healthy cooperative relationships. But to do this, we start with the relationship we currently have with ourselves.

We may talk about ourselves as being "negative, wrong or bad," "childish, selfish or immature," or "stupid, foolish or stubborn." We are simultaneously the "accuser and the accused," the "persecutor and the victim," the "punisher and the punished." Sometimes we identify with the critic and other times we identify with the one being criticized. Sometimes, we find another person who has an identical inner conflict and proceed to act out one part, while we play the other. And although we may find the perfect person to project that self onto, we are actually both parts. We are the relationship. To ignore this fact means spending years, if not a lifetime, picking people with whom we try to resolve an interpersonal conflict that is actually intrapersonal.

What is behind the statement, "You are being selfish"? It is probably a desire on the part of the speaker for the other person to be more attentive to his/her needs. The statement, "You are lazy" indicates a desire on the part of the speaker for the other person to be more active. The same can be said for statements, such as, "You are being insensitive," "You are cruel," "You are being stubborn." Rather than ask for what we need, we "attack" the other person by labeling them, "selfish," "lazy," "insensitive," or "stubborn" and maintaining an adversarial relationship. This also happens with parts.

Perhaps one part is a critical parent who demands adherence to rules by saying, "You should, you shouldn't, you have to, you must, you better" and scolds and punishes when the rules are not followed. And the other part is a rebellious child who sabotages any attempts to act responsibly and maturely. So what do we do? We can find someone who is willing to play the "critical parent" to our freedom-seeking rebel (who also wants to be loved) or find someone who will take the role of the "rebellious child" so we can be the responsible and mature authority (who can decide to give or withhold love). When we do this, we are playing out our inner conflicts through our interpersonal relationships and ignoring and disowning our own intrapersonal conflict, blaming our reactions on the other person and getting to feel like the righteous victim.

1. Identify The Incongruity and Separate into Two Distinct Parts

So how do we resolve the intrapersonal conflict? Sometimes the client makes it easy for us by stating directly that, "on one hand there is a part of me that want to quit smoking yet on the other hand there is a part of me that really enjoys the experience and does not want to give it up." When this happens, the parts have been identified and separated into two distinct selves. On the other hand, if he/she has identified with one side, we need to use the verbal skills previously described, to help him/her access the other side. To do this, we need to be an objective observer. If he/she is calling himself/herself "lazy, selfish, bad, negative, etc.," we must be alert so as not to buy into the narrative being presented by one side. It is no different than being the third party when the people involved in a conflict are each trying to get you to take sides against the other one. If you don't remain neutral, you can't help them. If one part succeeds in seducing you into taking his/her side, you will lose rapport with and the trust of the other part and render yourself ineffective. To help an individual resolve his/her conflict, you must get him/her to take on the objective observer position. To help yourself resolve your own inner conflicts, you must learn to take on this perspective as well – a perspective that exists outside the box containing the conflicting parts.

Suppose you are accusing yourself of being lazy. There are two parts. One part is doing something that the other part is describing as being lazy. The so-called lazy self may in turn rebel against the attacking self. Of course, the self who is making the accusation usually doesn't see him/herself as an accuser or attacker. And since it is so easy to fall into our usual habits and slip into our usual selves, we must establish and maintain an objective self, thereby creating a new habit.

2. Establish a Distinct Location for Each Part

So far we have only heard from one part talking about the other and we need to hear from both parts. You might say, "On one hand you have this so-called lazy part and on the other hand..." The answer may be something like, "On the other hand I want to take action, to do what needs to be done and complete projects." So we might then play polarity and say, "Then why not do it, go ahead, take action and complete the projects? Just do what needs to be done." The answer that follows might be something like, "I want to do that, but I sabotage myself. I start zoning out, becoming forgetful, getting distracted, procrastinating and doing other things that I shouldn't be doing."

In this scenario, we know that there is a part that wants to take action and complete projects and another part that forgets, distracts and procrastinates. We must maintain an objective position so as not to be convinced or seduced into thinking that one part is the positive part while the other is negative. The person, currently identified with one side, may try to get us to take sides. Once we have heard from one part, we will need to hear from and understand the other(s).

As we said before, often when we begin working with parts, one is seen as being "positive/good" and the other is seen as being "negative/bad." So when you hear a statement like, "I have a self destructive part that I need to eliminate," you can recognize that the "I" speaking is the current identification and considers himself/herself to be good while the part being labeled self-destructive is seen to be bad and needs to be dominated or eliminated. It is actually this way of looking at the conflict that perpetuates the conflict. To interrupt this pattern, it will need to be reframed. The parts are not in rapport. And to help them establish rapport we first need to get in rapport with each of them. Whenever we work with a client in conflict, we think about rapport with all parts. Rather than referring to each part as an "it," we will use the pronouns "he" or "she." "It" refers to a thing. We are not establishing rapport with a "thing." We are establishing rapport with a "self." If you lose this perspective, you will lose rapport. When meeting a new self, we are meeting a new presence. We begin by acknowledge him/her for being present.

Once we have separated these selves by going from a simultaneous incongruity (same time/same location) to a sequential incongruity (different time/ different location), we are ready to represent the two selves as existing at the same time, but in different places. So we set up two chairs and ask the client which self will be sitting in which chair. Once we have set up the chair identities and explain that we will be talking to each self individually, we ask the client to sit in the chair he/she feels most connected to right now. We intentionally ask him/her these questions to give him/her control over the process. Eventually we will have appropriate names for each self, but initially we can simply think of them as the one being called lazy and the one doing the labeling. As we learn more, we will have more accurate and more respectful labels.

We will proceed with how a coach or therapist might work with a client, but you can also imagine how you can modify it to work with yourself. And for readers who are coaches and therapists, you might want to imagine how you can adapt this technique for working with couples.

3. Positive Intention and Outcome for the Individual: What Do You Want for Yourself?

We begin with the self that the client most identifies with. In this case it would be the one that wants to take action. We ask, "What do you want?" When stepping into each self we ask the explorer to speak in the first person using the word "I." If he/she begins to speak "about" the self using the words, "it," "he," "she" or "this part," we redirect him/her to using "I." Only when the explorer is in the observer position will we ask him/her to use the words, "he" or "she" when referring to the two selves. It is important to maintain these distinctions. Here are some possible responses for the self that wants to take action. Listen for criteria words.

I want to be successful.
I want to accomplish my goals.
I want to move forward.
I want to learn, to develop new skills and become more

experienced.
I want to take responsibility.

We thank the self and let him/her know that we will talk with the other self and that he/she can listen in. We say this very congruently so each self feels respected. We then stand up with the client and get him/her to break state and go to the next chair.

Then we establish rapport with the second self and ask the same question, "What do you want?" Here are some possible responses from the so-called "lazy part." Again listen for criteria words.

I want to do nothing.
I just want to relax and enjoy life.
I want to be comfortable and stress free.
I don't want to think of the future.
Life is too short. I want to live life now.
I want to be free.

By asking each self what he/she wants, we are discovering his/her "positive intention" or purpose. So on one hand we have a self that wants to "relax, enjoy life, be comfortable, free and live in the moment." On the other hand we have a self that wants to "succeed, accomplish his/her goals, move forward, learn and develop skills, and to take responsibility."

When doing this correctly, each self will have its own distinct appearance and voice. Each one will have his/her own criteria and beliefs. In some cases each may have his/her own primary representational system (e.g. one being visual and one being auditory). But in any case, each one will be congruent. When speaking to one self, if you get an incongruous message where the appearance or voice of the other shows up, you need to stop and separate them once again. And in some cases, a third self will show up and will need to be given his/her own chair. If the coach/therapist does not calibrate this and the selves become incongruent and indistinguishable, the technique has been compromised and will not work. Making sure that each self remains in his/her own chair may be one of the most challenging aspects of this technique and therefore attempting to do this technique with yourself may prove to be beyond your present skill level.

4. The Naming Ceremony

As we said earlier, we will at some point need to "reframe" the selves by giving them each a new name that reflects his/her criteria. We suggest that you allow each self to determine the name he/she wants to be called rather than assigning names. If we do suggest a name, we make sure the self congruently embraces it.

Names for the "lazy" part might be the "Comfort Self", the "Here and Now Self," the "Present Self" or the "Centering Self" while some names for the "accusatory self" could be the "Success Self," the "Achievement Self," the "Future Oriented Self" or the "Responsible Self."

Once you have established the new name, it is important to use it when referring to each self. To simplify things, we will be using the "Here and Now Self" and the "Responsible Self."

5. Finding The Common Purpose: Chunking Up

Once we have established what they each want (their positive intentions), we learn what they have in common. What is it that they both want? Do they both want health? Balance? Empowerment? Happiness? Some common responses are, "We want him/her to have a good life," "We want him/her to be happy," "We want him/her to be proud of himself/herself," "We want him/her to respect himself/herself." This is an example of chunking up. It is identifying a common purpose. It is something that they can both agree to fight for, together. Of course, it is all too common to see enemies brought together by something to fight against. It may also be useful to have them step into the future and imagine what the rest of their life will be like if they do not change and continue to interact in this way. The common enemy they face may be "dis-ease." Whatever it is, it can be exactly what they need to be motivated to work together as a team.

After learning the self's positive intention, we also ask, "What do you want for the individual?"

6. Negotiating Between The Selves

Once we have identified their positive intentions, what they want both for themselves and the whole self, and their common purpose, we are ready to begin the negotiations. During the negotiations the coach/therapist will be asking the client to move among the three positions, (1) The "Here and Now Self" (2) The "Responsible Self" and (3) The "Observing Self."

What Do They Think of Each Other?

It might already be obvious what the selves think about or how they feel towards each other. Are they angry at each other? Do they appreciate each other? Are they scared of each other? Is there trust? Are they contemptuous of one another? Do they still see the other as the problem? Knowing this information will determine what needs to be done. Helping them develop trust and communicate appreciation and respect will be necessary if they are going to move forward as a team.

If it is not so obvious, you can ask them to speak directly to one another and communicate what they think. You might hear things like, "You are too bossy," "You are mean," "I don't like the way you speak to me," "I hate you," "You don't care," and "You don't understand." Knowing these things will help in the next step of the negotiation.

You might ask questions such as, "What do you need from the other in order to feel safe, trust, appreciation, respect, understanding, etc.? How can the other demonstrate his/her willingness to work together as a team?"

What Do They Want From Each Other?

To move the negotiations forward at this point, we suggest having each one look directly at the other and ask, "What do you want from me?" The answer will usually need to be chunked down and sensory based (not open to interpretation). And here are some possible responses.

The "Responsible Self"

I want you to stop interfering with my attempts to move forward in life. I want you to stop wasting time surfing the Internet, texting, checking personal e-mails, and other social media. Stop impeding our progress. I want you to let me be in charge so we can get ahead in life.

The "Here and Now Self"

I want you to stop stressing me out. I want you to back off and chill out. I want you to let me relax and enjoy life instead of filling my head with negative stuff, calling me lazy, irresponsible and immature and making me feel bad about myself.

While this may not be a familiar way of communicating, it is an effective way. And it is up to the coach to show them that it is in both their self-interest to learn a different way of interacting.

At times, the anger and animosity can be so strong that they just want to eliminate the other. When this happens, we often ask each self to have the fantasy of imagining what life would be like without the other. There would be no conflict. You would be in complete control. When we ask this question, sometimes the first reaction is elation. But whenever we ask him/her to continue the fantasy into the future, the elation wears off and something disturbing, missing and unecological is revealed.

In this case, the "Responsible Self" might imagine a "successful" life, but having a life devoid of fun, intimacy and enjoyment. And the "Here and Now Self" might see a life filled with ennui, stagnation and boredom. Our intention in doing this is to make it clear to each self that both are acting in the interests of the larger Self and rather than eliminating the other self or continuing to keep up the ongoing conflict, it is in everyone's interests to negotiate a mutually satisfying solution.

7. Acknowledging the Other

At this point, we ask each one to "speak directly to his/her counterpart and tell him/her what you appreciate about him/her and thank him/her for his/her contributions."

For example, the "Responsible Self" might say, "I appreciate that you want to enjoy life, have fun and be connected to people. Thank you for wanting to make sure I do not live my life regretting that I never lived it." While the "Here and Now Self" might say, " I appreciate that you want to grow and learn and build a better life where we can have more options available. Thank you for wanting to make sure I do not live my life regretting never having challenged myself, never knowing what I was capable of achieving."

When mediating, we make sure we have rapport with both parts and use the Meta Model to get clear statements regarding what each of them wants. If one part asks for support and the other part agrees to be more supportive, we need to make sure there is no ambiguity. So we chunk down to learn how specifically the support needs to be received and how support will be given. For example, in this case, the "Responsible Self" might agree that he/she will no longer look at the other as being, "lazy," "immature" or "doing nothing" and instead see him/her as being "youthful," "playful" and "free spirited" and that he/she will be responsible for arranging specific times for play and relaxation when play and relaxation will be the only thing on the agenda. And the "Here and Now Self" agrees to only spend time surfing the Internet, checking social media, and responding to personal emails during an agreed upon time.

We remind each one of what is at stake if they break their agreements and what is to be gained by honoring their agreement. We tell them not to make any agreements to which they cannot or will not fully commit.

The agreement needs to be stated in the positives, within their control, measurable, contextual, and ecological. Whatever arrangement they agree upon, we set up a specific time for them to evaluate their agreement and find out what they are each willing to agree on that would both serve both their individual as well as their mutual criteria.

Once they have a final statement of what they are agreeing to do, we check for congruency. Even if we detect the slightest sign of incongruity, we check it out. If there is any hesitation or resistance, we need to address it now and resolve it by incorporating the positive intention.

8. Parts Integration

Once they have come to an agreement that works for both of them, we are ready to do the "visual squash" which is a way of integrating the two selves. The explorer stands in the Meta position facing the two chairs and raises both hands, placing the "Responsible Self" in one hand and the "Here and Now Self" in the other. Then he/she slowly brings his/her hands together, as the two selves merge. We then guide him/her to bring the integrated self into his/her body. As we do this, we might verbally combine the criteria of both parts by suggesting, "you are now learning to develop the new skill of living life fully and responsibly right now and enjoying the success."

This is important because we want the individual to incorporate both selves, and to feel whole as the technique concludes. Once it is completed, we ask him/her how he/she is thinking and feeling now about what had been troubling him/her, whether it was a decision, a habit or some emotional discomfort.

This spatial reframe process has many steps. It usually takes around 45-60 minutes. On occasion, during the process we will adapt the spatial reframe by having the client remain seated and feel himself/herself shifting into one self, then shaking it out, and then shifting into the other. The questions we ask are the same. We do this when the client prefers not to move or if the client is uncomfortable with the idea of roleplaying. Although they still role play, they may feel more comfortable sitting in one chair. It is important to be flexible and work with the client's preferences.

NLP Momentary Practice

What is something you say you want to do, but don't do? Get to know your selves, their positive intentions and what they want. Find a mutual outcome. Notice any changes in your thoughts and feelings as you continue. Ask your creative parts to discover new possibilities for how they can work together more effectively and efficiently.

Summary of the Spatial Reframe

1. Identify and describe the inner conflict. Calibrate.
2. Identify each "self" establishing a distinct location for each.
3. Find out what each "self" wants. Both his/her positive intention and what he/she wants for the whole person.
4. Establish an outcome that they can both agree upon. This is a common purpose that both "selves" want for the whole person.
5. Negotiate between the "selves."
6. Create an observer (Meta) position.
7. Reintegrate the "selves."

Are we really made up of parts, selves, sub-personalities, or whatever you want to call them? Who knows? We don't know, even if some of our parts think they do know. What we do know is that this metaphorical way of thinking about our inner conflicts can be quite effective in transforming our experience, resolving inner struggles, reducing stress, eliminating emotional turmoil, making decisions and feeling whole. The techniques presented in this chapter are just two of the many ways we teach people how to care for themselves. After a session using the spatial reframe, we typically get responses like, "I didn't realize that these selves could actually work together as a team." "I discovered that they both want the same outcome for me." " I feel more whole." "I feel more balanced." "I feel more alive." "I feel comfortable in my own skin." "I feel like myself." "I like myself."

CHAPTER 24

Aligning Perceptual Positions: Developing Healthy Boundaries

Out beyond ideas of wrongdoing and rightdoing, there is a field. I'll meet you there.
-Rumi

After having an upsetting conversation with someone, do you hear the conversation still playing in your head? Are you still picturing the interaction in your mind's eye? Do feelings and emotions still persist?

If you did hear a voice, whose voice was it? Is it the voice of what you were thinking at the time? Is it what you actually said or what you would have liked to say? Is it what you remember the other person saying or what you thought they had been thinking?

If you are still picturing the scene, from what perspective are you viewing it? Do you view it from your own eyes? Do you view it from a perspective where you can see both you and the other individual? Or are you seeing it through the other person's eyes?

Do the feelings and emotions that you still feel belong to you, the other person or someone from the past? Or is it a combination? Are they adult feelings or feelings of a younger self?

In this chapter we will be exploring the answers to these questions.

Interpersonal conflicts are unavoidable. Some people can be quite adept when it comes to engaging in a conflict while others do everything they can to avoid a confrontation. How we approach a conflict, how we experience it as it is happening and how we think about it afterwards make a significant difference in the results we get. It will influence how responsive we are to the needs of others and to our own. And it will determine whether we stand up for ourselves, show empathy, be objective, and act responsibly.

Whenever we are interacting with others, there are two distinct perspectives, theirs and ours. And each has his/her own point of view, criteria and beliefs, wants and needs and distinctive behaviors. And there is a third perspective that we refer to as the "objective observer" or "witness." It is an outside perspective that does not take sides. We call these three Perceptual Positions 1st Position (or Self), 2nd Position (or Other) and 3rd Position (or Observer).

Imagine being interrupted in the middle of an argument and asked which of the three perspectives you are in. Would you know? And if you did, could you seamlessly shift from that perspective into another? Most of us have an unconscious default setting. Yet it is in our ability to take on each of these perspectives that gives us the means to be in touch with our feelings and thoughts and express them clearly (SELF), have and demonstrate empathy and compassion for others (OTHER), see the larger picture and have the wisdom and insight to creatively problem solve (OBSERVER).

NLP Trainers and early developers of NLP Steve and Connirae Andreas took this one step further by pointing out that while people may think they are in one of the positions, they may not. For example, if you ask someone to describe an interaction he/she recently had, he/she might say, "I am seeing the situation through my own eyes, but I still feel the other person's anger." This means that visually he/she is in the 1st position, but kinesthetically he/she is in the 2nd position.

If he/she says, "Even when I take a step back and look at the two of them fighting, I can't help but ask myself what I am doing wrong." In this case while he/she might be looking at him/herself from the 3rd position, he/she still hears the familiar self-talk of the 1st position.

When interpersonal conflicts arise, while we may think we are experiencing a single aligned position, we may actually be experiencing a combination of two or all three of them at the same time. This can result in confusion as to whose thoughts and feelings we are actually thinking or feeling. When people talk about picking up negative energy, it is not always easy to identify the source. And in our attempt to feel safe, we may react by putting up walls, launching into attack mode, shutting down, running away and/or blaming. Only by having healthy boundaries, in which we do not feel threatened can we remain centered (SELF), have empathy (OTHER) and work towards resolution (OBSEVER). An alternative to feeling threatened, being a victim and blaming others is to take responsibility by developing healthy boundaries.

The following, technique known as "Aligning Perceptual Positions," can help you find that place "beyond wrongdoing and rightdoing." With it, you can learn how to build healthy boundaries, to safely express yourself, to listen comfortably to others, and maintain a high degree of objectivity. We consider each position to be a distinct territory to be visited and explored. But instead of building walls, we will be creating boundaries.

Aligning perceptual position involves moving among these three different realities. Being in the first position (SELF) means being completely in touch with and owning your own thoughts and feelings, while the other's thoughts and feelings do not interfere. Stepping into the second position (OTHER) means temporarily suspending and leaving behind your own judgments and attitudes and exploring what is going on in the mind and body of the other person. Accessing the third position (OBSERVER) means being on the outside looking in, being in a state of nonattachment to either perspective, simultaneously holding two realities with the possibilities of exploring creative solutions.

Being in the OTHER position and being understanding does not mean agreeing with them. But whether you are agreeing or disagreeing with someone, you might first want to understand. Often when we take exception with another person's actions, we remain in SELF and do not consider what thoughts or feelings led them to do what they did. And we have all been in the position where we were wrongfully accused of thinking and feeling something that we were not thinking or feeling.

There are so many couples we have worked with where both individuals have been operating solely in SELF (1st position), refusing to take OTHER (2nd position) while angrily demanding that their partner be in OTHER. This can be quite amusing when viewed from the outside OBSERVER (3rd position), but not a laughing matter when viewed from the inside. However, when we can get them to step outside themselves and see what we see, they too can find their sense of humor as well as discover new ways to resolve the conflict. Show us two people who are able to move among the three positions and we will show you a relationship with healthy boundaries.

Aligning Perceptual Positions Technique

How do we Experience our Experience?

We start by asking the client or explorer to describe how he/she remembers an interaction in which he/she did not have healthy boundaries. There are various ways of identifying such an experience. You can say:

Think of an interaction:

1. In which you did not stand up for yourself.

2. Where you put up a wall or numbed your feelings to protect yourself.

3. That you avoided.

4. In which you were not being yourself.

5. Where you refused to listen.

6. Where you attacked or felt attacked.

7. In which you felt overly sensitive or vulnerable.

8. Which never got resolved.

If you are fine with how you responded, then pick something else. We want you to choose a situation in which you want an alternative way of responding.

Gathering Information

Information about the content is unnecessary and irrelevant when learning to align perceptual positions. We are only interested in the form. The more emotional the content, the more likely it is for us to get lost in the content. Keep in mind that the explorer may not understand this, so it is the guide's responsibility to direct him to the relevant information. The initial set of questions is to learn how the individual is experiencing the experience. We are not attempting to change anything at this time, only to establish the submodalities of the experience. The questions are grouped into three categories, visual, auditory and kinesthetic. While it may not be necessary to ask each and every question, it is important to get at the structure of the experience.

Visual: From what perspective are you seeing what you are seeing? Here we want to know the specific vantage point. What are you seeing? How are you seeing? Is it being viewed from the outside? From what distance is it being observed? At what angle is it being viewed? At what height is it being seen? Is it being looked at from the client's eyes? Is it being watched from the other person's perspective?

Auditory: What do you hear? Where do you hear it? How do you hear it? Whose voice do you hear? Ask for some of the content, but only listen for the following pronouns, "I," "Me," "My," "You," He," "His," "Her" She," "We," or "They."

Kinesthetic: What do you feel? Where do you feel it? How do you feel it? Whose feelings are you feeling? Who do they belong to? Are they yours or somebody else's?

Here is an example of submodality information you might get when asking these questions.

I am seeing the interaction from above myself and 2 feet behind and a little over to the right side. I can see the back right side of my head and body. And I see the other person about 6 feet away. I hear myself thinking, "This is really upsetting me." This thought is located at the top of my head. I also hear the other person's voice saying, "You are an idiot." It is located in in my left ear. And I feel impatience in my belly.

From the above description, we can tell that the individual, while seeing it from a location close to his/her body, is not in his/her body. And there are two voices. One voice is his/her own voice located in his/her head using the personal pronoun, "me" and the other voice with the person pronoun "you" is in his/her ear, not in the other person's mouth or lips. And finally there is a feeling of impatience in the belly, but we do not know to whom the impatience belongs.

Now we are going to teach you how to align your experience in each position. Sometimes all you have to do is tell someone, "Be in your own body," or "Step into the other person's shoes," or "Find an outside place from which to observe the interaction." However, more often than not these instructions are insufficient. We want reliable consistent results, so we need to use precise language to get precise information. In this way we will get to experience the Aligned SELF, the Aligned OBSERVER and the OTHER.

The OBSERVER position is the first position we will align.

Developing the Aligned "Observer" Position

Aligning Visual Observer

When we work with couples, we do not sit next to one person; we sit in a location equidistant from each person. One way to find the observer position is to imagine sitting in an audience and viewing two people on stage. We might ask, "If this was a scene from a play, what would be the title?" One of our clients called her play "The Mother and Daughter Duel."

So we now direct the explorer to:

Look at the two people from a place that is equidistant from each one.

Find a point exactly between the two and defocus your eyes so that you can see both people.

Now adjust your eye level, so that you are not above or below, not looking down at or up, but on the same level as the two people.

Aligning Auditory Observer

We already know that there are two voices, one is saying, *"This is really upsetting me."* The other says, *"You are an idiot."* The former voice is located at the top of the head.

So we direct the explorer to:

Listen to the two people from a place that is equidistant from each one and move each of the voices into the throat, chest or vocal chords of the respective individuals.

Any remaining voices will be those of the Observer and will use the pronouns, "he," "she," "they" or the names of the people. If John were the explorer, he would refer to himself as John, "he" or "him." If John slips into using "I" when he is observing himself, it is important to redirect him back into using the appropriate pronouns.

The Objective Observer is a witness. So if any voices critical of the individuals come up, they will need to be moved back to the person to whom they belong. The observer voice will be describing what he/she, the observer, sees and hears.

Aligning Kinesthetic Observer

We now ask the explorer to identify who is feeling the impatience and move those feelings into the body of the person feeling it. In addition, we ask the explorer to identify any other feelings that are present and move them to the person who is feeling them.

What remains will usually be neutral feelings or feelings of compassion. Then we ask the observer to locate and feel his/her center of gravity.

Now having experienced the "**Aligned Observer,**" we ask the explorer to locate times in the past when the Aligned Observer Position would have made a difference and have him/her go back in time with the Aligned Observer Position now available. You can suggest that, "The unconscious is generative and adapts quickly, so you don't need to go through every past experience for the unconscious to integrate these suggestions." Then, "When you feel complete, go into and experience some future situations that will benefit from this perspective." Now we ask him/her to describe how the Aligned Observer Position makes a difference.

Developing the Aligned "Self" Position

Aligning the Visual Self

The description, "*I am seeing the interaction from above myself and 2 feet behind and a little over to the right side. I can see the back right side of my head and body,*" indicates that while the individual is very close to his body he is not exactly "in" his/her body. So we lead...

Ask the explorer to adjust his/her visual point of view so that he/she is seeing exactly out of his/her own eyes, not a little above, not a little behind, not a little to the side, but right out of his/her own physical eyes.

Adjust the eye level along with the head tilt, so that he/she is not looking down at or up at the other person, but directly across from him/her at the same eye level.

Aligning the Auditory Self

The description, "*I hear myself thinking, "This is really upsetting me." It is located at the top of my head. I also hear the other person's voice saying, "You are an idiot." It is located in in my left ear,*" indicates both his/her voice as well as the other person's voice. We first check to see that the words, "This is really upsetting me" is his/her voice. If it is, we align the voice by having him/her move it to the location of his/her throat, chest or vocal cords. The resulting statement might be, "I am upset." You can think of this step as "finding your own voice."

If it is not his/her voice, we ask him/her to move it out of his/her body and into the body of the person to whom it belongs. Then we do the same with the voice saying, "*You are an idiot.*" Have him/her move the voice into the body of the person to whom it belongs.

Sometimes we encounter voices that attack our very essence or our value as a human being. Robert Dilts has used the phrase "thought viruses" when describing these statements. Steven Gilligan, in his "Self Relations" work describes these voices as "alien influences." These are statements that directly or indirectly say, "You are worthless, insignificant, stupid, disgusting, hopeless, etc." Or in other words, "You are not OK." As with viruses, they are not a part of who we are as human beings, so we suggest externalizing them, by having them go out of your body to wherever they came from. These are messages that do not "belong" to anyone.

We often suggest putting up a gorilla glass window between you and the other person or alien influences so when they speak, their words will bounce off the glass with a sound of their choosing. If you are a fan of Stephen King, you might want to use a dome. And we invite our clients to use their creativity to develop their own "force fields" or "psychic sheathing" that will provide the needed emotional safety and security.

Aligning the Kinesthetic Self

Once we have aligned the visual and the auditory, we are ready to align kinesthetically. To do this we ask him/her to notice the feelings in his/her body and ask, "To whom do they belong." People are often surprised to realize that they have taken on someone else's feelings (or energy), either those of the person they are with or someone from the past. So we direct him/her to send or move these feelings back to the person to whom they belong, so that the only feelings left in his/her body is his/her own. At this point we ask him/her to locate and bring his/her awareness to his/her "center" while feeling his/her own feelings now flow through the body. Some of you may not consider feeling other people's "energy" a choice. You may experience it as a special gift or a curse (or both). It is a choice once you learn how to do it differently.

The resulting experience is called **"The Aligned Self."**

Having experienced the Aligned Self Position, we ask if there were times in the past when it would have been useful to have the Aligned Self Position available. It is rare that someone will say no. We then suggest that he/she go back in time and imagine what it is like to now have the choice of the Aligned Self Position in other situations. Since there are so many possible situations, it is not expected that the client will re-experience each one, but it is helpful for him/her to select one or two. You can again say, "The unconscious is generative and adapts quickly, so you don't need to go through every past experience for the unconscious to integrate these suggestions." As he/she does this, we allow time for processing, and then say, "When that feels complete, go into and experience some future situations that will benefit from this perspective." Now we ask him/her to describe how the Aligned Self Position makes a difference.

The "Other" Position: Stepping Into Someone Else's Shoes

When we invite the client to step or leap into the other's position, it is not to align the other, but to do our best to understand what and how he/she is experiencing you and the situation. Establishing healthy boundaries through the Aligned Self and Aligned Observer will makes it easier to step into the other's position, since the client now has a safe and secure place to return. And being comfortable, curious and willing to learn about the other's experience will lead to new insights and meaningful realizations. Still, some people will resist going into the other's position. They may feel that the person is toxic and do not feel comfortable with the idea of stepping into that experience.

While honoring their choice to decline, we will still discuss with him/her the potential benefits of "briefly" stepping into the Other Position as well as any disadvantages of not doing so. We also remind him/her that "visiting" the Other Position is time-limited and only needs to last a few seconds or minutes. But if he/she is determined not to go into the Other Position, we will end the process by going back to the Self Position.

Although the technique is called Aligning Perceptual Positions, it is not the goal to align the other. One potential benefit is to discover what the other person is seeing, hearing, thinking and feeling. We are suggesting that you can suspend your own model of the world and be open to seeing the other person's point of view. We are asking you to shift into his/her world.

But can we really do this? Can we really step exactly into someone else's model of the world? We don't know, but we do think of the phenomena as an asymptote. In algebraic geometry, an asymptote is defined as a line that is tangent to a curve at infinity. The line keeps get closer and closer to the curve, but will only meet at infinity. By attempting to step into another's perceptual position, we are getting "closer and closer" to merging with the other. The more we have been paying attention to the other person and recognize his/her patterns, the closer we get to experiencing the world through his/her eyes and ears. Empathy is an ongoing process that requires checking in with the other person. However, while we may never know for certain if we actually get there, we can at least keep making our best attempt.

Integrating the Perceptual Positions into your Life

After asking the explorer to temporarily suspend his/her judgment and experience the other position, we lead him/her back to the observer position. Then before guiding him/her back to the Self Position, we take a moment to ask him/her to acknowledge what he/she has learned from both the Self and Other Positions. At this point we once again guide the explorer into the past to relive a number of past memories moving comfortably and effortlessly among the three distinct positions. Then guide him/her into the future to do the same.

Lastly, we check in with the client about the original situation. "How has it changed? What do you think will happen the next time you are in a conversation with this person?"

The Aligning Perceptual Position Technique is very useful for boundary issues. Here are the basic steps.

1. Identify a situation where you feel like you lost your sense of self.
2. Describe your experience and identify the submodalities.
3. Align the Observer Position: Generalize to the past and to the future.
4. Align the Self Position: Generalize to the past and to the future.
5. Return to Observer Position.

6. Return To Self Position: Generalize moving among all three positions in the past and future.

7. Discuss the original situation.

8. Futurepace: How will you experience similar interactions in the future?

NLP Momentary Practice

Identify a person with whom you lack clear alignment and good boundaries. Practice the eight steps of the Aligning Perceptual Position technique.

CHAPTER 25

Changing Personal History: What You Know Now, You Can Now Know Then

"There are so many things in human living that we should regard not as traumatic learning but as incomplete learning, unfinished learning."
-Milton H. Erickson

Where does our past exist? Scientists have identified the hippocampus and the amygdala, parts of the brain's limbic system, as being the places where we encode, store and retrieve memories. These stored memories influence how we think, feel and behave. We are, in effect, at the effect of these stored memories. Yet we do not have to "stand by" and feel powerless. While we cannot change what actually happened in the past, we can actually change what is happening there, now. By "there" we mean the area in our brain that stores these memories. It is the place where we can go to complete and finish the learning. So while "it" influences us, we can influence "it."

So "how" do we transform our memories to complete and finish the learning? The first thing to do is to reframe them as Erickson did, as an "incomplete, unfinished learning" instead of some disability that we just have to live with. Then we need to identify the specific memories that need completing. And we will also need to identify the "inner resources" required to accomplish the task. Accepting the presupposition that we have the inner resources needed to complete the learning will take us from a victim mentality to one of empowerment. Once we have identified the needed resources, we will anchor them and transfer them to the specific memories. We do not ask people to repeat going through the same unpleasant memory again. They have already done it and it serves no purpose to go through it again in exactly the same way we did it before. What does make a difference is going through it resourcefully. This means accessing the necessary and sufficient inner resources for transforming and completing the experience. Are you prepared to take this journey through time and space to finish something that began a long time ago? Memories are not ingrained, as many people believe; they are malleable. Experientially, we will be travelling through time and space to alter these memories to help ourselves. We will be liberating ourselves by first locating the specific incomplete memories currently stored the brain, and then empowering ourselves by utilizing the brains neuroplasticity to modify the memories.

We can spend our lives avoiding situations that might elicit the strong negative feelings associated with these unfinished experiences. In doing this, we miss out on the very experiences that move our lives forward. Once we transform our past, we can transform our present by getting to face up to the people, activities and situations that we had been running away from or fighting against. This time doing it with resources that will protect and empower us.

Changing Personal History

The technique we are about to present is entitled "Changing Personal History." While there are many variations, updates and enhancements we have made to this technique included in our NLP Master Practitioner and Ericksonian Hypnosis training programs, this is an excellent way to start learning some basic skills for healing our past.

To begin, we suggest looking for times in your life when you are feeling fine, confident and self-assured and suddenly something or someone triggers you into some negative debilitating thoughts or feeling state. It could be shame, fear, regret, overwhelm, rage, sadness, etc. These states can lead to behaviors that interfere with or thwart our attempts to make things happen.

This technique, as with the phobia/trauma technique (see chapter 27), in which we are altering memories of the past, are best done with an experienced NLP practitioner. It requires remaining disassociated and maintaining an objective perspective, which is something that most of us do not do when dealing with highly emotional issues. The experienced practitioner will immediately see if you are falling back into the negative experience, stop the process and re-establish the dissociation. Here are some examples of where and when you might use this technique.

Anger Management: Someone tells you what do and you become enraged.

Anxiety: When you are about to ask for what you want, you become anxious.

Fears: You are fearful of making presentations.

Sensitivity: You become overly sensitive to things people say and do.

Overreactions: You overreact to specific people, events and situations.

Being asked to look at and confront the people and things we've been programmed to avoid can understandably bring up resistance. To be willing to examine memories that have been connected to emotions such as fear, sadness, shame and anger there will need to be two things present. First, we need to be reassured that we can safely revisit these past memories. And second, we need an incentive. We need to recognize that by transforming these memories, we will enjoy the benefits that come with living our life free from the restraints of our old programming. Instead of surviving and getting by, we can look forward to thriving and seeking out new challenges and opportunities for personal and professional growth.

1. Locating the Unfinished Memories

To locate these unfinished memories, we need to first look at our current life, identifying what we are not getting done or how we are negatively reacting to particular situations. One way to do this is to divide our life into categories. Think about what is happening in your personal life, which includes intimates, friends and family.

Create another category that is about your professional life that includes your work place, colleagues and customers. If you want, you can add the category of health and identify whether you are taking care of your overall health including weight, nutrition, sleep and exercise. You can also divide your life into decades, or in the space of five years depending upon your age. As you divide your life chronologically you will begin to recall particular stories that represent the limiting belief or feeling that you are dealing with. Lastly, look at the latest interactions with others in any of these categories. What isn't working? If there is something that you are avoiding or putting off, there is most likely some limiting belief or persistent feeling that is getting in the way.

Once we have identified the negative feeling or limiting belief, we anchor it. This anchor will help us locate the past memories that are associated with the feeling or belief. We will explain to our client that it is like a portal to go through to find and collect the memories that formed and reinforced the negative feelings. As we hold the anchor, we suggest to the client that he/she let the anchor take him/her back into the past to find memories that are in some way connected to the feeling. If he/she "tries" to do this consciously, we ask him/her to stop trying. Rather than being actively involved in the search process, we ask that he/she be open and receptive and allow the unconscious to do the searching. And as soon as a memory "pops up" we have the client signal us and we release the anchor and have him/her open his/her eyes and come back to the here and now.

Clients are asked to only identify the memory, not to associate into it. They are asked not to talk about the memory at this time, since doing so might associate them into the experience and we do not need to know the full content. What we do need is a few words that will uniquely identify the specific memory, like, "In 1984 in the kitchen," or "12 years old in the playground." We repeat the process, firing off the anchor and releasing it until we get somewhere between four and six memories; however, even one memory is enough to heal. Although a memory may arise that had not been in the client's awareness for some time, it is not necessary for them to be new discoveries. But it is important to be patient and wait for specific times and places to be recalled. We write down the age and context or store it in our short-term memory, because in the next step we will need to come back to each memory. Now we are done with this anchor and will no longer be using it.

Once the client is finished with collecting events that relate to his/her limiting belief or negative feeling, we bring him/her back to the present and have him/her do the "NLP shake." It is important to bring him/her back to the present and reconnect with the here and now to establish a positive connection with the coach and remind him/her of the purpose of the exercise-healing his/her past to reshape his/her future.

2. Using Resources to Heal the Past

The coach now takes the lead and asks the client to view the memories lined up chronologically in front and slightly above him/her. Leave it up to the client to place the earliest memories on the left or on the right. In the early days of NLP, the metaphor was either of photos hanging in a dark room or pinned to a clothesline. This utilizes the submodalities of framing, size (small), distance (far), movement (stillness), and height (high). We have also used the metaphor of a museum to create the same submodalities. We ask the client to imagine visiting a museum and the memories that he/she identified are framed on a wall, far away from him/her. The images are disassociated so that the client is seeing himself/herself. Using disassociation along with the other submodalities keeps the client in an observer perspective and prevents him/her from being flooded by any unpleasant emotions connected to those events. This is also known as a visual-kinesthetic disassociation. We continually point upward (visual accessing) and outward (creating distance), and label the memories from left to right in chronological order. You can also choose to use a digital display on a computer screen.

In any case, always be prepared to modify the submodalities to maintain the dissociation, whether it means moving the frames further away, making them black and white or making them smaller.

3. Identifying and Accessing Resources

You are now about to identify the resources needed for each memory. Here are some variations of questions to ask that will help identify the needed resources.

What inner resource(s) does the younger you need?
What inner resource will allow the younger you to complete the experience?
What resource will heal the past experience?
What inner resource will empower the younger you?
What do you know now that you did not know then?
What resource state will allow him/her to be OK going through the experience?

Although the inner resource could be a behavior, such as "saying no," it is more often a state of being or state of mind, like "love," "acceptance," "safety," "self worth," or "inner strength." In asking the questions, we are looking for and listening for congruence.

When looking for appropriate resources it is possible that the explorer will select a different resource for each memory or have one resource that can be used throughout. Frequently, the resource is something that a child would not yet have, due to developmental readiness. However, you know now what you didn't know then and you are giving this resource as a gift to the younger self to ultimately help him/her (you) heal and move forward more resourcefully into the future.

Now it is time to remember a time when you've experienced the resource, i.e. confidence, and anchor it. We usually suggest creating a self-anchor, but the guide can also anchor with a touch or words. Once the client has established the anchor and tested it, we continue with the next step.

4. Being The Ally From The Future

We hold the resource anchor, while guiding the explorer to look at the first event and watch (being disassociated) the younger self go through the experience with the inner resource. We can also become an ally to the younger self, traveling back to the past event as a resourceful adult. It is essential to maintain clear boundaries between the adult self and the younger self. And it is important to pause long enough to give the client enough time to visit. This relationship resulting from bringing together the two selves will transform the memory. Obviously, we are not changing the past; we are changing our present representations of the past. So we are, in effect, healing the present.

5. Building Resourceful Memories

We suggest that once the explorer has completed his/her visit to the first memory, he/she gives us a nod to signal that it is complete. Next we might say something like, "Now let the younger self take on the wisdom and resourcefulness of the present self and re-experience the event with this new perspective." The resource can be "sent" to the younger self by continuing to hold the anchor, with words, with sound, and/or with energy. Again the coach stops talking and waits for the client to report that the younger self has successfully gone through the event with the needed resources. If any additional resources are needed, this is the time to add them. And finally, we ask the explorer to associate into the experience of the younger self, so as to experience it from the perspective of the younger self.

We are not suggesting that the explorer change the facts or event of his/her life. But we are changing the way we look at, think of and feel about the situation and most importantly the way we experience ourselves.

By bringing the resource back into their past we are changing the way the mind and body hold the memory and retraining or reprogramming the brain for a resourceful response to future events that used to trigger the old negative reactions. For example, a client programmed to feel "bad" and "undeserving" when she was with men can change her program creating new coding in her unconscious by bringing the resources of "self worth" and "self esteem" to her younger self.

Once the explorer goes through the experience with the resource(s), we stop again and ask him/her to describe what happened. When we get a congruent response with words like, "I am feeling empowered," or "I feel complete," or "I can be myself," then we know we can move on to the next event and repeat the process. If there is any indication of an incongruent response, accompanying statements like, "It was just OK," or "I felt a little better," "It was sort of helpful," then we will look for the resource that will truly make a difference. We only move on when we get a congruent, "yes." Otherwise we look for additional resources. If the response is "that was much better," we might ask, "Is there some additional resource that you want to give the younger you so that it could not be any better?" People are often willing to settle for less than complete. With each memory, we encourage the explorer to "go for it" and not to settle for less.

6. Testing Your Work and Futurepacing: Healing the Future

Having used the anchors to bring the resources to each distinct memory, we now guide the client to once again look up at the museum gallery and go through each memory again, this time without the anchor. We do this to test the work, observing how the client now experiences the memories that used to upset him/her. We ask him/her to let us know when he/she is done. If the explorer remains resourceful and does not fall back into the stuck state, then the test is successful. Anything less than this requires repeating the technique with stronger or additional resources.

It is important to note here that there are times when the current self has not yet experienced the resources that the younger self needs. This will require advanced skills on the part of the guide to assist the explorer in accessing a resource state that is not yet within his/her experience.

When the explorer has completed this process, ask him/her to think of a future situation that in the past would certainly have triggered this old belief or negative feeling. Sometimes a client feels attached to using his/her self-anchor. We remind him/her that just as he/she never needed a self anchor to elicit the previous negative feeling state, he/she will not need one now. If the resource does not automatically "kick in" without the self-anchor, then the work is not done. The sights and sounds of the situation should be sufficient anchors. The technique is designed to make the situation itself the anchor for the resourceful self. It's fine if he/she wants to temporarily use the self-anchor to rehearse and practice, but the final test happens when the new program is running without any conscious thought or attention.

When the session is over, there is time for discussion and reflection. Sometimes this is when we do another test, perhaps saying or doing something that would have previously triggered the negative response. So if the person's trigger was being told what to do, we tell him/her what to do. If their trigger was being told, "no," we tell him/her "no." Typically people laugh when they realize that they are no longer triggered in a negative way and are very appreciative that they have moved on. Frequently, they do not realize it until afterwards, when we point it out.

Demonstration of the Changing Personal History Technique With a Client

Here is an example of using this technique with one of my (R.H.) clients who felt that she was once again getting into an unhealthy relationship.

She wanted to make better choices about men, but always found herself with a "bad boy." When a client uses the phrase, "always," I know that he/she is referring to something happening over time. When I checked in with her, she confirmed that she had repeatedly dated people who did not show her love. As I began to gather information about her "bad boy relationships," I learned that she "found herself" in relationships in which she would either be verbally or physically abused. Her feeling over time was that she didn't deserve to be in a healthy relationship because she herself was "bad."

I asked her to recall a time when she experienced herself as being "bad."

She thought about a recent time when she been attempting to stop drinking alcohol while her boyfriend kept finding reasons why she should drink with him. I asked her to remember one of those dates with him when she was feeling that she was "bad," and "undeserving" so I could anchor the state.

I often apologize to the client when anchoring such an uncomfortable state and explain that we will be using it as a portal, passing through it to find other memories that exemplify this experience. Using the anchor, I led her to other experiences as a way to uncover events with the same theme. I am not necessarily looking for repressed memories, but for memories that are somehow connected to her feeling "bad," and "undeserving." She recalled a previous boyfriend, another previous boyfriend, and then a time when she was eight years old visiting her father in the hospital. As she recalled each memory I asked her to give an age and a title, and then continued on the search for any other examples.

It is important to guide the client to understand that he/she is collecting memories and not living through each experience. He/she doesn't have to tell you the content, just the title and age. The client was surprised that the memory shifted from her previous boyfriends to her father. It was not that she had repressed this memory; it was that she hadn't made the connection regarding her feeling "bad," and "undeserving," with that particular story. As a coach, I accept all stories that come up. Once the client was finished gathering her stories I brought her back to the present and asked her to do the "NLP shake."

In this particular session the order of the memories was: the 8 year old with dad in hospital, 16 years old with boyfriend in high school, 20 years old with boyfriend at the beach, and 30 years old in current situation.

Each story was placed out on a wall and I asked her to look at those stories and determine what resources would have been helpful for her at the time. A phrase that I used was, "What do you know now that you did not know then?" When she looked at those stories she said, "I know now that what other people do is about them, not me." When we asked her what resource would embody that knowledge she replied, "Inner Power." So I then led her to recall a time she had her "Inner Power" and had her create a self-anchor.

Being The Inner Ally

With this anchor of "Inner Power," I guided her to look at the first event when she was 8 years old with her father in the hospital. I encouraged her to become the future ally that this 8 year old did not have. "Take your time to find the way to time travel back into the past. Science fiction writers do it all the time and so can you. Bring this 'inner power' resource with you and let her know that you are here to give it to her." I continued by saying, "Now let the younger self take the wisdom from the future ally and re-experience the event with this resource."

Once the client went through the experience with the resource, we stopped and I asked her what it was like. She reported, "I wish it had happened that way," and "I feel better now." In this session she felt very clear that she now has the "inner power" and reminded herself that she can say "No," to the current man in her life and other men like him.

Testing your work and future pacing

My client thought about a future situation when she might meet a man who would be flirting with her and she projected inner power into this future scenario. She felt very hopeful about her next relationships and shared that she no longer felt that she herself was 'bad' and that she respected herself and deserved to be treated with respect.

NLP Momentary Practice

Select a feeling that you have over time that limits your self-esteem. Ask yourself to identify two to four memories that support this limiting feeling. Write the events on post-it notes and put them on the wall chronologically. Identify a resource for each one. Self-anchor the resource and as a future ally bring the resource to each memory, remembering to also relive each memory with the resource. Review each memory after having re-experienced it with the resource. Select a future situation where you would like to have this resource and let yourself be there now.

Reclaiming Personal History: A Bonus Technique to Boost Your Self-Esteem

In this technique, we will once again revisit the past. But this time we are not looking to change anything. We are just going to gather resources. In previous techniques, when we needed a resource, we retrieved it by going back in time to a specific event when we were experiencing that resource. Now we are going to expand our search by identifying and collecting numerous examples of the same resource that occurred at different moments in our life.

The Reclaiming Personal History Technique is a way of getting greater access to an elusive resource state that we have already experienced at various times. For example, in the process of becoming professionals, many of us have lost our sense of playfulness and forgotten how important it used to be and still is.

Other examples include losing confidence, losing motivation and losing our sense of humor. This exercise will help you find your confidence, your motivation or your sense of humor. It is not lost; it was just misplaced. We learned this reframe from Dr. Jacqueline Hott (Rachel's mother, Steven's mother-in-law), a sex therapist, who said, "When a patient complains about losing his erection, I tell him it is not lost, just misplaced, and it only needs to be relocated."

The Reclaiming Personal History technique provides an opportunity to organize and catalogue our resources. In this way, we can continue to gather evidence about our successes and feel positive about our past. Doing this exercise periodically can keep our Self-Esteem current.

For this technique, we ask the client to remember one time when he/she had the resource he/she wants to reclaim. For example, one client wanted to have more levity. She described levity as a feeling of lightness and not taking herself and life so seriously. So she selected a memory of a time when she had levity with her family. Then we created a self-anchor.

Holding the self-anchor, I invited her to let the unconscious search through her past for other times when she has had levity. (This is the same process as Change Personal History, but now we are searching for resource examples). Each time she found an example of levity, I asked her for the age and a title. She found "age 40 at work," "age 35 at a picnic" and "age 22, laughing with her family." After finding these memories she released the anchor.

Stacking Same Resource on One Anchor

Next I invite her to hold her self-anchor and associate into each event. As the guide, I suggest that she go deeply into the earliest experience at age 22, while calibrating to confirm that she is in the resource state, breathing more deeply and starting to giggle. By the time she had been led through ages 35 and 40, she is laughing. The experience became one of lightness and laughter. She attached all the memories onto the one self-anchor and reclaimed levity back into her life. Next she identified contexts where she is too serious and used her self-anchor to bring levity into these situations.

NLP Momentary Practice

Select a resource you already have, but would like to have access to it more often and more intensely. Create a self-anchor and use it to recall 3-5 additional memories when you have experienced this resource. Write them down. Then associate deeply into each memory while holding the self-anchor. Applying the anchor, think of a future situation where you would like to have access to this resource.

CHAPTER 26

The Swish Technique: Instantaneous Change

"You have power over your mind – not outside events. Realize this, and you will find strength."
-Marcus Aurelius

It takes four to six hours for our body to digest food. It takes about one minute for blood to circulate through the body. But it only takes milliseconds for us to react to visual and auditory stimuli. The brain works fast. It happens so fast that the conscious mind only finds out about it after the fact and, at best, can only attempt to reverse the effects. Let's say we become instantly enraged when someone insults us. When this occurs, we have no time to react otherwise. We might react with an onslaught of verbally offensive remarks, do bodily harm to the offending party or we can hold back and contain our rage. In any case, our button got pushed, we feel enraged and the only choice we have is how we are going to behave.

Most of us, when reflecting upon a situation that caused emotional distress, ask, "What could I have done differently?" or "How should I have behaved?" One answer is, "Instead of blowing up and cursing, I could have been more civil and bit my tongue." Another is, "Instead of holding back and remaining silent, I should have expressed my feelings and told him what I really thought."

But there is a second set of some very different questions that we could ask instead, such as, "How do I want to be in these situations?" or "Who do I want to be when faced with these circumstances in the future?" Some possible answers could be, "I want to feel safe and secure," "I want to be a compassionate person," "I want to be amused," or "I want to be unfazed and remain centered."

There are two main distinctions between the two sets of questions. The first distinction is about time. The former set of questions focuses on the "past" and asked how we could have or should have acted differently. The latter set focuses on the "future" and how we want to be different. As you know by now, NLP is not concerned with what was, but with what can and will be. Even in the change history technique (Chapter 25), we changed how we experienced the past only to change how we will be experiencing the future.

The second distinction is about what we are changing. The first set of questions focuses on changing "behavior" while the second set is about changing "our state of being." In many situations, changing our behavior is sufficient, but in others, the more deeply satisfying transformation involves changing our internal state as well as our external behavior.

Consider the person who automatically responds to an insult with amusement. Instead of having to choose how he/she is going to express or contain his/her rage, he/she gets to choose how he/she is going to express or contain his/her amusement. So for some of us, choice is seen as choosing from a number of different behaviors while being stuck in some negative state, while for others it is really about choosing the state of being. Choice means different things to different people.

While some of us may become enraged and hold a grudge for a very long time, many of us learn to let go of it and think about the person with compassion and forgiveness. There is also the difference between learning how to get out of a stuck state and learning how to avoiding getting into it in the first place. NLP can accomplish both of these. Whether we are programmed to respond with rage or with amusement, we are still programmed. And our response requires no effort. So our question is, "How would you like to effortlessly respond within milliseconds, before you even know it?" Another way of asking is, "How do you want to reprogram yourself?"

Which brings us to our next technique. Remember the Stuck Meta Resource Technique from Chapter 10? It starts out where we identify the situation propelling us into a Stuck State, then moving us to the Meta Position and finally entering into the Resource State. This technique chains together a series of states using locations as anchors. The technique we are about to present, named the Swish Technique, which unlike the Stuck Meta Resource Exercise which gradually moves you from the trigger to the resource using anchors, will quickly (milliseconds) take you from the initial trigger directly to the resource state using submodalities (Chapter 6).

As we have discussed, the anchoring and reframing techniques can be instrumental in helping an individual change his/her behavior. In our NLP Coach Practitioner Certification Training, we teach a variety of techniques (there is no one magic button technique), so that trainees have many tools among which to choose. The Swish Technique can be very helpful for contexts where we are locked into a habit, for example nail biting or cigarette smoking. The reason why it is called Swish is because of the sound that frequently accompanies the implementation of the technique.

The Swish Technique can also be used for eliminating unwanted habits. For example, grabbing a cookie out of the cookie jar, lighting up a cigarette, or reaching for a beer. At an NLP conference, Steve Andreas once described doing the Swish technique with someone who had a self-concept attached to a behavior. For example, "I am an overeater," "I am a smoker," or "I am an alcoholic." And this is why, when it comes to the resource, instead of asking, "What do you want to do?" or "How do you want to feel?" we will be asking, "Who do you want to be?"

Jack Canfield refers to the Stimulus-Response reaction as a Stimulus-Organism-Response. What he is saying is that the stimulus itself does not cause the response. There is something happening in the brain that gives meaning to what is being seen and/or heard and directs the nervous system to follow a specified path. And it happens so quickly. So what we are about to do is teach the brain to follow a new path in which it will re-interpret the stimulus and re-direct the nervous system to a highly desirable resource state, at a speed at which it is already accustomed to be operating.

The Swish Technique

First we identify the stimulus. To do this we can ask, "What, specifically, do I see or hear that lets me know it's time to react?" or "What, exactly, is it I see or hear such that I can't not react in this way?" or "What is it I actually see in the situation just before I start having the feeling and doing the behavior I don't like?" In describing this technique, we will be assuming a visual stimulus. Afterwards will explain how it can be done with an auditory stimulus as well.

So let's assume the stimulus is someone rolling his eyes and shaking his head. And the response is a combination of being devalued, feeling small and getting aggressive. It could just as easily be "an alcoholic" being offered a beer or "a nail biter" looking at an uneven nail. The image of what you are actually seeing (associated) is called the Cue Image.

So the first step is to have the client associate into the situation, seeing what he/she is seeing. We will use the context where a client sees someone looking at him while rolling his eyes and shaking his head. We ask him/her to see it as he/she actually sees it from his/her own perceptual position by asking, "What is it you actually see in the situation just before you start having the feeling and doing the behavior you don't like?"

1. Develop A More Desirable State (or Behavior)

We know how the client habitually reacts; we now want to know how he/she wants to respond. What we are looking for is a "self-image." Who is it that he/she wants to be, when someone rolls his/her eyes and shakes his/her head? It can be a self he/she is already familiar with or one that he/she would like to be. This can include specific behaviors, qualities and/or states of being.

The client is then guided to see this self as a resourceful disassociated self-image. Whatever resource self-image the client decides upon, it must be compelling. To be compelling, the client must have an irresistible attraction to the disassociated image of himself/herself. This image can be literal or symbolic. For example, a person can see an image of himself/herself being loving and compassionate or he/she can see a beating heart symbolizing love and compassion. I (R.H.) have used the image of seeing myself on top of a mountain with my hands on my hips as a compelling desired state of confidence and achievement.

The image of who you want to be (disassociated) is called the Self Image.

The Self Image we will be using in this example is one in which he/she is breathing comfortably with a balanced stance, looking self-assured, confident, with soft eyes and a smile.

2. Playing with Submodalities

The Swish Technique may only take milliseconds to do, but getting it set up right requires some time. We next find two powerful "analog" submodalities that will significantly increase and decrease the intensity of both the cue image and the self-image. There are two kinds of submodalities; one is digital, the other is analog. To simplify the distinction, first think of a digital watch that only shows numbers, like 8:00 AM or 2:45 PM or 23:30 hours. Then think of a watch that has the sweeping hour hand, minute hand and second hand. This is analog. With analog there is movement along a continuum. With digital there is none. The time "jumps" from 8:00 AM to 8:01 AM to 8:02 AM. Another example is the light switch. The "digital" switch only turns the light "on" and "off." The "analog" switch is a dimmer switch that controls the degree of brightness. Some visual digital submodalities are 2D or 3D, color or black and white, still or moving. Visual analog submodalities include size, brightness and distance. In the Swish Technique we only use analog submodalities.

Starting with the cue image, ask the client to experiment with analog submodalities to determine which ones most strongly influence the intensity of the experience. Does making it brighter increase the unpleasant feeling while making it dimmer decrease the feeling? Does bringing it closer increase the unpleasant feeling while moving it further away decrease the feeling? Or does making it bigger increase the unpleasant feeling while making it smaller decrease the feeling?

Then do the same thing with the resourceful self-image. Does making it brighter make it more compelling while making it dimmer less compelling? Does bringing it closer make it more compelling while moving it further away make it less compelling? Does making it larger make it more compelling while making it smaller make it less compelling?

We are looking for the two most powerful analog submodalities that have the same effect on both the cue image and the resource self-image. These are called the driving submodalities. Let's suppose we find that for both the cue image and the self-image, bringing them closer and making them brighter significantly intensify the feelings, while moving them further away and making them darker significantly decrease the intensity. Once have identified the two driving submodalities, we are ready to do the Swish. As you will see, using two submodalities instead of one will make the stimulus response irreversible.

3. Time to Swish

This is a technical moment and it is important to explain to the client what the next steps will be. You will explain that you will be asking him/her to see the cue image (seeing a person rolling their eyes and shaking their head), "close up and bright," as if they are actually there in front of you. Then explain that he/she will be visualizing the compelling disassociated self-image (self assured, confident, smiling, soft eyes, breathing easy with a balanced stance) dark and in the distance. Once this is set up, we are ready to do the Swish.

But before you do it, describe to your client that the brain works "faster than you think." It only takes milliseconds, as fast as blinking your eyes. So we are going to have the brain learn at its normal super speed. Now go ahead and have your client set up the two images as described and explain to him/her that he/she is about to reprogram his/her response. Let him/her know that you are going to count to three and at three you will say "Swish," fast and loud. Hearing this signal, he/she will, as fast as possible, have the cue image get darker and darker as it moves farther and farther away into the distance while simultaneously the self-image grows brighter and brighter as it gets closer and closer. Some people need to do a brief rehearsal at a slower pace to get the coordination of the cue image fading into the distance and the desired image emerging into the foreground.

We also suggest that as you set up the technique, you sit next to the client, because you want to direct his/her attention so that he/she is looking at the images, not at you. You can use your hands to guide the Swish, one hand being close to the person indicating the cue image while the other hand is further away and pointing in the distance. So when you are doing the Swish, your hands can reverse positions. Each time the Swish is done, stop, drop your hands and have the client do the "NLP Shake." This is important because we will do the swish several times and if done continuously without interruption, you might inadvertently create a loop in which he/she cycles back to the cue image.

4. Now Close Your Eyes and Make Three Swishes

Everything we have done up until now had been in preparation for what comes next. Have your client set up the images as described and prompt him/her to do the Swish by saying, "One, Two, Three, Swish!" This is to be done three times, each time making it faster and faster! After each swish, make sure the client does the "NLP Shake." After making the three swishes, ask him/her to think of the cue image.

Calibrate the client's response and ask him/her to report his/her experience. If done correctly, the client will immediately associate into the resource state as soon as he/she thinks of the cue image. You can also prepare for the future (futurepace) by having him/her think of the future and place him/herself in a variety of settings where someone is doing the former cue, which was rolling his/her eyes and shaking his/her head.

You can be as creative as you like when setting up the exercise. If both of you are familiar with sci-fi space travel, you can use the image of two starships passing each other traveling at warp speed. Some clients have liked the imagery of the desired self-image coming to them like a circus lion crashing through the scrim of the hoop.

For this technique, as with many others, the more you experience you have guiding and being guided, the easier it will be and the more effective you will become guiding yourself.

Here are some variations of the Swish Technique:

1. What do you do when distance and brightness are not the driving submodalities?

Suppose the driving submodalities are size and clarity. You would follow the same procedure as we described, but instead have the cue image start large and clear while the self-image is small and unclear. You can place the self-image in the lower left corner of the screen containing the cue image. So when the cue image shrinks and fades in clarity, the self-image enlarges and becomes increasingly clearer.

2. What do you do when the cue that initiates the negative reaction is not visual?

The Swish Technique can also be adapted to the auditory and kinesthetic modalities. Let's say it is a voice that initiates the reaction. Instead of using visual analog submodalities, we use analog auditory submodalities, such as volume, distance or speed. And instead of a self-image, you can use a "self-voice," in which you hear your own voice incorporating the qualities that would make it compelling, such as gravitas, calmness or playfulness.

If the trigger is a touch, you can use submodalities such as pressure, location or temperature. And instead of a self-image, it can be a self-touch that carries with it an empowering energy.

Before doing this technique find out if the reaction or behavior that you are about to change has a positive intention. If it does, we suggest first doing a Six Step Reframe.

NLP Momentary Practice

Identify a trigger that throws you into a negative state or a behavior that you would like to stop doing. Identify what happens right before you begin to do the behavior. Identify a state of being that you would like to have along with a behavior you would like to do. See yourself in this resource state. Play with the submodalities and determine the driving submodalities. Create a swish. Do it at least three times (more if necessary), and remember to break state by doing the good old "NLP Shake" in between the swishes. Now think of the stimulus. If the new response kicks in, you have a new program.

CHAPTER 27

The Phobia Technique: Fear Itself

"Expose yourself to your deepest fear; after that, fear has no power...You are free."
-Jim Morrison

Meta Model Question: "How, are we going to expose our selves to our deepest fears?" Answer: Safely, securely and with some selective submodalities.

When we went back in time in the "Change Personal History" exercise we went back well prepared with all the needed resources. And here we will do the same. Only this time we are going to do it to cure a phobia.

A phobia is a strong persistent fear of animals (e.g. dogs, birds, mice), places (e.g. elevators, airplanes, heights), things (e.g. needles, blood, chemicals), activities (e.g. swimming, public speaking, vomiting) and people (e.g. dentists, clowns, lawyers). The list is a long one and includes many that you may not have heard about unless you happen to have had or know someone who has had one of them. New phobias continue to develop along with technology such as nomophobia, an abbreviation for no mobile phone phobia (the fear of being out of mobile phone contact). Remember the good old days when all we had was ornithosclidaphobia (fear of dinosaurs) and pyrophobia (fear of fire).?Some common phobias we have worked with over the years include acrophobia (heights), aquaphobia (water), arachnophobia (spiders), claustrophobia (being closed in), emetophobia (vomiting), erythrophobia (blushing) and gephyrophobia (bridges).

Facing Fear: Just The Two of You

My (S.L) relationship with fear

At some point in my life, I decided that I was going to live life fully. And while being afraid is part of being alive, I knew that giving into my fears – by altering my behavior to avoid the things I feared – I would not be living fully.

But I did not do it by using willpower to push through the fears. Actually, I do not think of fear as an "it" to be overcome. I think of the "me" that's scared and needs to be supported – listened to, cared for and reassured. And I want to make sure he feels safe and secure. I do not see him as flawed. I do not shame him for being afraid. I do not call him cowardly. I value him and give him the attention and appreciation he needs and deserves. Over the years, I have developed a caring, loving and respectful relationship with myself. I let myself know when a particular course of action appears reckless or needs to be carefully thought through before taking action. As long as I remain in charge, the fearful me will not be alone. And our relationship is key.

In my practice, I have heard many clients describe being afraid of expressing their needs and wants to their partner. They are afraid that their partner will become angry, get upset, be critical, abandon or hurt them. They do not feel safe. But when avoiding these real or imagined consequences becomes a pattern, it destroys any trust and intimacy that exists and only perpetuates feelings of insecurity and resentment. The same can happen to our intrapersonal relationship.

It has been my quest to create a safe, supportive, loving relationship with myself, so I can respond resourcefully and stand up for myself in the face of another's anger, upset, criticism or withdrawal. So whatever happens, I can still count on me to be there for me.

In my younger days when I was afraid to approach an attractive girl, I reassured myself and I approached her, knowing that whatever happened I would be ok with me. And I got to have a lot of dates. It was much better than spending my time imagining all of the things that I was afraid would happen.

When I was 18, I wanted to travel, but was afraid of being alone. So I responded by booking a flight to Europe where I did not know anybody and travelled on my own for two months. I was my own travelling companion.

When teaching at an alternative high school in Bushwick, Brooklyn, back in the 1970s, I decided to confront my fear of standing in front of a class having nothing to say. So I came to class with no lesson plan, prepared only to stand in front of the students without saying a word, looking around the room, listening, breathing and waiting until I became curious and comfortable. I survived. And it made for a wonderful and quite memorable learning experience for all of us. I could not have planned it better.

When I dreamt of being an expert NLP trainer, the idea of exposing myself to a discerning New York audience was intimidating. So I did it. I have now trained thousands of New Yorkers in NLP and Hypnosis. I also worked through my fear by taking an improvisational comedy class and performing at a Manhattan comedy club.

My fascination with horror movies at an early age is a metaphor for confronting my fears. I watched with eyes wide open. I remember my fear of drowning that surfaced the day before my first scuba dive and the fear of falling before skiing down a mountain.

If I had given in to my fear of living alone, I would not have enjoyed my time as a single man. And if I gave in to my fear of commitment to marriage and parenthood, I would not have such a deeply satisfying relationship with my partner, Rachel, our son, Daniel and our daughter, Maya.

This pattern has followed me into my sixties as I currently bike to work over the Williamsburg Bridge and through the streets of lower Manhattan and spend quite a bit of time in the hot and humid Bikram Yoga studio.

But it is really not about me. It's about the strategy I was using. And you can use it too.

When studying NLP, I realized that the strategy I was using was being utilized in the NLP Phobia Technique. Phobias are extremely intense and debilitating fears that we go to great lengths to avoid. When we have a phobia, we cannot "not" react to the stimulus or the thought of the stimulus without having an overwhelming fear. And still the solution lies in facing these fears accompanied by the resources necessary to keep us safe, calm and feeling secure.

According to Richard Bandler, a phobia is a "one step learning process." And if it has been learned, then we can learn how to respond differently.

Whether you have a phobia or a strong fear that gets in the way of feeling safe and secure, this technique will be useful. This technique can also be used for PTSDs (Post Traumatic Stress Disorders) and is referred to as the NLP Trauma (or Phobia) Technique. However, if you have been traumatized, we strongly suggest doing this technique with a licensed psychotherapist, knowledgeable in NLP. Many of our trainees and clients with traumas and phobic responses have found their intense negative reactions dramatically decreased or eliminated completely after going through this technique.

I (R.H.) had a phobia of birds since I was a kid. After doing the phobia cure in 1983 when I was a student in the NLP Practitioner Training, I was able to go to Central Park in New York City and walk comfortably through a flock of pigeons. That was a great achievement for me and made a big difference when I travelled to Venice and Rome where the plazas are full of pigeons. My comfort around birds has continued to this present day. My final "test" was holding our pet parrot on my finger. Interestingly, some friends and family who remember my fears still refer to the past and are genuinely surprised when I tell them I no longer have this phobia.

When we have a phobia, we not only have the phobic response in the presence of the actual object. It also happens when we think of the object. And while we cannot always avoid the object or the thought of the object, we can learn how to change the way we think and feel about the object and towards ourselves. And this is what we are going to do.

As part of our NLP Master Practitioner Training, we work with our students to come up with specific behavioral tasks so they can confront their fears, expand their choices and to discover who else they may be. One task we gave ourselves was to write this book, something we had never done before. There is something quite powerful about making a commitment to do something that we believe will bring up doubts and fears.

Making and keeping a commitment to face our fears requires developing a bond between a self that is strong, loving and encouraging and the self that is full of fear.

The Phobia Technique

To successfully do this technique, there are two states that need to be anchored. The first is a state of here and now "safety and security." Anchoring this deep sense of wellbeing is essential. The second state is one of "disassociation," or "an objective observer." It is a place where you are able to see and hear yourself in the phobic situation without feeling any of the unpleasant feelings. It is "not" a state of avoidance, withdrawal, numbness, coldness, aloofness or indifference. And while it is a place of objectivity and open mindedness, it can also be a place of warmth and compassion. So before we do anything, we want to have these two resources firmly anchored in place.

1. Access Safety and Security: Anchor #1

Where do we go to feel safe? Is it an actual location, a sacred space, a monastery, a secluded beach or a room full of family and friends? Does it happen with a special person, a loving grandparent, a dear friend, or special teacher? Is it an animal? A dog? A cat? Is it a memory or created? First and foremost, guide the client to find this place.

Once the client has established the safe place, we create an anchor. This is anchor #1. Make sure it is a unique anchor and have him/her test it. Creating a safety anchor is important in this technique so that the client feels comfortable before, during and after the process. In addition to anchoring it to our voice and a touch, we usually have the client create a self-anchor so that they are in control.

2. Identify Your Fear From a Distance: Anchor #2

Having created the safety anchor, we will use a movie theater metaphor to create the disassociation anchor. While much has changed since the inception of NLP, we still have, for now, movie theaters. As an alternative, we have had our clients imagine a computer monitor or a hand held device. The disassociation anchor involves three steps and is therefore referred to as "3 Step Visual-Kinesthetic Disassociation." We suggest to the client that he/she imagines himself/herself sitting in a movie theater, and then floating out of his/her body and into the projection booth. From the projection booth, we have the client look at himself/herself sitting in the audience, while the self that is sitting in the audience observes a blank screen where his/her younger self will soon be appearing. We say this several times. Once it is clear that he/she is disassociated, we anchor it. This is anchor #2.

The idea of disassociating and observing one's self was introduced when we discussed submodalities in Chapter 6. We used it with the Change Personal History Technique (Chapter 25) as well. This extra step in the process of disassociation trains the client to become separated from the self with the phobia, fear or trauma that up until now has had a strong emotional hold over him/her. So when he/she looks dispassionately at the memory and feels comfortable, we know we are making progress.

We ask the client to think of the earliest memory of having had the phobic response. The memory will have a beginning (before anything unpleasant happens), a middle (the event itself), and an end (when everything is over). Robert Dilts named this the sandwich experience.

Once the client has both his/her safety anchor and his/her disassociation anchor, we tell him/her that he/she will be in charge of starting and stopping the movie. The first step will be to place on the screen a black and white image of the beginning of this earliest memory "before" anything unpleasant happens. We then ask him/her to go to the projection booth and nod when he/she is ready to start the movie of the event. When he/she signals, we fire off both anchors and remind him/her to use his/her self anchor, so that he/she is safely ensconced in the projection booth, watching himself/herself in the audience, watching the younger self over there on the screen going through the experience in black and white. It is okay to repeat this statement several times in a slow and low volume voice.

If the client begins to cry or demonstrates that he/she is becoming upset, it is best to stop the process, check that the anchors are holding and if necessary encourage him/her to make whatever submodality adjustments (e.g. distance, size, brightness) that bring back the feeling of safety and security. It is fine to stop the process, bring him/her back to the here and now, and ask about what he/she was experiencing. As long as both anchors are doing their job, crying is perfectly acceptable.

As the client watches from the projection booth, we encourage him/her to observe himself/herself and learn and appreciate something about himself/herself that he/she had not yet realized. We tell him/her to give a head nod when the movie has ended. Then we ask him/her what he/she discovered about the self that he/she was observing.

At this point you can release anchor #2. This is an opportunity for him/her to connect with the self in a loving and caring way. We encourage him/her to visit with the past self and express appreciation for what he/she had gone through. We say something like, "Take a moment and find a place where the adult you and the younger you can have a safe and caring interaction. Let him/her know that he/she made the best choice he/she could make at the time and have adult reassuring you give the younger you whatever it is he/she needs, now. Once you do this, let me know when you feel complete."

We then bring the client back to the here and now, and see what happens when he/she is asked to think of the situation that had been causing the intense fear to determine if the phobia is done or significantly diminished. Depending upon his/her response, we either conclude that we are done or continue with the next part to eliminate the phobia completely.

I (S.L.) worked with a client who had a snake phobia. His earliest memory was a childhood experience of accidentally disturbing a nest of snakes when crawling underneath his country house. After going through these steps most of his discomfort when thinking about snakes was gone, so we continued with the next part.

3. Changing Submodalities: Color, Backwards and Speed

Having already established a safety anchor, a disassociated state and an appreciation for the self that went through the event, I added, "Now this time (1) use your safety anchor, (2) float up to the projectionist's booth, and (3) watch the movie in black and white, starting from the beginning before anything happened, through the middle where the event is taking place and arriving at the end when the event is over and you are fine. This time when you get to the end I want you to nod and pause the movie, just like you would when you are watching a DVD." I waited until he signaled, then continued, "Okay, now I am going to release the dissociation anchor and have you 'step into' the end of the movie and as you do, it will turn from black and white to color and start moving backwards very fast – really fast. Do it now – right now!"

The use of speed, color and reversing direction (going backwards) helps the client let go of the way he was thinking about the event. I repeated this several times, having him associate into the end of the memory, then in color and with extraordinary speed go in reverse to the beginning. I did this three times in total, making sure he did the "NLP Shake" in between each one. After completing the three rounds, I asked him to think of encountering a snake. When he did, the fear and anxiety were no longer triggered, even when he thought about his childhood experience. He was quite amazed by the results, as most people are. He shared that he was feeling safe and was still hearing a firm yet gentle inner voice saying, "Now just be careful and remember to watch where you are going." And he was fine with that.

4. Testing The Work

Ideally the final step is to expose the client to the actual thing that had been triggering the phobic response. We have done this with clients who have fears of heights and elevators. Many years ago, before 9/11, I (R.H.) had a client who was afraid of heights. After doing the phobia technique with her, we went to the top of the World Trade Center. She managed very well going to the highest point as possible. She was thrilled with the change. After doing this process with another client who had an elevator phobia, we took a ride in the building's elevator. On the way up she asked if the elevator had been updated because her perception had changed. One of our trainees worked on her fear of dogs. After the demonstration I walked onto the street and together we approached dog owners and their dogs. She was very surprised at her comfort level being close to dogs and speaking with the dog owners.

Some people have questioned whether the effects of the NLP techniques are just temporary or long lasting. Whenever we can, we like to follow up with our students and clients to check in on their progress. So we decided to include this report from one of our students who was our demonstration subject for the phobia technique.

"A few weeks ago, during my NLP training, I volunteered to be the subject of the technique we were learning that day: the phobia technique. I've always had a fear of heights, and although I have learned to control this under most circumstances, certain specific physical symptoms such as sweaty palms, a feeling like the floor was made of JELL-O, and rapid heartbeat, would always present themselves.

Rachel Hott went through the technique with me and at the end I was curious to see when and where I could test this. A week later, on a trip to Rio de Janeiro, the perfect opportunity came up. We visited the Sugar Loaf Mountain (in Portuguese, Pão de Açúcar), a place I had been to many times before and where the physical symptoms always came up. Going up 1,300 feet on a clear Plexiglas walled cable car seemed like a good test, and having a baseline to compare seemed perfect. To my surprise, none of the symptoms showed up. Even being at the edge of the cable car and at the top of the mountain didn't instigate any of the previous physical symptoms."

Update (09/21/2013):

"A few months after the experience at Sugar Loaf Mountain, I was looking for a new office space in Manhattan and came across a building that had an open stairwell on the side of the building. It was an open concrete staircase, not one of those metal ones typical of New York. I went out to the ledge and looked down. It was pretty high up, well over ten stories high. Again I experienced none of the physical symptoms I used to have before. However, this time I had some time to be with this feeling and noticed that what I was experiencing was best described as an absence... it was as if something was missing. I found this curious and as I became more attuned to this experience of absence, suddenly some of the symptoms showed up. As silly as it may sound, my first thoughts were 'Ah, there you are...' followed immediately by 'Thanks, but no thanks...' As I continued looking down the symptoms went away.

I have since experienced this again a few times, the symptoms showing up 'tentatively,' such as when suddenly walking over a sidewalk grating where I can see a 20 foot drop, and the feelings going away almost immediately as I say, 'Thanks, but no thanks...'"

Practice Thinking in New Patterns: Editing

The following is a variation of Trauma/Phobia technique taught by Robert Dilts when working with PTSD. We have added it to our repertoire. It gives the client another way of holding onto a positive body memory. Essentially every step of the Trauma/Phobia Technique is the same except for some editing. I (R.H.) was hired to work with a company who had been downtown at the World Center site on 9/11. Working with individuals using the Trauma technique, I asked them to edit their memory as follows, "Now that you have worked on this event, imagine that you are the editor and you could change the movie any way you want. What would you do?" Some of the individuals imagined that it was just another Tuesday in September, and nothing occurred. Others saw themself as some powerful superhero fighting the planes. While none of that did or could happen, it helped them view the event differently so their body memory was no longer holding onto the fear and despair that they had felt that day. Then

I added, "Now watch the movie the way you would have wished it would have happened. You can do it any way you like, in color, in black and white, fast or slow, close or far. Just let it happen." They all reported and demonstrated breathing comfortably.

Similarly to Change Personal History technique, we were not changing the facts of an individual's experience. He/she still knows the facts. But when you encourage someone to edit, you are helping him/her to release the way his/her body holds onto the memory. Right now as you are reading this chapter your mind is aware that you are reading and your body is involved in that process. What would happen if you tell your mind that there is no floor underneath you or that there is a big gaping hole that is opening up under your seat? If you have a vivid imagination and use it, your body will begin to experience fear and/or discomfort even though it isn't true. We are doing the same thing just in reverse. Our clients have had some terrible experiences, and their body is still holding onto the trauma. To promote healing, we help our clients release the feelings and connect to resourceful feelings while still retaining the facts. This is not a simple process and not one that we recommend trying out on yourself or someone else if you do not have proper guidance and supervision. We suggest that if you or someone you know is dealing with a trauma or phobia that you find an experienced NLP professional to help guide you through this process.

The NLP Research and Recognition Project, developed by Dr. Frank Bourke and Dr. Richard Liotta, has been using the trauma technique to work with veterans who suffer from PTSD. Two of our students were selected to participate as NLP coaches in the research. This research is ongoing and if you want to find out more please go to the website, nlprandr.org.

NLP Momentary Practice

Create a safety anchor. This is a wonderful anchor to create for any situation.

Then create a three-step dissociation anchor. From the perspective of the projection booth, see yourself sitting in a theater. Then create a movie of yourself that is based on something you did this past week. Then combine the two by being the self in the projection booth, watching your self, sitting in the theater, watching your self on the big screen. Once you have successfully done this think about where, when and with whom either one or both of these anchors would be useful. (Do not use a phobia or trauma at this point. You are still practicing.) Finally, while holding the anchor(s), go into the future and experience what it is like now.

CHAPTER 28

Strategies: The Way We Do The Things We Do?

"For the musician, before he has begun his work, all is in readiness so that the operation of his creative spirit may find, right from the start, the appropriate matter and means, without any possibility of error..."
-Paul Valery

How do we remember someone's name? How do we choose a partner? How do we ask for what we want? How do we say, "no"? How do we do what we do?

Some of us are aware of how we do the things we do. Most of us are not. We do what we do without knowing how we do it.

In the beginning (of NLP), Bandler and Grinder modeled three therapists: Milton Erickson, Virginia Satir and Fritz Perls. Bandler and Grinder were not interested in learning "why" these wizards in the field of Psychology got the results they got from their patients. They were not interested in theories. What they were interested in was "how" these three successful psychotherapists got the results they got with their patients, so that they could transfer these "strategies" to others. When we ask a client or a trainee what they do well and how they do it, we are engaging in the process of modeling. Strategy elicitation is one form of modeling. It involves learning the precise steps a person goes through to achieve his/her outcome.

For example, they found that people who are excellent spellers have similar "spelling strategies." They all have a "visual" representation of the word that they have memorized. If they see the word misspelled they automatically compare it to their "stored" representation and get an unpleasant feeling; if it does not look right it does not feel right and they "know" it is not correct. If you ask them to spell a word they will first visualize the word. If it matches their stored visual word they will get a good feeling. When they get a bad feeling, it becomes feedback, letting them know they have to change the spelling until they get a match that produces the good feeling. That's when they know they got it right. I (S.L.) remember my mother writing down a word to see if it "looked" right. For most good spellers, seeing it in their mind's eye is sufficient. People who use an auditory strategy in which they "sound out" the words instead of visualizing them will not be successful because words in English do not always look the way they sound. In other languages, such as German, words do look the way they sound, so an auditory strategy can be effective.

List Your Abilities

So, what are you good at? What do you do well? Steve is great at solving problems. Rachel is great at getting things done. We have strategies that we have practiced over time. One of Steve's strategies involves looking at everything as a puzzle and maintaining a belief that there is a solution. One of Rachel's strategies relates to her awareness of time – seeing the future very close to her, knowing that time will pass quickly. Part of Rachel's strategy is to say out loud to others what she is going to do, thereby committing to the goal. Thus this book has been written.

In our training sessions we have had many demonstrations of trainees' strategies. We have learned about cleaning while listening to great music, enjoying making mistakes, turning criticism into feedback, being patient and feeling good to be alive while sitting in traffic, getting motivated for exercise by creating a compelling self image and choosing to eat healthy food by having a kinesthetic awareness of emptiness or fullness. Whatever you do, whether you do it well or poorly, there is a strategy, which for most of us is unconscious. Our NLP students enjoy engaging in the process of eliciting strategies, learning how people accomplish what they do, so that they can do it themselves and teach it to others. If you do not know how to forgive someone, find someone who is excellent at forgiving and get his or her strategy.

NLP trainer Steve Andreas told us about a strategy he uses to fall asleep. He visualizes a beach where the ocean waves are approaching. Then as he becomes aware of his self-talk, he writes down every word in the sand and watches it washed away by the waves. Find out more about his sleep strategy along with other articles about strategies for sleeping well and eating healthy at www.nlptraining.com/articles.

Exploring Strategies: How Do You Memorize?

We would like you to try the following exercise that we use in our training to learn about strategies. Read the following list of words and memorize them; *master, experiment, transformation, warmth, adventure, solution, fun, balance, love, success, challenge, destination.*

Now take out a blank piece of paper or go to an electronic device and from memory "write down" the words. Once you have done this, ask yourself, "How did I remember the words?"

What strategy did you use?

Did you picture the actual words with each letter spelled out?

Did you see images associated with each word?

Did you make up a story containing images of each word? If so, were they still photos or moving images? Were the images in a frame or were they panoramic? Was it in 2D or 3D? What other submodalities were involved? Were you in the pictures?

Did you have feelings associated with each word?

Were you saying the words to yourself or out loud?

Did you "tell" yourself a story?

Did you see the words in the story?

What else did you do to retrieve those words?

Ask a friend, colleague or family member to do this memory exercise. And ask him/her how he/she memorized the words. Use any of the above questions to get the information. If he/she is not familiar with NLP, his/her answers may be mostly about content. So you will need to ask questions to find the submodalities. For example, if for the word "experiment" he/she says, "I see a laboratory with test tubes, microscopes and people in while lab coats," you can ask if it is a photograph or movie. Is it 2D or 3D? You can ask if he/she is in the scene or watching it from the outside, etc. Some people link one movie to the next. For example, one of the lab technicians may pick up a test tube and drink the contents and transform into a monster. That could indicate "transformation." He or she may then become the monster and feel "warmth" spreading throughout his or her body and leave the laboratory to go on an "adventure" to find a "solution." Other people may make very separate and distinct images with no flow from one scene to the next.

And remember that this is not about the content. We are exploring how we "form" our thoughts.

In our training, once the participants learn how they do it, we give them another list of words and ask them to "try on" another student's strategy. Only after going through this exercise, do people appreciate just how differently we each process information. It also prepares our trainees to learn to model other's abilities.

Looking for Models

When we teach strategies, we ask trainees two questions, "What are you good at?" and "What ability would you like to have?" After making a list of the various answers, we look for "perfect matches." So if Elena is good at making decisions and George is good at remembering names and Elena would like to learn how to remember names and George would like to improve his decision making, then we have a "perfect match."

Most people take their skills for granted because they seem so natural and require so little effort. Of course that is part of the skill – to do it naturally, effortlessly and unconsciously. Some of the skills that people shared over the years include: organizing a closet, inspiring children to learn, telling stories and jokes, exercising daily, maintaining a healthy diet, remaining calm in a crisis, composing music, negotiating a deal, saying "no," planning a party, taking in a compliment, giving feedback, responding to criticism, learning a language and engaging in conflict.

In the following example, we will be indicating in parenthesis the representational system (V, A or K) that the model (the person with the ability) is using. This can help separate the form from the content. The most successful strategies use all three representational systems.

Auditory External: Refers to the sounds or words in the environment that the person is hearing.

Auditory Internal: Refers to the sounds or words that the person is hearing that are not occurring in the external environment (this includes self talk).

Visual External: Refers to what the person is seeing in the external environment.

Visual Internal: Refers to what the person is imagining in his/her mind's eye.

Kinesthetic External: Refers to what the person is feeling externally. This includes tactile sensations like touch, texture, warmth, pressure as well as movement.

Kinesthetic Internal: Refers to what the person is feeling internally. This includes emotions and visceral body sensations.

The following is an example taken from a demonstration I (R.H.) did in our NLP training with one of our students to learn how she went about buying the right gifts for friends and family.

Strategy Elicitation:
Buying Gifts for Friends and Family

At every NLP Practitioner training course, we ask one of our students to come up to the front of the room and we elicit his/her strategy. The first and most direct question here is, "How do you buy gifts for family and friends?" Of course the answer is often unconscious for the model, so we usually ask the model to remember and re-experience a specific time and place (in this case, when she was buying a gift for a particular person), and then unpack or unwrap the experience. The exemplar described how she was shopping with a friend when the friend said, "Oh, I like those colors on that scarf." She explained that, "When I hear (auditory external) someone describe something that he/she likes, I always hold onto that piece of information, knowing that I will use it in the future." She listens (auditory external) for what is important to friends and family. When she hears (auditory external) it, she says (auditory internal) to herself, "I will remember that" while having a feeling (kinesthetic internal) that she can keep it in her mind's eye (visual internal) for a future time when she sees (visual external) something that matches.

So the strategy begins well before the special occasion occurs. She will be on the lookout (visual external) for those colors throughout the year. She does not wait until the event, but maintains a search overtime with the birthday or celebration date in sight (visual internal). She continued, "I think (visual internal/her eyes went up to her left) about this person and all of the activities he/she liked to do so that I can put the colors together (visual internal) with that." This strategy sustains over time until she finds the colors (visual external) that match (visual internal). It is important for her to give something to someone that matches that person. If she doesn't find something in time for the gift giving, she gives (kinesthetic external) a joke present with a note saying something about how this is not really the present she would have liked to give but the real present will soon show up.

Since this was only one example, I (R.H.) asked her for other instances. Although each had its differences, what they had in common gave us the formula for her strategy for buying presents in general. The formula seemed simple. She listens to the person whenever she is with him/her (auditory external). She tells herself (auditory internal) to remember any particular highlights (visual internal) that he/she liked. Then she reviews other things she knows about him/her (visual internal). She keeps a lookout any time before the gift giving time period (visual external). She notes the event on the calendar and attempt to find something that matches (visual external). When she does eventually see something (visual external) that matches (visual internal), she has that good feeling again (kinesthetic internal) and buys it (kinesthetic external). If no match happens before the event, she uses humor (auditory external).

I (R.H.) successfully used this strategy to buy Steven presents for his 60th birthday. I surprised him with two presents, a private yoga session with a Bikram teacher and a Thai massage. Using the exemplar's strategy, I figured out birthday presents that matched the things that were most important to him at that time in his life.

"Give a man a fish and you feed him for a day. Teach a man how to fish and you feed him for a lifetime." (This idea was taken from a passage in the 1885 novel <u>Mrs. Dymond</u> by Anne Isabella Thackeray Ritchie.)

Modeling to Teach Others

You may be in the leadership position and want to be a model for others, but don't know how you do what you do. Would you like a strategy for learning to elicit your own strategy and teaching it to others?

The T.O.T.E (Test-Operate-Test-Exit)

Here are some steps to figuring out how you do what you do.

Step 1: Test

This step is a comparison between what you want to see, hear or feel and what you are currently seeing, hearing and feeling. For example, if you are a hairstylist, you have both the image of what the person's hair currently looks like as well as a vision of what it is going to look like. Hopefully the stylist has an effective strategy asking questions and listening to the answers so that both stylist and client are seeing "eye to eye." In this case the comparison is visual. For other strategies, it could be auditory or kinesthetic.

Step 2: Operations

This is a series of steps that the person goes through to arrive at, in this case, the final look. It will involve a specific series of actions internal and external, in this case the selection of scissors and sequencing of cutting.

Step 3: Test

This step is actually the same as the first step. It is a comparison of what, in this case, is being seen to what it is "supposed to" look like.

Step 4: Exit/Feedback

When the hairstylist sees that the way the hair look matches their internal representation, he/she is done. When the way the hair looks does not match the way he/she wanted it to look, he/she continues to go through a similar set of operations or a different set until there is a match. The more flexibility you have, the greater likelihood of success. When there is a match, the strategy exits. Usually there is another representational system involved. So when it matches, there is a "feeling" of satisfaction or an internal voice that says, "yes." When he is done, the barber I (S.L.) go to exclaims, "A new man." That signals he's done.

Of course, the "final" step may be to hand a mirror to the customer once the stylist is satisfied, to determine his/her satisfaction. This may be another test to determine if the customer looks and sounds satisfied. If they are, then it is really done. If not, there may be some verbal feedback from the customer to guide the stylist to make further changes. Hopefully they are on or eventually arrive at the same page. Of course, the customer has his/her own strategy for choosing a hairstylist and deciding whether to stay with him/her or not.

To elicit a strategy, it is a good idea to identify one instance when the model is demonstrating the ability. All strategies start with a *Test/Comparison Phase* where the model identifies what he/she wants to see, hear or feel differently. Then we learn the sequence of thoughts, feelings and behaviors that he/she goes through. This is the *Operation Phase*. Then we come back to the *Test/Comparison Phase* that he/she is using to determine whether or not he/she has achieved his/her goal. The last step is called the *Feedback/Exit Stage*. It is a yes/no stage. In this step you either exit the strategy because (yes) your criteria has been met or (no) it has not been met, and use it as feedback to go back to the original sequence of operations or do something different – a secondary set of operations. The example of our student using humor when she needed more time to gather information to buy presents is an example of a secondary operation. Once the gift was found, the strategy was complete and she exited. This is known as the **T.O.T.E.** that stands for Test, Operation, Test, Exit.

Questions To Ask Your Self or Others

Operation Stage:

Remember it is best to have him/her first re-experience a time(s) when he/she did this strategy. After that ask him/her:

"How do you begin?"
"What steps do you go through to achieve your outcome?"
"How do you do...?"
If there is a gap in the sequence that you do not understand, ask them, "How do you get from point A to point B?"
"What happens if you do not get your outcome?"
"What is important to you about doing or having this ability?" (Criteria)

Test Stages:

"What standard do you use to determine whether you have achieved your goal?"
"What do you need to 'see,' 'hear,' or 'feel' to know whether or not you are getting your outcome?"
"What underlying emotion is present while you are doing this strategy?"

Feedback/Exit stage:

"How do you know when you have successfully achieved your outcome?"
"What lets you know if you have not achieved your outcome?"
"What do you do if you haven't achieved your outcome?" (Secondary Strategy)

Practicing The Strategy

As we said earlier, we have all been unconsciously modeling others throughout our lives. As a child we modeled the people who happened to be around us. As an adult, we can choose whom to model. Learning to elicit the strategy is only part of the goal, the other piece is taking it on as your own. Just because you ask an advanced skier how to manage the black diamond slope does not mean that you can immediately go down a black diamond slope. But in many cases, you can rehearse in your mind and body the strategies that you have elicited and incorporate them into your life. As Rachel did with the gift giving strategy, you can adapt someone's strategy to your own style.

Installing a Strategy: Reprogramming Your Software

After eliciting a strategy, think about the sequence of steps that you have learned and review it internally. Imagine a situation where you want to have that ability and see through your own eyes (associated) what it's like. It is also important to remind yourself that you are only taking on a specific ability, not all of the other person's behaviors, beliefs or identity.

Sometime there is just one piece that will make the difference. For example, you might elicit an elaborate strategy from someone who eats healthy. But what stands out for you is that before he/she eats, he/she imagines himself/herself having already eaten it. Then stepping into this image and feeling what it feels like, asking himself/herself, "Is this how I want to feel?" This part of the strategy may be all you need to modify your own and receive the benefits. If you find yourself eliciting a strategy and getting confused or stuck and not knowing what to do at certain moments, go ask the exemplar what he/she does. We measure our success by our ability to get the results we want, not necessarily doing it the same way the exemplar does it.

Also, keep in mind that it might be easier and more effective to have someone else with NLP experience guide you through the steps.

When working with clients, a common theme is learning how to build and maintain an intimate relationship. So we have them identify someone they know who is enjoying a healthy intimate long-term relationship and give them tools to model that person. We can then be resource people to help them learn to learn.

NLP Momentary Practice

Identify someone who has an ability that you would like to have. Let him/her know that you recognize that he/she does something that you would like to do too. Let him/her know that you are learning how to elicit strategies by asking questions and would like to spend some time with him/her to learn about how he/she does it. It is important that he/she know it is not his/her job to already know how he/she does it. That is your job. Practice the strategy questions. And remember it is essential to remain curious throughout the process. Then "try on" the strategy. For an additional resources about modeling, look at David Gordon and Graham Dawes' book, *Expanding Your World*.

The New Behavior Generator: How to become your "Ideal Self"

There is another technique that we use to help our trainees and clients learn to model. It is called The New Behavior Generator.

In our training we have discussed that sometimes a trainee/client will say, "I don't have the resources I need" or "I don't have the ability." We can ask him/her to "Pretend you have the ability," (As in Frame) or "What are three resources that create that resource?" (Chunking Resources), and lastly we can say, "Do you know someone who does have that resource or ability?" (Modeling).

What distinguishes the New Behavior Generator from Strategy Elicitation is that we do not ask any questions to determine how the other is thinking or feeling. We only pay exquisite attention to the details of their behavior (visual and auditory).

I (R.H.) had a client who was a vice president at a large corporation. He wanted to have what he called, "dynamic relaxation," at work. He stated that although he did not have it, he knew someone at work who did. I had him identify a time when he had observed this individual doing dynamic relaxation. With eyes closed, I guided him to carefully observe the other, noticing how the other is doing what he is doing, how he is moving and how he is speaking. I tell him that when he has learned all that he can learn through studying the external behavior that he let me know with a head nod. Once he had done that, we discussed what he has learned about the person.

The next step was having him observe himself doing exactly what he just observed from the exemplar. I said, "Now watch yourself doing dynamic relaxation just like your friend at work, but now it is you and you have learned how he does it, so you can watch yourself and see he moves, acts and express himself. And when you have done this, let me know with a head nod."

Then he and I discussed what the experience was like. At this point, some people are not completely comfortable with the "new behavior." If this happens, we ask the client to modify the behavior in whatever way he/she needs to, so that it looks, sounds and feels right for him/her.

The last step is to be "in" the experience. So I said, "Step in or float into what it is like to already have dynamic relaxation, fully and completely. See through your eyes and hear through your ears, discover your thoughts and feelings as you relish in this experience of dynamic relaxation. When you have fully experienced dynamic relaxation and are ready to complete this process let me know with a head nod." After that we again discussed his experience and determined where and when he wanted to have this new resource/ability available in the future, and then we futurepaced.

NLP Momentary Practice

Think of resource you believe you do not have and select a model that has this resource. Practice the New Behavior Generator Technique.

CHAPTER 29

Metaphors: Once Upon a Lifetime...

"Transcendence is something between a metaphor and a miracle."
-Mason Cooley

Storytelling has been around for centuries, passed down through oral tradition, written works of prose and poetry, music and dance, stage performances, movies and TV. Stories have been used to communicate ideas, influence people and as a means of entertainment. They are told by sages, teachers, coaches, psychotherapists and motivational speakers to impart knowledge and insight. The NLP developers did not invent storytelling. However, they did model an exceptional storyteller in Dr. Milton Erickson.

As we have mentioned, Erickson was a psychiatrist and hypnotherapist and his goal was to heal his patients, or more accurately, to help them heal themselves. Within his hypnotic trance inductions, he would use personal stories of things he knew (e.g. gardening and overcoming obstacles). At times he would suggest that a student take a hike up Squaw Peak, a mountain near his Phoenix office (since renamed Piestewa Peak, named for Lori Piestewa, a Hopi-Hispanic woman, who was killed in the Iraq war) to find a particular bush or flower. In that case, he created a task that was a living metaphor for the client.

Throughout this book we have been using "direct communication" to be clear and specific when asking Meta Model questions and eliciting present state and outcome state information. Using therapeutic metaphors to create change is an example of "indirect communication." Sometimes these stories will be shallow metaphors where their meaning is obvious to the client, and they understand why they are being told the story. However, sometimes the stories will be deep metaphors, which parallel the person's life, but whose meaning is not obvious.

What's a Metaphor For?

In 1981, we (R.H. and S.L.) had the pleasure to attend a metaphor workshop taught by David Gordon. David is an early NLP developer and author of <u>Therapeutic Metaphors</u>. David has built an international reputation not only as a metaphor trainer, but also as a model modeler. Years later in 2000, we sponsored David Gordon to come to New York City to teach a metaphor workshop. He taught us a formula for creating metaphors that we will discuss later in this chapter.

During the 1981 metaphor workshop (which was only our second encounter), we found ourselves working together in a small group. Our assignment was to share stories. Rachel told Steven a story about King Arthur that she had heard on National Public Radio (NPR) earlier that year. Here is one version of the story.

What Do Women Want?

Young King Arthur was ambushed and imprisoned by the monarch of a neighboring kingdom. The monarch could have killed him, but was moved by Arthur's youth and ideals. So the monarch offered him his freedom, as long as he could answer a very difficult question. Arthur would have a year to figure out the answer and if after a year he still had no answer, he would be put to death.

The question was, what do women really want? Such a question would perplex even the most knowledgeable man, and to young King Arthur, it seemed an impossible query. But, since it was better than death, he accepted the monarch's proposition to have an answer by year's end.

He returned to his kingdom and began to poll everyone: the princess, the priests and the wise men. He spoke with everyone, but no one, not even Merlin the magician, could give him a satisfactory answer.

Finally he was advised to consult an old witch, for only she would have the answer.

But the price would be high, as the witch was famous throughout the kingdom for the exorbitant prices she demanded.

The last day of the year arrived and King Arthur had no choice but to talk to the witch. She agreed to answer the question, but he would have to agree to her price first.

The old witch wanted to marry Sir Lancelot, the most noble of the Knights of the Round Table and Arthur's closest friend!

Young Arthur was horrified. She was hunchbacked and hideous, had only one tooth, smelled like sewage and made obscene noises. He had never encountered such a repugnant creature in all his life.

He refused to force his friend to marry her and endure such a terrible burden, but Lancelot, learning of the proposal, spoke with Arthur and told him that nothing was too big of a sacrifice compared to Arthur's life and the preservation of the Round Table.

Hence, a wedding was proclaimed and the witch answered Arthur's question thus:

What a woman really wants is..."sovereignty" – being in charge of her own life.

Everyone in the kingdom instantly knew that the witch had uttered a great truth and that Arthur's life would be spared.

And so it was, the neighboring monarch granted Arthur his freedom and Lancelot and the witch had a wonderful wedding.

The honeymoon hour approached and Lancelot, steeling himself for a horrific experience, entered the bedroom. But what a sight awaited him. The most beautiful woman he had ever seen lay before him on the bed. The astounded Lancelot asked what had happened.

The beauty replied that since he had been so kind to her when she appeared as a witch, she would henceforth be her horrible deformed self only half the time and the beautiful maiden the other half.

She then asked him which would he prefer, beautiful during the day or beautiful at night.

Lancelot pondered the predicament. During the day meant that he could have a beautiful woman to show off to his friends, but at night, in the privacy of his castle, she would become an old witch. Or, would he prefer having a hideous witch during the day, but by night a beautiful woman for him to enjoy wondrous intimate moments?

Noble Lancelot responded by saying, "The choice is yours."

Upon hearing this, she announced that she would be beautiful all the time because he had respected her enough to let her be in charge of her own life. Sovereignty rules.

It wasn't until a month later that we began dating. Many years later Rachel discovered that that story had a tremendous impression on Steven, as he had learned what was most important to Rachel: to have choice. Later on in our relationship, Rachel discovered that Steven was frequently sharing that story with our students, as it continued to have special meaning for him.

One of the first exercises we do to create the power of storytelling is to share personal stories. Each one of us has many stories to tell. Sometimes it is a story told by a family member or one that we heard from a friend. And sometimes it is our story. When trainees are asked to prepare a story to share with the class they initially think that they have to come up with an amazing story. But we encourage them to simply think of a story that has impacted them in some way. Some students bring in poems; others tell about life adventures. One student came in with a song. She told us that she had been a chorus teacher for an elementary school. The chorus was practicing the song, *I Believe I Can Fly*, by Bianca Ryan. Our student said that she had asked for a volunteer to sing the solo. No one volunteered until a hand shot up from a boy who was new to the school. She gave him the solo. Then, as they practiced singing the verses, he suddenly collapsed. She ran for help, called 911 and he was taken to the hospital. The boy died that evening. Unbeknownst to our student, the young student had a heart condition that had not been reported to the school. The song was his swan song. While she shared that story, our group was silent and moved. We were touched with the beauty and power of life, death and innocence.

At the end of each training day, we also tell a story. But we do not tell the class what it means. Each of us gets to enjoy our own personal meaning. But the day our student spoke about her young student's death, instead of using the teaching tale that we had planned for the day, we printed copies of the lyrics and the group sang the song together. It was a moment of transcendence.

NLP Momentary Practice

Think about this song and story. What does it mean to you?

Select a personal story and share it with others. Ask someone to share a meaningful story with you.

One of my (R.H.) students was an executive coach who taught people to believe in their ability to create powerful futures. She told the story about her own experience with the book, The Secret, by Rhonda Byrne. The Secret was published in 2005. It was a book that encouraged the reader to state their outcome and believe in the power of the universe. Ultimately, her story was about the power of beliefs. Our student said that so many clients were telling her about The Secret that she felt pressured to read it. However, she felt overwhelmed with work and family life and didn't think she really had the time to read and thoroughly learn it well enough to use it with her clients. She continued to think about it, and one day while she was driving to the supermarket, she had an idea. She said, "I realized that I could listen to CDs of the book while I am driving around doing errands." As she parked her car, she continued to think about her CD idea. When she came back from the store she saw that there was a plastic bag under her car tire. She picked it up and there in a plastic bag were all of the CDs for The Secret. Needless to say, she listened to them. When our class listened to that story, many of us had chills down our spine. The story illustrated the power of belief and mystery.

Another example of how to use personal stories comes from a time when I (R.H.) was working with a client who had a fear of flying. So I decided on my next flight to attempt to create a phobia. I thought about my client's fear, which was about not having a way out, but I kept finding myself thinking of other things. Mainly I discovered that either I was involved in a book or thoroughly distracted with thoughts unrelated to planes. I told my client about my inability to be fearful. While it was not a deep metaphor, my client reported weeks later that my personal story helped her when she flew on an airplane.

Sometimes stories that people share are about a book or movie. For example, the story of the Wizard of Oz spoke to the unique resources that we each already have. Then there is the story of The Ugly Duckling where an outsider perceived as being ugly leaves her community and finds another that embraces her and sees her beauty. Stories will touch you and speak to your unconscious mind.

How do you build rapport using someone's metaphors?

A client of mine (R.H.) used war metaphors when talking to his 14 year old son, with expressions like, "You are your own worst enemy," "I think we should kill the idea," and "Let's bring in some reinforcements." His son liked creative writing, so I suggested to him that instead of using war metaphors, that he change his language to something related to writing. For example, "How about if we turn the page and begin a new chapter?" "How can we edit our behavior?" or "What would be an appropriate theme for this experience?" Does this idea of matching someone's language sound/feel/look familiar? The concept is similar to identifying someone's representational system from Chapter 9 and matching key words and criteria from Chapter 15.

We learned the application of building rapport with someone's operating metaphors from Charles Faulkner, an NLP trainer also well known in the financial world for modeling traders. He wrote a chapter in the book, Market Wizards. When I (R.H.) worked at American Management Association (AMA), I learned about the corporate culture and realized that the majority of the metaphors used were either about war or sports. That was in the 1980s. Now in the 21st century, war and sports are still being "tossed" around and "battered" about. Other metaphors have begun to be used in our culture, for example, metaphors about family, gardens, animals and food, but war and sports are still "winning" out.

When we match someone's operating metaphors, we are listening for how they describe an experience. Typically in our private work, clients will describe problems at work, with themselves or with their significant others and family. Within a couple, one person might react by saying, "You are so controlling. You act like my mother." And the response back could be, "Well, I have to act like your mother because you are acting like a child." Each person is speaking in the same operating metaphor. They are using family as the representation of their experience. Yet even though they are speaking the same metaphoric language, they are not getting along. A coach could use their metaphor language to lead them to a solution. For example, "Let's have a family meeting and remember that since you are both members of this family you have to be clear on your roles. As two loving partners, what was it like when you felt spoken to as a child and what did it feel like to be disrespected?" You can then follow up with, "How will it change your relationship when you are respectfully speaking to each other, adult to adult?" In this case we are staying in their metaphor and adjusting it towards a way that a family would work to resolve a conflict.

When individuals use different operating metaphors, it is our goal to translate and help them understand what each person is saying. For example, in a business setting, a manager who was male talked about teamwork and expected everyone he managed to work towards winning and making it to the championship. Clearly he was using a sports metaphor. Yet one of the members of the team said, "I want to make sure that each one of us, like a flower in the garden, is acknowledged for our individual qualities and that we provide something to the environment that is unique." Now the NLP coach interpreted for each person. To the sports person the NLP coach said, "The point your player is making is that he wants each member of the team to be acknowledged as a most valuable player and that their special talents will significantly impact the final score. He wants to have a winning team people where camaraderie makes a difference." Then the NLP coach turns to the other person and explains, "Your manager is like the gardener who is tending meticulously to the garden, making sure that each of the flowers is getting the needed attention, nutrients and sunlight. He wants each of you to fully blossom. And as the master gardener, he is striving to cultivate the number one (Madison Square) garden party. If speaking this way does not come to you right away, it's fine. You just may be one of those late bloomers just waiting for a chance to break into the big leagues."

In our classes, when we practice matching someone's metaphors, we set up improvisational interactions between two people, with a third person becoming the translator. Initially we ask our trainees to think about all different operating metaphors. We begin with war and sports, and then continue to generate as many as possible. Sometimes a trainee will say nature and then another person will say trees. The categories can be large or small. The possibilities are endless. After we put up about at least 15 suggestions we begin the improvisational role-playing. Two trainees come to the front of the room and we assign a different metaphor to each one. Then we give them a scene to enact. For example, "You are two friends and you are planning to go on a vacation." Then they interact using the different operating metaphors. A third person, in this case the trainer, translates what each person is saying using the other's metaphor. This exercise can be a lot of fun when you let yourself exaggerate how people speak. However, once you become aware of operating metaphors, you will find that it will be easy to shift metaphors when speaking with others. Ultimately, this will help you to build and maintain rapport and become more influential.

After this exercise, we explore the types of metaphors that can be used to describe the training group itself. For example, we will say, "We are an NLP group that has worked hard and played hard together for many days, but what are we metaphorically?" Some responses have been, "We are travellers on a journey," "We are wizards studying the structure of magic," "We are a circus troupe." Once a theme has been selected, we then go around the room and describe how we are that theme. As a circus, the training staff can be the Ring Masters, and participants claim being the acrobat, the lion tamer, the tight rope walker, the strong woman, the clown, the elephant, etc. It is a lot of fun and reinforces the power inherent in learning to use metaphors.

Create Stories To Motivate and Inspire Others

As previously stated, David Gordon, NLP developer, created a structure that is useful for basic storytelling. Many of our students say that it reminds them of Joseph Campbell's Hero's Journey. The metaphor structure follows the idea of creating something parallel to the client's present state and desired outcome. We begin with his/her present state. Then the storyteller creates a crisis followed by a miracle. Then he/she ends the story with the desired outcome. Now let's explore using each of these pieces to create a healing metaphor.

In Chapter 20, we learned about present states and outcomes. When we listen to a client's present state and desired outcome, we ask ourselves, "What is his/her present state similar to?" Our goal is create a parallel story that relates to the present state and desired outcome. For example, a client states that he doesn't know how to stick to his commitments. He finds himself saying that he will do something, starts to do it, but doesn't follow through. His outcome is to be reliable to himself and others. When we begin to create a metaphor for him, we think about what is similar, parallel to the present state and outcome.

One of the ways to begin exploring what is parallel to something is to ask, "How is x like y?" In this example, "How is not sticking to commitments like a tree, like a house, like a baseball player?" If you want to use a metaphor about a person, we suggest that you keep the gender the same as the person with whom you are working. In creating a story, we use the formula Present State->Crisis-> Miracle-> Desired State. The coach is pacing (matching) the person's experience, and then exaggerating the experience (that is the crisis part,) and then adding a miracle, which will be a thought (cognition) and action (behavioral), before arriving at the desired outcome. In this situation the storyteller is making suggestions to the person both directly and indirectly about what he/she may have to do to achieve his/her outcome. Some therapists make up stories on the spot or spontaneously adapt a story they have heard before, while others spend some time between sessions to construct an appropriate metaphor.

In creating a story, you can begin with an outline of the four pieces. In our training we ask the group to become story consultants, within the demonstration. We will interview the demonstration client and then after gathering the information about his/her present state and desired state, we stop and ask the group, "What is his/her present state like? What is his/her desired outcome like?" We take three ideas and put them up on the board using the structure Present State->Crisis-> Miracle-> Desired State. We write the present state and desired state metaphors first, since this is what the client has given us. It will be the storyteller's poetic license to create the crisis and miracle. We then ask the demonstration client to select one of the ideas. Then before we tell the story, we begin with a relaxing trance. And as the relaxation deepens and he/she begins to connect within we continue with "Once upon a time…"

Crafting The Metaphor

Here is one example of a metaphor crafted for a male student. While the sequence in the story is Present State->Crisis-> Miracle-> Desired State, we will describe the present and desired state first since that is what we do first in creating the metaphor.

The Present State is "I don't stick to commitments."

We created a story about a carpenter who is planning to build a house, but continues to fall asleep and the house remains unfinished. When people come by to visit they have to eat in a room with holes in the ceiling.

The Desired State is "I want to be reliable to my self and others."

The next piece is to select a desired outcome that fits with the carpenter. The client wants to be reliable (to himself and others). Now we have the ending that the carpenter finishes one room and can invite friends over to enjoy the fruits of his labors.

The Crisis

Unfortunately, the carpenter is unable to get to any of his projects and at one point while working, he realizes that by rushing the nail he was hammering was going into the wood at a crooked angle. Then he realizes another error – that he was leaving an uneven edge when cutting the wood. As mistakes mount up, the carpenter finds that he is sleeping more and more, and ignoring the foundation. And one day the floor caves in.

When you read this, did you notice how the crisis exaggerated the present state and made things even worse? This is a tricky moment in storytelling because you are actually leading the person to a greater stuck place; however, the miracle will be the uplifting moment. The crisis is meant to be a dramatic moment when the protagonist is pushed to his/her limit. Many people who have made changes in their life know this as "rock bottom." The crisis moment is communicating to the unconscious that something must be done. Taking action and having a thought are essential for change. The thought is the beginning. The action drives the story. This is when the miracle occurs.

The Miracle

The carpenter, being in a state of shock and unable to move, finds himself buried under a sea of rubble. All he can do is stare directly in front of him. And in the dim light, he spies a solid piece of wood that he had cut cleanly and nailed carefully. As he looks at that piece of wood, he realizes how simple it had actually been for him to do that one task. And he realizes for the first time what people had been telling him for many years, but he had never really heard. All he has to do is do one thing at a time until the job is completed. That's all. The only real mistake he made was in not seeing this. With that realization, he frees up his arm and reaches out, taking the piece of wood into his hand. As the wood is dislodged, he sees the light shining down through the floorboards where there appears to be just enough space for him to crawl out. So upward he carefully crawls, one movement at a time. At last, as he nears the surface, he hears someone calling his name and sees a hand reaching down towards him. He reaches up and grabs the hand.

The miracle is the moment we give the protagonist the power within to make something happen. It is important that once the crisis has occurred the protagonist experiences a perceptual change and takes action toward the outcome. If in the crisis, there is someone else who lends his hand, it is the protagonist who reaches out to take it. The goal for the metaphor is to empower the person to take action.

Desired Outcome: Ending

Now we return to the person who had crawled out of his rut and keeps moving upward and onward, discovering the value of doing and completing one thing at a time which results in following through with what he says. After resting for a couple of days to regain his strength, he is determined to put his new awareness to good use and proceeds to build the house. As his project is nearing completion, he invites his friends to see the first finished room so that they can enjoy the fruits of his labors.

At the end of the story, we suggest that the demonstration client take all the time he/she needs to integrate these suggestions, trusting that the unconscious mind will discover new ways of moving forward. We then reorient him/her back to the here and now. Once he/she opens his/her eyes, we take a pause and ask if there is anything he/she wants to share.

Typically the responses are, "Wow," "Now I know what needs to be done," or just silence with deep breathing. Then, as we always do when we complete a demonstration, we ask the group if they have any questions for us or for the demonstration client. In our private work after the story is told, we discuss the client's experience. Sometimes we will co-create the metaphor with the client and say, if this was a story, what would be parallel to your experience? We co-create the story and then tell it to him/her while he/she is in a relaxed trance state.

NLP Momentary Practice

Think about a present state that you want to change. What is it like? Design your own personal metaphor using the structure Present State->Crisis-> Miracle-> Desired State. Write it and have someone read it to you.

CHAPTER 30

Technique Guidelines: What To Do When

NLP is an attitude and a methodology that leave behind a trail of techniques.
-Richard Bandler

Techniques are procedures that we go through to accomplish specific outcomes. Anyone can simply memorize and regurgitate the steps of the techniques in this book, but not everyone communicates with the NLP attitude or with knowledge of the NLP methodology.

There are many ways not to do NLP.

If you are not curious, you are not doing NLP.
If you are worried about failing or getting frustrated, you are not doing NLP.
If you think people don't have or cannot develop the resources they need, you are not doing NLP.
If you are in downtime, you are not doing NLP.
If you are focusing on negative intentions, you are not doing NLP.
If you are blaming and making people wrong, you are not doing NLP.
If you confuse the map with the territory, you are not doing NLP.
If you are "trying" to do NLP, you are not doing NLP.

When you find yourself maintaining a state of curiosity, when everything becomes feedback, when you firmly believe that we do have all the resources, when you effortlessly shift into uptime, when you naturally wonder about the positive intentions of any behavior, when you fully grasp that the meaning of your communications are the responses you are getting, when you can distinguish between map and territory and when you stop trying to do NLP, then you will be doing NLP.

One of the things we do in our NLP training courses is give people experiences that take them from unconscious incompetence to conscious incompetence, then to conscious competence and finally to unconscious competence. Serious students of NLP recognize the importance of practicing both the skills and techniques while receiving feedback, so that eventually they no longer have to think about them.

Before arriving at the point of intuitively knowing which NLP technique to use and when it's time to invent or discover (model) a new one, it is useful to have some guidelines.

Which NLP techniques can I use to accomplish specific goals?

If you want confidence, you might use the technique of "anchoring" to transfer the resource from where you have it to where you want it.

If you wanted to overcome a fear of mice, you might choose the "Phobia" technique.

If you wanted to stop procrastinating, you might do a "Six Step Reframe."

Whatever issues you want to work on, whether it is to start exercising, make healthy food choices, improve sleep patterns, have better sex, stop procrastinating, improve your relationships, etc., the same basic foundations principles apply. First, identify your outcome. Determine what you want and follow the steps for a well-formed outcome: stated in the positive, within your control, identify the context, describe your evidence and how you would measure your results and evaluate the ecological ramifications on you and your environment. Then identify your present state: what is happening now with this situation. After identifying the outcome and the present state, you get to choose what techniques to use.

The techniques in the chapters are like recipes. Once you begin to practice your skills, you will discover that the recipes can be changed depending upon the person with whom you are working, which includes yourself. We recommend that at first you practice the "recipes," as taught, and then, add your own variations.

The more familiar you are with each of the techniques and the more experience you have guiding others and being guided yourself, the more adept you will be in getting the results you want.

Here are some brief descriptions of when and where you might use the NLP techniques described in this book. Remember, if something is not working, be prepared to do something else. In alphabetical order they are:

Aligning Perceptual Positions (Chapter 24)
To be used when having difficulty establishing boundaries, saying "no," understanding people, finding perspective, getting in touch with emotions or generally having problems with interpersonal relationships.

Anchoring (Chapter 22)
To be used when immediate access to a specific resourceful state is needed. It will also be essential in doing most of the NLP techniques that call for anchoring.

Anchoring Opposites (Chapter 22)
To be used to undo an existing "negative" anchor. In other words, to neutralize unpleasant, unwanted feelings.

As If Frame (Chapter 7)
To be used to "fully experience" or "associate into" a specific outcome. It can either create the needed resource state or help identify the steps needed to get there. The "As If frame" can also be used to test ecology.

Association (Chapter 21)
To be used when there is a lack of connection to feelings and emotions. It is also a prerequisite for anchoring.

Chaining (Chapter 22)
To be used as "stepping stones" to get from a specific "stuck state" to a specific "resource state." The "Stuck Meta Resource" technique is one example of a chain.

Change Personal History (Chapter 25)

To be used when an emotion is triggered that becomes so overwhelming that it interferes with the ability to responding effectively to the present situation. It will be evident because you will have had this emotional reaction over time.

Chunking Resources (Chapter 22)

To be used to access a resource that we have not yet experienced, but have experienced its components.

Disassociation (Chapter 21)

To be used when it is important to examine and learn about an experience without becoming "lost" in it. To be used to create objectivity and to explore new options. The three-step dissociation is appropriate for phobias.

Future Pacing (Chapter 22)

To be used to transfer a new learning and resources to future contexts and to test to determine if they are working.

Metaphors (Chapter 29)

To be used to communicate with the unconscious mind. Use to communicate indirectly with others, to symbolically guide them from their present state to their desired outcome.

New Behavior Generator (Chapter 28)

To be used to access a resource that we have not yet experienced ourselves, but have seen others demonstrating it. This is an excellent precursor to modeling and strategies.

Phobia Model (Chapter 27)

To be used to treat phobia or other overwhelming fears. It can also be used to treat trauma.

Reclaiming Personal History (Chapter 25)

To be used when we have forgotten about past resource states and need a powerful reminder of just how resourceful we were, are and will be.

Six-Step Reframe (Chapter 23)

To be used with limiting or destructive habits or behaviors, and unexplained symptoms. It is also an excellent technique for responding to resistance, objections and interference. It contributes to appreciating our selves and building self-esteem.

Spatial Reframe (Chapter 23)

To be used for internal conflict, incongruent behavior, mixed emotions and inner turmoil. To be used when our "parts" are not communicating. This is useful for mediating and negotiating with teams, couples and families.

Strategies (Chapter 28)

To be used when current strategies are not working or are outdated. To be used to think and act more effectively and efficiently. Strategy elicitation is one aspect of modeling.

Stuck-Meta-Resource (Chapter 10)

To be used to gain perspective, access inner resources and create a new resourceful response to a situation that has previously triggered an unresourceful state.

Submodalities (Chapter 6)

To be used to transform our way of experiencing the world. To be used to increase or decrease the intensity of a feeling that is being generated from an internal image or an inner voice or coming from an external stimuli. Submodalities are the building blocks of our subjective experiences and are part of every NLP technique.

Swish (Chapter 26)

To be used to reprogram our "stimulus-response" habits. To redirect our unconscious mind from "non-useful" thinking and feeling to "constructive" thinking and feeling.

Often we will use a number of these techniques in sequence or in conjunction with one another. It is also important to understand that these techniques can be adapted and changed. Top chefs are always exploring new recipes and experimenting with different ingredients.

You have been reading about the basic ingredients of NLP. Many more essential NLP techniques along with enhanced skills and additional patterns are part of our NLP II Master Coach Practitioner Training curriculum.

Make Up Your Own Techniques

Much of this book emphasizes change and transformation, so we want to warn you about getting overly focused on changing the things we want to change without stopping to appreciate what we already have. I (R.H.) have developed my own gratitude practice. I start off in a comfortable position and take a few moments to think of something I am grateful for in my life. I include things like being thankful for my health and the health of the people I love. With each member of my family I get more specific about what I am thankful for.

I then send appreciation to the part of me that I call my "enhanced well-being part," (you are welcome to create a part too), and thank it for taking care of me. I then thank my immune system for taking care of me and ask it to let go of any existing cancer cells and then I send a healing white light throughout my body.

Lastly, I ask if there are any past wounds that need healing and send light to the wounded selves. And even after doing a change personal history, I will continue to send healing energy to my younger selves. I always end my practice by sending myself love and acceptance.

NLP Momentary Practice

Write down your outcome and present state, look at this list and identify two techniques that would be helpful to achieve your outcome.

Begin a daily practice where you begin to utilize the skills of NLP.

Create your own gratitude ritual.

We would love to know what results you get. You can contact us at info@NLPtraining.com or The NLP Center of New York Facebook page.

CHAPTER 31

The End: A New Beginning

"For me there is only the traveling on the paths that have a heart, on any path that may have a heart. There I travel, and the only worthwhile challenge for me is to traverse its full length. And there I travel – looking, looking, breathlessly."
-Carlos Castaneda (Don Juan)

As teachers of NLP and Hypnosis, we want to engage the imagination of our students so that they in turn will be an inspiration for others. We are not interested in producing technicians who memorize scripts. We seek to awaken a deep passion for learning about ourselves and developing compassion for others. For us, life is a place of wonder and possibilities. And it keeps getting "curiouser and curiouser..." Whether this book was your first exposure to NLP, a refresher or the next step in your NLP learning process, we hope you enjoyed reading it and found it to be both informative and useful.

As we indicated earlier, it was our intention in this book to give both an overview of NLP and to describe some of the ideas, skills and techniques that are part of our NLP Level I Coach Practitioner Training. But there is so much more. In our next book we plan to explore the advanced patterns of NLP, which we teach in our NLP II Master Coach Practitioner Training. They include Meta Program Patterns, Neurological Levels, Time Line Reimprinting, Sleight of Mouth Patterns, Changing Limiting Beliefs, States of Excellence, Modeling and much more.

You have now learned "about" numerous NLP skills and techniques for communication and change. When you are ready to actually learn them, we are here. From the feedback we have received since starting our training programs in 1986, we believe that we have one of the best and most comprehensive NLP training centers in the world.

Each year we offer many options for taking NLP Level I Coach Practitioner Training. There are classes on weekdays, weekends, evenings as well as a summer intensive. The same is true for NLP Level II Master Coach Practitioner Training and Ericksonian Hypnosis Training. Our training NLP and Ericksonian Hypnosis Training meet the strict guidelines set up by the International Association of NLP (IANLP) and the National Board of Certified Clinical Hypnotherapists (NBCCH), respectively. While there is much to be gained from reading and watching videos of NLP presentations and demonstrations, it will pale in comparison to participating in one of our live training programs. Be prepared to participate – fully. Not only will you get to see demonstrations of everything you read in this book, but you will also have the opportunity to integrate what you are learning by getting to experience the roles of guide, explorer and observer. Learning NLP requires both being receptive and interactive while receiving high quality feedback.

When participating in our NLP training you will be invited to join our ongoing practice groups, where you will have the opportunity to meet fellow NLP explorers and work with different trainers. We have found that the more you practice NLP, the more it will integrate into your life.

If you are in the New York City area, please come to one of our previews to see the center and meet the trainers. You can register online at nlptraining.com.

And check out our free NLP Mobile Map App that will help you locate NLPers throughout the world. If you are already an NLP Practitioner or Master Practitioner and would like to be on the NLP Map, let us know.

Thanks for joining us on this delightful journey we call NLP. And let us know what you found most valuable in reading the book and what results you are getting.

You can contact us at info@nlptraining.com or visit us at nlptraining.com.

Connect with us on Facebook: We hope you had as much fun reading this as we did writing it.

Rachel and Steven

Rachel and Steven, certified NLP Master Practitioners and Trainers, are co-founders and co-directors of The NLP Center of New York. Since 1986, they have trained thousands of students while leading NLP and Hypnosis certification training courses for both personal and professional development. They are certified by the National Board of Certified Clinical Hypnotherapists (NBCCH) and authorized and endorsed by Connirae Andreas to conduct Core Transformation seminars. They have recently launched the NLP Map App that can locate NLP Practitioners around the world.

Rachel B. Hott, PhD is a NYS licensed Clinical Psychologist who also holds a Master degree in Dance/Movement Therapy. Rachel has been trained by Jack Canfield to facilitate self-esteem trainings. She has also studied with Stephen Gilligan in the field of Self Relations. Her specialization areas include Performance anxiety, Sexuality, Life Transitions, Addictions and Healthy Lifestyles including weight control, sleep, pain management and exercise. She also incorporates Thought Field Therapy and Eye Movement Desensitization and Reprocessing (EMDR) in her therapeutic repertoire. She has been a course leader for American Management Association as well as a private consultant for executives. Rachel has presented at numerous conferences including the Ericksonian Hypnosis Congress.

Steven A. Leeds, LMHC is a NYS Licensed Mental Health Counselor, who holds Masters degrees in both Counseling Psychology and Secondary Education. He began studying NLP and Ericksonian Hypnosis in 1980 with John Grinder, Richard Bandler, Robert Dilts, Leslie Cameron Bandler and Virginia Satir and has studied extensively with both Stephen Gilligan and Jack Canfield. Since 1986, Steven has designed and conducted NLP and Ericksonian Hypnosis training in the United States and abroad. His areas of specialization include transpersonal psychology, healthy relationships, habit control, and state management. Steven works as a psychotherapist/ coach with individuals and couples. He was a founding member of the International Association of NLP.

32754331R00203

Made in the USA
Lexington, KY
31 May 2014